Conceptual and Historical
Issues in Psychology

The PsychologyExpress series

→ **UNDERSTAND QUICKLY**
→ **REVISE EFFECTIVELY**
→ **TAKE EXAMS WITH CONFIDENCE**

'All of the revision material I need in one place – a must for psychology undergrads.'
Andrea Franklin, Psychology student at Anglia Ruskin University

'Very useful, straight to the point and provides guidance to the student, while helping them to develop independent learning.'
Linsay Pitcher, Psychology student at Anglia Ruskin University

'Engaging, interesting, comprehensive . . . it helps to guide understanding and boosts confidence.'
Megan Munro, Forensic Psychology student at Leeds Trinity University College

'Very useful . . . bridges the gap between Statistics textbooks and Statistics workbooks.'
Chris Lynch, Psychology student at the University of Chester

'The answer guidelines are brilliant, I wish I had had it last year.'
Tony Whalley, Psychology student at the University of Chester

'I definitely would (buy a revision guide) as I like the structure, the assessment advice and practice questions and would feel more confident knowing exactly what to revise and having something to refer to.'
Steff Copestake, Psychology student at the University of Chester

'The clarity is absolutely first rate . . . These chapters will be an excellent revision guide for students as well as providing a good opportunity for novel forms of assessment in and out of class.'
Dr Deaglan Page, Queen's University, Belfast

'Do you think they will help students when revising/working towards assessment? Unreservedly, yes.'
Dr Mike Cox, Newcastle University

'The revision guide should be very helpful to students preparing for their exams.'
Dr Kun Guo, University of Lincoln

'A brilliant revision guide, very helpful for students of all levels.'
Svetoslav Georgiev, Psychology student at Anglia Ruskin University

Psychology Express

Conceptual and Historical Issues in Psychology

Brian M. Hughes
National University of Ireland, Galway

Series editor:
Dominic Upton
University of Worcester

Prentice Hall
is an imprint of

Harlow, England • London • New York • Boston • San Francisco • Toronto
Sydney • Tokyo • Singapore • Hong Kong • Seoul • Taipei • New Delhi
Cape Town • Madrid • Mexico City • Amsterdam • Munich • Paris • Milan

Pearson Education Limited
Edinburgh Gate
Harlow
Essex CM20 2JE
England

and Associated Companies throughout the world

Visit us on the World Wide Web at:
www.pearson.com/uk

First published 2012

© Pearson Education Limited 2012

ISBN 978-0-273-73728-5

British Library Cataloguing-in-Publication Data
A catalogue record for this book is available from the British Library

Library of Congress Cataloging-in-Publication Data
Hughes, Brian M.
  Psychology express : conceptual and historical issues in psychology / Brian M.
Hughes.
    p. cm.
  Includes bibliographical references and index.
  ISBN 978-0-273-73728-5 (pbk.)
  1. Psychology--History. 2. Psychology--Philosophy. I. Title.
  BF81.H796 2011
  150--dc23

                              2011019425

10 9 8 7 6 5 4 3 2 1
15 14 13 12 11

Typeset in 9.5/12.5pt Avenir Book by 30
Printed by Ashford Colour Press Ltd, Gosport

Contents

Supporting resources

Visit www.pearsoned.co.uk/psychologyexpress to find valuable online resources.

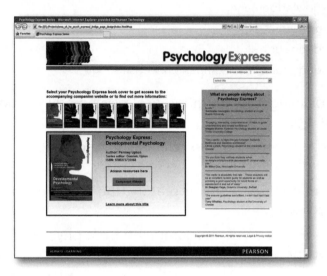

Companion website for students

→ **Get help in organising your revision**: download and print topic maps and revision checklists for each area.

→ **Ensure you know the key concepts in each area**: test yourself with flashcards. You can use them online, print them out or download to an iPod.

→ **Improve the quality of your essays in assignments and exams**: use the sample exam questions, referring to the answer guidelines for extra help.

→ **Practise for exams**: check the answers to the Test your knowledge sections in this book and take additional tests for each chapter.

→ **Go into exams with confidence**: use the You be the marker exercises to consider sample answers through the eyes of the examiner.

Also: The companion website provides the following features:

● Search tool to help locate specific items of content.

● E-mail results and profile tools to send results of quizzes to instructors.

● Online help and support to assist with website usage and troubleshooting.

For more information please contact your local Pearson Education sales representative or visit **www.pearsoned.co.uk/psychologyexpress**.

Acknowledgements

Author's acknowledgements

I am grateful to all at Pearson Education for their work on this book. I am particularly grateful to Dominic Upton, Series Editor, for his support, guidance and encouragement, and to the appointed reviewers for their feedback.

Thanks also to Marguerite, Louis and Annie for tolerating my distractions.

Brian M. Hughes
February 2011

Series editor's acknowledgements

I am grateful to Janey Webb and Jane Lawes at Pearson Education for their assistance with this series. I would also like to thank Penney, Francesca, Rosie and Gabriel for their dedication to psychology.

Dominic Upton

Publisher's acknowledgements

Our thanks go to all the reviewers who contributed to the development of this text, including students who participated in research and focus groups, which helped to shape the series format:

Dr P. Mani Das Gupta, Staffordshire University
Dr Niall Galbraith, University of Wolverhampton
Professor Paul Gardner, University of St Andrews
Dr Simon Hampton, University of East Anglia
Professor Simon Handley, University of Plymouth
Dr Rachel Manning, University of the West of England
Dr Hugh Miller, Nottingham Trent University
Professor Cheryl Pitt, Buckinghamshire New University
Senior Lecturer Tim Robins, University of Glamorgan
Professor Jan Schijvenaars, Fontys Sporthogeschool, the Netherlands

Student reviewers:
Sarah Turner, Psychology student at the University of Chester
Aimee Roberts, Psychology student at Anglia Ruskin University

Introduction

Not only is psychology one of the fastest growing subjects to study at university worldwide, it is also one of the most exciting and relevant subjects. Over the past decade the scope, breadth and importance of psychology have developed considerably. Important research work from as far afield as the UK, Europe, USA and Australia has demonstrated the exacting research base of the topic and how this can be applied to all manner of everyday issues and concerns. Being a student of psychology is an exciting experience – the study of mind and behaviour is a fascinating journey of discovery. Studying psychology at degree level brings with it new experiences, new skills and knowledge. As the Quality Assurance Agency (QAA) has stressed:

> Psychology is distinctive in the rich and diverse range of attributes it develops – skills which are associated with the humanities (e.g. critical thinking and essay writing) and the sciences (hypotheses-testing and numeracy). (QAA, 2010, p.5)

Recent evidence suggests that employers appreciate the skills and knowledge of psychology graduates, but in order to reach this pinnacle you need to develop your skills, further your knowledge and most of all successfully complete your degree to your maximum ability. The skills, knowledge and opportunities that you gain during your psychology degree will give you an edge in the employment field. The QAA stressed the high level of employment skills developed during a pyschology degree:

> due to the wide range of generic skills, and the rigour with which they are taught, training in psychology is widely accepted as providing an excellent preparation for many careers. In addition to subject skills and knowledge, graduates also develop skills in communication, numeracy, teamwork, critical thinking, computing, independent learning and many others, all of which are highly valued by employers. (QAA, 2010, p. 2)

This book, is part of the comprehensive new series, Psychology Express, that helps you achieve these aspirations. It is not a replacement for every single text, journal article, presentation and abstract you will read and review during the course of your degree programme. It is in no way a replacement for your lectures, seminars or additional reading. A top-rated assessment answer is likely to include considerable additional information and wider reading – and you are directed to some of these in this text. This text is a guide providing an overview of your course, helping you formulate your ideas, and directing your reading.

Each book within Psychology Express presents a summary coverage of the key concepts, theories and research in the field, within an explicit framework of revision. The focus throughout all of the books in the series will be on how you should approach and consider your topics in relation to assessment and exams. Various features have been included to help you build your skills and knowledge, ready for your assessments. More details of the features can be found in the guided tour for this book on page xii.

By reading and engaging with this book, you will develop your skills and knowledge base and in this way you should excel in your studies and your associated assessments.

Psychology Express: Conceptual and Historical Issues in Psychology is divided into 13 chapters and your course has probably been divided up into similar sections. However we, the series authors and editors must stress a key point: do not let the purchase, reading and engagement with the material in this text restrict your reading or your thinking. In psychology, you need to be aware of the wider literature and how it interrelates and how authors and thinkers have criticised and developed the arguments of others. So even if an essay asks you about one particular topic, you need to draw on similar issues raised in other areas of psychology. There are, of course, some similar themes that run throughout the material covered in this text, but you can learn from the other areas of psychology covered in the other texts in this series as well as from material presented elsewhere.

We hope you enjoy this text and the others in the Psychology Express series, which cover the complete knowledge base of psychology:

- *Biological Psychology* (Emma Preece): covering the biological basis of behaviour, hormones and behaviour, sleeping and dreaming, and psychological abnormalities.

- *Cognitive Psychology* (Jonathan Ling and Jonathan Catling): including key material on perception, learning, memory, thinking and language.

- *Developmental Psychology* (Penney Upton): from pre-natal development through to old age, the development of individuals is considered. Childhood, adolescence and lifespan development are all covered.

- *Personality and Individual Differences* (Terry Butler): normal and abnormal personality, psychological testing, intelligence, emotion and motivation are all covered in this book.

- *Social Psychology* (Jenny Mercer and Debbie Clayton): covering all the key topics in Social Psychology including attributions, attitudes, group relations, close relationships and critical social psychology.

- *Statistics in Psychology* (Catherine Steele, Holly Andrews and Dominic Upton): an overview of data analysis related to psychology is presented along with why we need statistics in psychology. Descriptive and inferential statistics and both parametric and non-parametric analysis are included.

- *Research Methods in Psychology* (Steve Jones and Mark Forshaw): research design, experimental methods, discussion of qualitative and quantitative methods and ethics are all presented in this text.

- *Conceptual and Historical Issues in Psychology* (Brian M. Hughes): the foundations of psychology and its development from a mere interest into a scientific discipline. The key conceptual issues of current-day psychology are also presented.

This book, and the other companion volumes in this series, should cover all your study needs (there will also be further guidance on the website). It will, obviously, need to be supplemented with further reading and this text directs you towards suitable sources. Hopefully, quite a bit of what you read here you will already have come across and the text will act as a jolt to set your mind at rest – you do know the material in depth. Overall, we hope that you find this book useful and informative as a guide for both your study now and in your future as a successful psychology graduate.

Revision note

- *Use evidence based on your reading, not on anecdotes or your 'common sense'.*
- *Show the examiner you know your material in depth – use your additional reading wisely.*
- *Remember to draw on a number of different sources: there is rarely one 'correct' answer to any psychological problem.*
- *Base your conclusions on research-based evidence.*

Explore the accompanying website at www.pearsoned.co.uk/psychologyexpress
→ Prepare more effectively for exams and assignments using the answer guidelines for questions from this chapter.
→ Test your knowledge using multiple choice questions and flashcards.
→ Improve your essay skills by exploring the You be the marker exercises.

Guided tour

→ Understand key concepts quickly

Start to plan your revision using the **Topic maps**.

Grasp **Key terms** quickly using the handy definitions. Use the flashcards online to test yourself.

→ Revise effectively

KEY STUDY

Little Albert

Watson famously demonstrated classical conditioning in an experiment involving an eight-month-old boy, referred to by the pseudonym Little Albert. Together with his student Rosalie Rayner (1899–1936), Watson succeeded in conditioning Albert to become fearful of a white rat by consistently presenting loud noises when the rat was present (Watson & Rayner, 1920). As the loud noises were frightening to Albert, they served as a powerful UCS. Watson also demonstrated stimulus generalisation by showing Albert to have developed negative reactions to other objects similar in appearance to the white rat, including Watson's own white hair. Although the study provided an effective demonstration of conditioning, it was also controversial. For one thing, Watson and Rayner did not seek to decondition Little Albert after the study had concluded. While extinction may well have occurred eventually, it is also possible that Albert's new phobias persisted following the experiment. By the standard of today's conventions, as formulated by professional bodies and universities, such procedures for research with a small child would be deemed unethical.

Source: Watson, J. B., & Rayner, R. (1920). Conditioned emotional reactions. *Journal of Experimental Psychology*, 3, 1–14.

61

Quickly remind yourself of the **Key studies** using the special boxes in the text.

Test your knowledge

3.3 What were the strengths and weaknesses of Wundt's approach to psychology?

3.4 How did psychophysics contribute to psychology's standing as a laboratory-based university discipline?

Answers to these questions can be found on the companion website at: www.pearsoned.co.uk/psychologyexpress

Prepare for upcoming exams and tests using the **Test your knowledge** and **Sample question** features.

Compare your responses with the **Answer guidelines** in the text and on the website.

Answer guidelines

✱ *Sample question*   Essay

Critically evaluate the impact of technology on behavioural neuroscience and behavioural genetics.

Approaching the question

The essay question asks for a critical evaluation, which requires a consideration of both the strengths and weaknesses of the proposition. It also refers to both behavioural neuroscience and behavioural genetics, and so both fields should be discussed.

Important points to include

As a critical evaluation is called for, it will be important to include both the strengths and weaknesses associated with the contribution of technology to these fields. While the strengths are frequently discussed (tending to involve

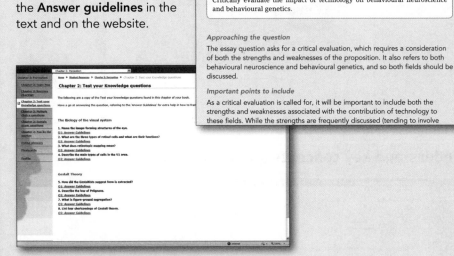

→ Make your answers stand out

Use the **Critical focus** boxes to impress your examiner with your deep and critical understanding.

CRITICAL FOCUS

The Turing test

Alan Turing made a number of important contributions to mathematics, psychology and computing. He also presented a number of highly influential concepts in the philosophy of knowledge and, in particular, the philosophy surrounding the notion of artificial intelligence. One of his most famous philosophical ideas relates to a hypothetical test that might be used to identify whether a machine has successfully demonstrated intelligence. This procedure, originally proposed in 1950, is now known as the Turing test. But simply, the Turing test involves a machine participating in a three-way conversation

Make your answer stand out

In discussing the role of computer metaphors during the history of cognitive psychology, it would be interesting to trace the development of actual computers in society during this time and to consider whether such technological developments influenced the ways in which computer metaphors were discussed and understood. For example, in Turing's time, computers were largely hypothetical devices, while today large numbers of people have personal computers in their own homes. As such, over time, cognitive psychologist's metaphors may have become skewed by practical developments in how publicly available computers have been designed. Try to think of examples of how modern computers differ from older ones, especially in terms of how users interact with them (for example, today's computers present information using

Go into the exam with confidence using the handy tips to **make your answer stand out**.

Guided tour of the companion website

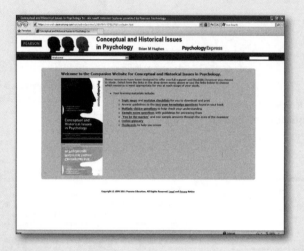

→ Understand key concepts quickly

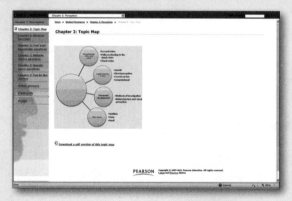

Printable versions of the **Topic maps** give an overview of the subject and help you plan your revision.

Test yourself on key definitions with the online **Flashcards**.

→ Revise effectively

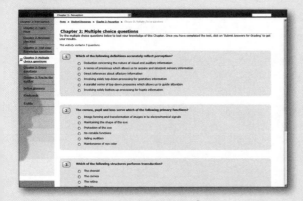

Check your understanding and practise for exams with the **Multiple choice questions**.

→ Make your answers stand out

Evaluate sample exam answers in the **You be the marker** exercises and understand how and why an examiner awards marks.

Put your skills into practice with the **Sample exam questions**, then check your answers with the guidelines.

All this and more can be found at
www.pearsoned.co.uk/psychologyexpress

Explaining people: theoretical psychology throughout the ages

1

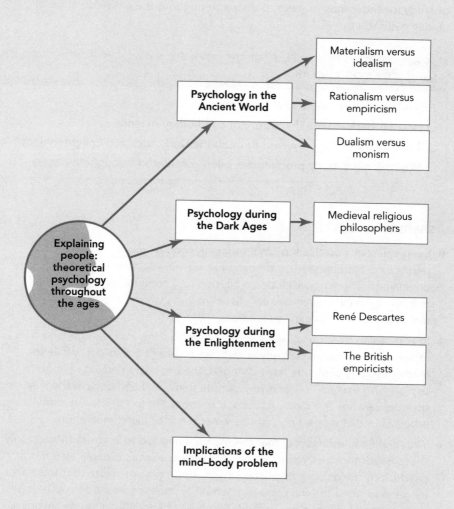

A printable version of this topic map is available from
www.pearsoned.co.uk/psychologyexpress

Introduction

History can tell us as much about the present and the future as it can about the past. By showing us how people have traditionally attempted to explain each other's behaviour, the history of psychology helps us appreciate the limits of the discipline as it is currently studied and practised. It also helps us consider the strengths and weaknesses of contemporary psychology, as well as its potential. While in many senses modern scientific psychology can be said to have emerged with the arrival of experimental research in the 19th century, a historical perspective suggests that psychology has been contemplated as a formal field of study for thousands of years, perhaps throughout the entire duration of human civilisation.

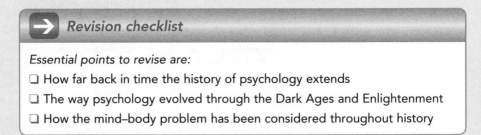

Revision checklist

Essential points to revise are:

❑ How far back in time the history of psychology extends
❑ The way psychology evolved through the Dark Ages and Enlightenment
❑ How the mind–body problem has been considered throughout history

Assessment advice

- Essay questions on this topic will ordinarily require you to consider how psychology has changed, and how it has remained unchanged from its very beginnings. There may well be an allusion to a common perception that psychology is exclusively a 'new' discipline, one which emerged along with the laboratory-based experimentalists in the 19th century.

- In addressing such questions, it is important to show insight regarding the long history of human curiosity about one another's behaviour. While the methodologies of inquiry have changed, the underlying agenda (i.e. to explore and explain how and why people think, feel and behave the way they do) remains the same. As such, it is important to refer to the formal scholarship that existed prior to the emergence of experimentation.

- You might sometimes feel that the material needed to address satisfactorily these issues requires you to be familiar with academic disciplines other than psychology, fields such as philosophy or anthropology. Note that this tells us some important things about psychology itself: namely that psychology is an extremely wide-ranging field, that it has been influenced by several other disciplines, and that it addresses questions that are of wide interest to non-psychologists.

Sample question

Could you answer this question? Below is a typical essay question that could arise on this topic.

> *Sample question* Essay
>
> Should the history of psychology include periods prior to the 19th century? Why?

Guidelines on answering this question are included at the end of this chapter, whilst further guidance on tackling other exam questions can be found on the companion website at: **www.pearsoned.co.uk/psychologyexpress**

Psychology in the Ancient World

In formal academic contexts, psychology refers to the systematic study of human (or animal) thoughts, feelings and behaviour. The word 'psychology' itself did not appear in English-language texts until the 17th century, shortly after the Latin equivalent *psychologia* had first appeared in 1590. However, it would be wrong to suggest that human (or animal) thoughts, feelings and behaviour were not studied systematically until this time. In fact, it is now typically noted that the subject matter of psychology was studied systematically by philosophers in the ancient Greek and Roman world. Ancient Greek and Roman philosophy often focused on the constitution of the universe and its contents, and introduced important distinctions that continue to be used to organise science today, such as those between 'real' and 'imaginary', 'living' and 'dead', and 'plant' and 'animal'. These philosophers were just as interested in the human mind (or spirit) and its physical properties, which led them to speculate about fundamental psychological phenomena like sensation and perception, personality, and motivation.

Key term

Ontology: a concept in philosophy that refers to the study of the nature of reality. It is concerned with explaining what reality consists of, what categories of entities exist in the universe and how they are organised, and the basis of deciding whether something can be said either to exist or to not exist. As well as with material objects, ontology is concerned with explaining the essence of such abstract entities as human thoughts and feelings. As such, to the early philosophers, questions about psychology were as much a part of ontology as were questions about biology or physics. Within philosophy, ontology is a major branch of metaphysics, the study of existence, truth and knowledge.

Several themes important to modern psychology were first explored by the ancient Greek and Roman philosophers. These included the ontological distinction between materialism (the notion that reality is grounded in physical objects, which exist independently and are available for us to perceive and think about) and idealism (the notion that reality, as we know it, consists only of our perceptions and ideas). Early philosophers such as Thales (624–545 BCE), and Parmenides (504–456 BCE) were materialists, while later figures such as Plato (429–347 BCE) and Aristotle (384–322 BCE) were idealists. Another important distinction was between rationalism, the position that knowledge is best produced by reasoning, and empiricism, the position that knowledge is best produced by experiences and observations. While Plato was a rationalist, his student Aristotle was more of an empiricist, and emphasised the importance of observation in knowledge production.

CRITICAL FOCUS

Empiricism

Empiricism refers to the notion that all knowledge is rooted in observation and experience. Within philosophy, it is an example of a 'theory of knowledge'. It emphasises the importance of evidence to support assertions because it suggests that such evidence should always be available (at least theoretically). Perhaps one way to appreciate the nature of empiricism is to compare it with its alternative, the notion that knowledge can be produced entirely from reason alone independently of any experience or observations about the world (or, alternatively, that innate ideas exist). Empiricism discounts such possibilities. The principle of empiricism is fundamental to the scientific method, which insists that all assertions be objectively testable against observations of the natural world. It is worth noting that in the context of science (and especially psychology) empiricism is often confused with the idea that research requires scientists to quantify their observations. This is flawed because not all observations need (or allow) quantification. While quantification is essential to science, the term 'empiricism' refers merely to the reliance on objective observation and the avoidance of intuition.

The way in which the ancient Greek and Roman philosophers considered psychology is often encapsulated in a field of philosophy known as philosophy of mind. For example, several of the materialists, most prominently Parmenides, applied their views about the nature of the universe to argue that that the mind is a non-independent by-product of the physical body. In contrast, both Plato and Aristotle argued extensively that human psychological function existed independently of physiological processes. Such views relate to a conceptual debate that has continued throughout the entire history of psychology, and which has been referred to as the mind–body problem. This refers to the question of whether the mind and the body are separate entities (the position known as dualism) or whether they are intrinsically one and the same entity (the position of monism).

These philosophers fall within the so-called 'Western tradition' of philosophy. Today, many authorities also point to the fact that consideration of psychological subjects was widespread in the ancient philosophical traditions in China, India and Egypt, and across the Islamic world.

Example of ancient Egyptian consideration of psychology

As well as within the Western philosophical tradition, psychological subject matter was considered by thinkers in other cultures. Some historians argue that ancient Egyptian culture was far better informed about some aspects of psychology than ancient Greek and Roman culture. One historical artefact, known as the Edwin Smith Papyrus, is particularly informative in this regard. This document comprises a lengthy written description of medical knowledge in Egypt dating back to around 1600 BCE. The document was written to aid Egyptian physicians in treating wounds suffered by soldiers in the battlefield. It describes the structure and function of the human brain with surprising accuracy, identifying the nature of meningeal arteries and the role of cerebrospinal fluid. The Edwin Smith Papyrus (named after the American antiquities collector who brought it to public attention) reveals that the ancient Egyptians possessed a far more advanced knowledge of the human brain than their European counterparts. While the papyrus itself was written some 1000 years prior to the life of Hippocrates, it is argued by some Egyptologists that the text was derived from previous documents dating back another 1000 years.

Test your knowledge

1.1 How is the distinction between materialism and idealism related to that between rationalism and empiricism?

1.2 What main difference characterised the epistemological approaches of Plato and Aristotle?

Answers to these questions can be found on the companion website at:
www.pearsoned.co.uk/psychologyexpress

? Sample question   Essay

Compare and contrast the concerns of the ancient Greek and Roman philosophers with those of contemporary psychologists.

Psychology during the Dark Ages

The 'Dark Ages' refers to the period of Western history that followed the fall of the Roman Empire (around 400 CE) and lasted until around the 16th century. The term was originally used to imply that this period was blighted by intellectual stagnation or 'darkness', although this view is now increasingly challenged by historians as the accomplishments of this period become better appreciated. It is true, however, that for various economic and social reasons, the Dark Ages were associated with less contemporaneously recorded history than the periods before or afterward. Developments in psychological thought during this time were often intertwined with religious philosophy, especially within Christian culture. Such debates often concerned the nature of virtue and its relationship to cognition.

For example, in Christian philosophy, Augustine (354–430 CE), John the Irishman (815–877 CE) and Pierre Abélard (1079–1142 CE) presented arguments to support their assertion that human morality stemmed from knowledge, and immorality from ignorance. In later centuries, figures such as Bonaventure (1221–1274 CE), Aquinas (1225–1274 CE), John Duns Scotus (1266–1308 CE) and William of Ockham (1288–1348 CE) continued to debate the nature of conscience and, specifically, whether human morality resulted from innate drives or intellectual choices. In addition, these theological philosophers each presented several arguments in favour of dualism, as did philosophers from the Islamic tradition, such as Avicenna (980–1037 CE), and from the Jewish tradition, such as Maimonides (1135–1204 CE).

It is important to note that the works of these thinkers are important to psychology because they presented more than just opinions about human behaviour; they attempted to use reason, argument and observation to formulate defensible explanations. However, it is certainly also true that their arguments rested largely on arbitrary assumptions furnished by their religion, such as the assumption that all humans were created in the image of a supreme deity.

Test your knowledge

1.3 How did religious philosophers explain the relationship between morality and knowledge?

1.4 In general, were the theological philosophers of the Dark Ages monists or dualists?

Answers to these questions can be found on the companion website at: www.pearsoned.co.uk/psychologyexpress

 Sample question   *Essay*

Is it fair to argue that the psychology of medieval philosophy was an attempt to use reason to justify mysticism?

Psychology during the Enlightenment

The 'Enlightenment' refers to that period of Western history that is broadly defined as beginning around the 16th century, with the publication of several important scientific works in Europe, and lasting until the start of the 19th century. This was a period when reason, as opposed to religion, began to be promoted as the fundamental basis for determining the truth of assertions. It is also considered to be the period that saw the birth of modern science. Given that psychology itself was very much concerned with the notion of 'reason', the Enlightenment marked a dramatic departure in how psychological subject matter was dealt with by scholars.

René Descartes (1596–1650 CE) is often described as the first Enlightenment philosopher, and is properly acknowledged as a pioneer of modern psychology (while also being an important mathematician, physicist and physiologist). As well as promoting a form of science that championed scepticism and methodological rigour, Descartes became important in psychology for his philosophical work on the mind–body problem. After studying the physiology of animals, he concluded that it was possible for organisms to function without a mind. In addition, on the basis that human perceptions can always be doubted, but that it requires a mind to do the doubting, he concluded that thought and physiology must be separate. He famously encapsulated this conclusion with the Latin phrase 'Cogito ergo sum' (or 'I think, therefore I am'). While Descartes was unambiguously a dualist, he argued that the mind and body interacted in a truly physical sense, suggesting that the pineal gland in the brain was the very site of this interaction.

 Sample question   *Problem-based learning*

Descartes' argument proposes that reflecting on one's thoughts proves that one exists. However, this is based on an assumption that all thinking things must exist. Is this a convincing assumption? Are there any examples of things that think but which do not exist independently? Consider the concept of 'groupthink' as it is studied by social psychologists. If a group of people can produce a decision that no one individual within the group would have produced on their own, does this suggest that there then exists some kind of group-level thinking entity other than the individual group-members themselves?

Other important Enlightenment philosophers included the British empiricists, such as Thomas Hobbes (1588–1679 CE), John Locke (1632–1704 CE) and David Hume (1711–1776 CE), who presented various arguments to the effect that knowledge arises from sensory experience rather than from innate thoughts. Such arguments stood in favour of monism. In continental Europe, many more Enlightenment philosophers produced work of relevance to modern psychology. For example, in Holland, Baruch Spinoza (1632–1677 CE) argued that human behaviour followed the laws of nature and so could be studied scientifically, as well as defending monism. Meanwhile in Germany, Gottfried Leibniz (1646–1716 CE), also a monist, developed extensive theories of language, perception and the unconscious mind. These philosophers were considered important to psychology, not only for having established new perspectives on the nature and function of the human mind, but also for promoting independent thinking and logical analysis, and for having established the basis for the scientific study of human thoughts, feelings and behaviour.

Test your knowledge

1.5 How did Descartes conclude that the mind existed independently of perceptions?

1.6 In what major way did the views of Descartes differ from those of the British empiricists, such as Locke?

Answers to these questions can be found on the companion website at: **www.pearsoned.co.uk/psychologyexpress**

 Sample question Essay

Why do you think scientific enlightenment would encourage monism?

Implications of the mind–body problem

We have seen that the mind–body problem presented one of the key conceptual debates in the psychology of the historical philosophers. Indeed, the mind–body problem is an excellent example of a debate from the history of psychology that highlights a conceptual issue that remains of wide philosophical concern and cultural importance today.

The mind–body problem remains controversial because of its implications for widely held cultural and religious belief systems. In broad terms, the dualist position is compatible with the view that the human spirit can continue to exist after a person has died, which reflects a key assumption of most formal religions.

On the other hand, a strictly monist position would seem to imply that, upon death, human beings essentially cease to exist. Monism argues that psychological life is itself a secondary product of physiological function: once physiological death occurs, a person's psychological existence comes to an end.

KEY STUDY

The folk psychology of souls

The monist position that psychological life is a by-product of physiological function raises several questions about why so many people develop strong feelings that personal 'life' continues after physical death; in other words, the belief that there exists an afterlife in which physically deceased persons continue to exist in spiritual form. Bering (2006) presented a major overview of research studies examining the psychological basis for this popular form of mind–body dualism. In one study (Bering & Bjorklund, 2004), children and adults were presented with a puppet show in which a mouse was killed and eaten by an alligator, and then asked a series of questions by the researchers. In their responses, young children were found to strongly demonstrate 'common sense dualism': they agreed that biological states such as hunger or tiredness no longer applied to the dead mouse, but they also agreed that the mouse was still able to 'feel' hungry or tired. The researchers found that older children and adults were less likely to agree that the (dead) mouse was capable of such psychological experiences. The pattern of findings was surprising because it implied that young children started out with these beliefs and then gradually lost them over time: this contradicts a commonly held view that belief in an afterlife is acquired by children through exposure to religious ideas in culture. Instead, it suggests that belief in an afterlife might be the default cognitive stance for human beings in general (perhaps relating to the practical limits of human cognition), rather than being solely the result of a particular type of upbringing.

Source: Bering, J. M. (2006). The folk psychology of souls. *Behavioral and Brain Sciences*, 29, 453–498.

Bering, J. M., & Bjorklund, D. F. (2004). The natural emergence of reasoning about the afterlife as a developmental regularity. *Developmental Psychology*, 40, 217–233.

Historians now argue that the very fact that monism runs counter to religious views regarding the immortality of human spirits has served, at various times, to influence the history of psychology. Firstly, it is likely that, for long periods of academic history, competing philosophical arguments were often promoted for theological rather than scholarly reasons. In this regard, it is important to note that throughout Europe and North America, colleges and universities were predominantly run as seminaries by religious orders right up until the 19th century. Many philosophers themselves held profoundly religious views which they were happy to accept as absolute truths, which in turn influenced the degree to which they attached credibility to monist and dualist arguments. Secondly, it is likely that some philosophers held monist views in private but presented dualist views in public, in order to conform to the pressures of wider society, their peers or their employers. Thirdly, even when monist arguments were sufficiently accepted by philosophers to warrant wide dissemination, the public at large were often very sceptical about them because they clashed with their own religious beliefs.

Some commentators argue that the mind–body problem still affects psychology today, and will continue to do so into the future. Many modern criticisms of psychological research can be traced to concerns about its monist implications. For example, research in cognitive neuroscience clearly demonstrates that a major component of psychological experience is directly consequential to physiological functioning within the brain, so much so that it is very difficult to imagine how psychological experience could possibly occur without living brain tissue. Because of a strong belief in an afterlife, some critics dismiss this research, and its therapeutic implications, as being inherently unreliable. Similarly, some members of the public are wary about psychology and the motivations of psychological researchers because they interpret such research as being hostile to religious belief. In turn, the general public might then dismiss recommendations arising from psychological research in other areas, on the grounds that the discipline as a whole cannot be trusted.

As such, the mind–body problem illustrates how familiarity with the history of psychology, and consideration of how conceptual debates have progressed throughout this history, can help shed light on contemporary debates and on psychology's possible future.

Test your knowledge

1.7 How do the implications of monism and dualism relate to commonly held religious views about the immortality of human personhood?

1.8 Does research linking brain activity and human cognition imply dualism more than monism, or vice versa? Why?

Answers to these questions can be found on the companion website at: **www.pearsoned.co.uk/psychologyexpress**

? Sample question   Essay

Has the mind–body problem inhibited or accelerated the success of psychology?

Chapter summary – pulling it all together

→ Can you tick all the points from the revision checklist at the beginning of this chapter?

→ Attempt the sample question from the beginning of this chapter using the answer guidelines below.

→ Go to the companion website at www.pearsoned.co.uk/psychologyexpress to access more revision support online, including interactive quizzes, flashcards, You be the marker exercises as well as answer guidance for the Test your knowledge and Sample questions from this chapter.

Further reading for Chapter 1

Topic	Key reading
Psychology through time	Green, C. D. (2009). *Where did experimental psychology come from? An impossibly brief history of the origins of experimental psychology, from Aristotle to Wundt* [Video]. Retrieved from http://www.youtube.com/watch?v=P81vx75JEaA
Aristotelian psychology	Aristotle (350 BC, trans. T. Bushnell). On the soul. In D. C. Stevenson (Ed.), *The Internet classics archive*. Retrieved from http://classics.mit.edu/Aristotle/soul.mb.txt
Teleology	Howard, G. S. (1990). Aristotle, teleology, and modern psychology. *Theoretical & Philosophical Psychology, 10*, 31–38.
Medieval psychology	Kemp, S. (1998). Medieval theories of mental representation. *History of Psychology, 1*, 275–288.
Ancient psychologists	Brysbaert, M., & Rastle, K. (2009). *Historical and conceptual issues in psychology*. London: Pearson.
Descartes	Fancher, R. E. (1996). *Pioneers of psychology*, (3rd edition). New York: Norton.
Monism and dualism	Bunge, M. (2007). Blushing and the philosophy of mind. *Journal of Physiology, 101*, 247–256.

Answer guidelines

✳ *Sample question* *Essay*

Should the history of psychology include periods prior to the 19th century? Why?

Approaching the question

The essay title is in two parts, although it should be clear that the latter part ('Why?') is its main focus.

Important points to include

You should note that, in order to address whether periods prior to the 19th century should be included in the history of psychology, an examination of history as a whole is important. In other words, you should describe what is positive about studying history, and then use this rationale to assess whether including periods prior to the 19th century contributes to such positive outcomes. Arguing simply that the periods prior to the 19th century were interesting and colourful, rather than truly informative, would be a much weaker strategy.

While you are free to argue the opposite, it is probably more straightforward to accept the proposition presented by the first part of the essay question. This then reduces your task to one of highlighting how the issues covered in this chapter are informative to us today. You should trace the history from the ancient Greek and Roman philosophers, through the Dark Ages, and into the Enlightenment. Omitting or glossing over one of these periods would be weak, because the essay question implies that all periods prior to the 19th century should be considered.

Make your answer stand out

The following two strategies should help make your answer stand out. The first strategy would be to incorporate global perspectives wherever possible, rather than confining your account to an Anglo-Saxon or Eurocentric context. You should at least allude to the ancient Egyptians and Babylonians, as well as the ancient Greeks and Romans, and to non-Christian as well as Christian philosophers from the Dark Ages. The second strategy is to emphasise both the subject matter and practice of scientific psychology. Most students will give comprehensive explanations of how perception, motivation and cognition were conceptualised by the philosophers discussed in this chapter. However, fewer students will show how their use of rigour, reason and (in many cases) empiricism set the scene for the scientific methods that underlie psychology today. Therefore, by explaining how this is the case, you can make your answer stand out.

Explore the accompanying website at www.pearsoned.co.uk/psychologyexpress

→ Prepare more effectively for exams and assignments using the answer guidelines for questions from this chapter.

→ Test your knowledge using multiple choice questions and flashcards.

→ Improve your essay skills by exploring the You be the marker exercises.

Notes

Ways of knowing: the scientific method and its alternatives

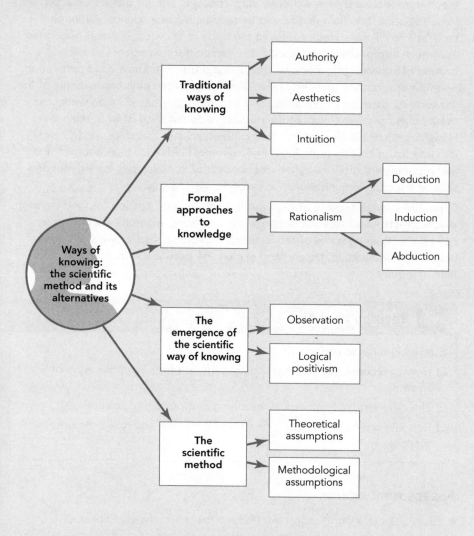

A printable version of this topic map is available from
www.pearsoned.co.uk/psychologyexpress

Introduction

While the specifics vary, virtually all definitions of the term 'science' refer to a practice of generating new knowledge about the universe we live in, using systematic methods of inquiry designed to maximise objectivity, reliability and validity. Central to such methods is the gathering of observations, the minimising of bias and the testing of predictions against data. Some definitions of science require the use of experimentation, although this term is itself subject to interpretation; while other definitions emphasise the development of hypotheses, theories, models and laws, although such concepts are not universally accepted to be required for a field of study to be recognised as a science. Although the term 'science' is also used to refer to the body of knowledge that is generated using such approaches, it is important to remember that science is more a *process* of knowledge generation than it is a *product* of knowledge generation. Scientific approaches have long been used to study the physical elements of the universe, its chemical composition, and its biologically-based inhabitants, and these fields constitute much of the popular understanding of what science is. However, science is also used to study subject matter that does not fit neatly into physics, chemistry or biology. For example, fields such as economics and anthropology are often classified as sciences (by, for example, publicly-funded science advocacy organisations), as indeed is psychology.

Often the scientific nature of psychology can generate tension for (and among) psychologists when scientific findings clash with folk wisdoms about human nature. Considering some of the historical and conceptual aspects of science helps us to understand, defend and exploit the potential of psychology as a field of inquiry.

> → *Revision checklist*
>
> *Essential points to revise are:*
> ❏ How traditional ways of knowing are different from scientific ways of knowing
> ❏ The different types of logical reasoning that pertain to science
> ❏ How the scientific method is described in theory, and how it operates in practice

Assessment advice

- Essay questions on this topic are likely to focus on how scientific methods differ from non-scientific ones. The comparison between the scientific and the non-scientific may relate to historical developments of ideas (e.g. how modern understandings of the solar system differ from older theories) or it may be based on contemporary philosophical disputes (e.g. how scientific explanations of the origins of the universe differ from religious ones). When addressing such questions, it is important to keep in mind the two following issues.

- Firstly, science is a 'process' rather than a 'product'; this means that science represents a philosophical orientation toward the definition and accumulation of knowledge, rather than the sum output of accumulated knowledge itself. This is why we refer to science as a 'way of knowing'. Science is frequently stereotyped in terms of its (purported) superficial characteristics, such as is encapsulated images of scientists in white coats using microscopes to examine specimens in laboratories. However, the meaning of the term *science* does not refer to the appearance of scientists, their equipment or their workplaces. Instead, the term *science* refers to the way scientists consider and value evidence, in terms of its objectivity, reliability, validity and so on.

- The second important issue to bear in mind when addressing this topic relates to the function of science. Science can tell us much about what happens in the universe, but it does not have (or claim to have) the capacity to tell us either why these things happen or whether they should happen. In other words, science does not address moral questions, and it is unlikely that ethical disputes can be directly resolved through scientific research. This is important because detractors of science often raise criticisms relating to the moral implications of scientific research.

- However, while such criticisms might be important to consider in terms of how scientific knowledge is used in contemporary society, they do not have a bearing on whether the knowledge generated by science is accurate or inaccurate.

Sample question

Could you answer this question? Below is a typical essay question that could arise on this topic.

 Sample question   *Essay*

'Despite the intricacies of the scientific method, the insights gained by scientific research in psychology are ultimately no more valuable than folk wisdom handed down by human communities through the millennia.' Discuss.

Guidelines on answering this question are included at the end of this chapter, whilst further guidance on tackling other exam questions can be found on the companion website at: **www.pearsoned.co.uk/psychologyexpress**

Traditional ways of knowing

When we think about how 'knowledge' is produced and then shared, it is useful to consider two particular contexts. Firstly, we can consider how individuals generate knowledge in their own minds over the course of their lives, such as when they develop an understanding of their families, their communities and the functioning of their immediate environment. Secondly, we can consider how large groups of people develop collective knowledge about conceptual issues, such as nature. This can include the ways academic scholars use systematic methods to investigate problems and formulate evidence-based solutions. While it is tempting to assume that most of the formal information we encounter about the world falls into the latter category, and so is produced in some kind of objective and reliable fashion, it is worth looking also at some of the other ways in which information can be generated and transmitted. Throughout history, we see that such methods are often less objective or reliable than we might hope.

One of the most influential sources of knowledge is authority. This is when we come to believe something because it was told to us by someone we consider to be a source of reliable information. At the level of the individual, knowledge derived from authorities can often be very important. For example, children acquire lots of important knowledge about their environments by believing things their parents tell them. In this sense, in biological terms, trusting in authorities can be viewed as an important survival skill. Similarly, scholars build an understanding of their specific fields by comprehensively studying the works of other specialists. Indeed, it is hard to imagine how human beings could realistically function without the facility to acquire huge amounts of second-hand knowledge from other people.

The problem with authority-based knowledge is that it is difficult to be sure when a particular source is in fact truly authoritative. In the history of science there have been numerous instances where conventional knowledge handed down by authority figures was later shown to be unreliable. Often, perhaps because of the social dynamics that affords authority figures status in the first place, such beliefs have been vigorously defended even after being objectively disproved. The most commonly cited examples of this relate to the scientific knowledge inherent in traditional religious worldviews, such as the Christian teaching that the sun orbits the Earth (the refutation of which led to the excommunication of the astronomer Galileo by the Catholic Church). In summary, as a way of knowing, reliance on authorities can be useful, but there is nothing inherent in authority that guarantees reliability.

Other traditional ways in which assertions become popularly believed relate to the extent to which they are attractive or satisfying to audiences. This includes the extent to which assertions are aesthetically pleasing, consistent with other beliefs or conform with intuitions. Again, this can be at the level of individuals or of society as a whole. It can also be noted that these traditional ways of knowing often interact with or corroborate each other. For example, an assertion by a respected authority might be considered more believable if it is compatible with a listener's other beliefs about the nature of the universe.

The main shortcoming of traditional ways of knowing is that they do not incorporate ways of checking the accuracy of what is claimed to be known. Whereas a social convention advising people to wash food before eating it might be based on accurate beliefs about what causes food poisoning, another social convention that directs people to shun members of a particular caste might be based on false beliefs about race and biology. As such, while scholars throughout history were quite successful in developing an understanding of the world around them, a good deal of the information they produced was misleading. This led many to focus specifically on the nature of objective, valid and reliable information, and how it might be most effectively produced.

Test your knowledge

2.1 In the context of knowledge transmission in human societies, what is meant by the term 'authority'?

2.2 What are the main shortcomings of traditional epistemologies?

Answers to these questions can be found on the companion website at: **www.pearsoned.co.uk/psychologyexpress**

 Sample question *Essay*

If authority is ultimately an unreliable source of knowledge, why is reliance on authority so prevalent?

Formal approaches to knowledge generation

A more formal way of knowing is encapsulated by the notion of rationalism. This refers to the process of demonstrating or determining the truth of an assertion by evaluating the logic of its underlying arguments. Some types of assertion are intrinsically true, and are known as axioms. An example of an axiom is the assertion that one plus one equals two. Other assertions are so well supported by our experiences that we are likely to consider them to be just as true as axioms, such as the assertion that the Earth is round. In science, assertions of knowledge are likely to be constructed from multiple smaller assertions known as premises, combinations of which constitute arguments. If we can establish that such arguments are sound and that their premises are valid, then we can conclude that the assertion itself is likely to be true and deem the associated knowledge to be reliable.

The use of logical reasoning to establish new knowledge has itself been studied for thousands of years. Further, because it relates to the way people think about information and make sense of their environments, it is inherently bound up with the field of psychology (in particular, with cognitive psychology). While there are many types of reasoning available, they tend to fall into three major categories: deduction, induction and abduction.

Deduction refers to the combination of premises of successively lessening generality to produce an irrefutably true conclusion. An example is the assertion that because all men are mortal, and because Socrates is a man, it can be concluded that Socrates is mortal. Deductive reasoning involves generalising from the broad-ranging (e.g. 'all men') to the specific (e.g. 'a man').

Induction refers to the combination of premises concerning samples from a larger group, the identification of a pattern across the premises, and a conclusion about the larger group that assumes that the pattern will continue. An example is the assertion that because this man is called Socrates, and because he is Greek, then it can be concluded that all Greek men are called Socrates. Inductive reasoning involves generalising from the specific (e.g. 'this man') to the broad-ranging (e.g. 'all Greek men'). The conclusion of an induction has a certain probability of being true (especially if the sample under consideration is large and representative), but is not guaranteed to be so.

Finally, abduction refers to the combination of premises about a given outcome and its possible preconditions in a way that concludes that the outcome was directly caused by those preconditions. An example is the assertion that because this man has a beard, and because some Greek men grow beards, then it can be concluded that the reason this man grew a beard is because he is Greek. The conclusion of an abduction has no particular likelihood of being true because, logically, there is always the possibility that some other preconditions (even ones heretofore unheard of in science) led to the outcome. Nonetheless, abductions are useful because, unlike deduction or induction, they can suggest new ways of explaining entities in nature and so are helpful for generating theories. Unlike abductions, deductions essentially restate what is already known, while inductions generate predictions about the future rather than explanations for the present.

Test your knowledge

2.3 What is the main difference between axiomatic assertions and empirical assertions?

2.4 Why is the concept of logical reasoning particularly important to psychology?

Answers to these questions can be found on the companion website at:
www.pearsoned.co.uk/psychologyexpress

Sample question   *Essay*

Explain the differences between induction, deduction and abduction. Which is most important for scientific reasoning, and why?

The emergence of the scientific way of knowing

The emergence of science, the idea that knowledge about our universe can be generated using systematic approaches of inquiry, occurred gradually over the course of the history of philosophy. At various times, some of the most significant figures in philosophy had emphasised methods of deduction, induction and abduction.

The development of deductive reasoning is often attributed to Plato, and its use in science is associated with figures such as Descartes and Isaac Newton (1643–1727). The development of inductive reasoning, and thus the use of selected observations to support knowledge production, can be attributed to Aristotle, with its introduction to science often associated with Francis Bacon (1561–1626). The fact that induction is not capable of guaranteeing true conclusions led to much discussion about how best to ensure that the knowledge generated would be useful. Philosophers such as David Hume (1711–1776) argued that only direct observations could be relied upon, highlighting the importance of empiricism while encouraging scepticism about generalisation from specific observations to other situations. Several philosophers sought to establish systematic methods of drawing successful conclusions from scientific observations, with contributions by William Whewell (1794–1866), Claude Bernard (1813–1878) and William Stanley Jevons (1835–1882) proving particularly influential. Later, the idea of abductive reasoning was developed and explained by philosopher Charles S. Peirce (1839–1914), who argued that abduction is fundamental to the way scientists formulate theories and hypotheses.

In the 20th century, philosophers sought to combine the practices of logical reasoning with those of empirical observation to argue that both were necessary for successful science. This approach became known as logical positivism and was particularly associated with a group of European philosophers, including Moritz Schlick (1882–1936), which became known as the 'Vienna Circle'. The main thrust of their position was that hypotheses needed to be verified by observations. However, other philosophers pointed out that such verifications could not ultimately establish the truth of an assertion. For example, the assertion that all swans are white could not be proved true by the observations of several white swans (even many millions), because there would always remain the possibility that a black swan might be observed in the future. In fact, should even one such black swan be observed, this would conclusively prove the assertion wrong, implying that falsification is more powerful than verification. This example involving swans, as well as the broader doctrine of falsificationism, was introduced by Karl Popper (1902–1994) in his 1959 book, *The Logic of Scientific Discovery*, which had a lasting impact on the practice of modern scientists. Popper was particularly concerned about the way some research traditions failed to emphasise falsification, and so constituted pseudoscience rather than science. From this position, researchers realised the importance of intentionally seeking counter-examples to their own theoretical positions, and of organising research studies in ways that deliberately seek evidence that, if presented, would support an alternative to their own favoured explanations.

 Sample question   *Problem-based learning*

Popper's position on falsification has often been criticised on the basis of its impracticality. Specifically, it is argued that when scientists encounter evidence that falsifies their predictions, it is impossible for them to determine what part of their worldview they should discard. More often than not, they respond by refining their worldview in a way that preserves their original hypothesis, albeit in a modified form. Imagine you are one of the astronomers who first noticed irregularities in the way Uranus orbited the sun. Previously, you would have believed that there were only seven planets in the solar system and that they followed paths that were predictable using Newton's laws of physics. How would you respond to the irregularities in Uranus's orbit? Would you allow yourself to conclude that Newton's laws must be wrong? In reality, astronomers retained Newton's laws and concluded instead that there must be an eighth planet. Eventually they discovered the existence of Neptune. What does their approach say about the usefulness of falsification?

Example of pseudoscience

A pseudoscience is a practice that has the superficial appearance of a science but which fails to meet the quality standards normally required of sciences. Most typically, pseudosciences will fail to adhere to the requirement that hypotheses be falsifiable, and so will make open-ended predictions that can be construed as true whatever the evidence says. Non-falsifiable hypotheses are usually phrased in ways that are vague or ambiguous. One of the most commonly described examples of a pseudoscience is astrology, which uses information about the position of celestial bodies in order to make inferences about entities on Earth. For example, an astrologer may assert that a person born on a certain day is more likely to be talented. Such a hypothesis can be considered vague because terms like 'talented' are not strictly and clearly defined. Moreover, it can be considered ambiguous because it refers to something that is 'more likely' than something else. This construction does not guarantee an outcome: the assertion will appear plausible whether or not the person turns out to be talented. Some hypotheses lack falsifiability because they are presented after the fact. For example, the astrologer may claim that people born in certain months are more talented and then offer famous historical figures as examples. Such retrospective reasoning does not *prove* the link between birth date and personal attributes (after all, it may just be the result of a series of coincidences) nor does it take account of contrary examples. Because of these problems, astrology is generally considered to be a pseudoscience. Pseudosciences are often characterised by their focus on controversial or sensationalist subjects (such as the existence of extraterrestrial or supernatural beings). However, sometimes areas of research that focus on mainstream subjects are also pseudoscientific, and some sub-fields of psychology (such as parapsychology and psychoanalysis) have frequently been accused of being pseudosciences themselves.

Test your knowledge

2.5 How is deduction related to empiricism?

2.6 Why can't verification prove an assertion?

Answers to these questions can be found on the companion website at: www.pearsoned.co.uk/psychologyexpress

 Sample question   **Essay**

Why is falsification considered to be more powerful than verification?

The scientific method

Many commentators refer to the 'scientific method' to describe the procedure used by scientists when generating scientific knowledge. Typically, the scientific method is said to involve the following sequence of steps: definition of a research question; collation of information about current understandings; formulation of hypotheses; development of procedures; gathering, analysis and interpretation of data; publication of findings; and replication. Moreover, the scientific method is often said to be characterised by certain philosophical assumptions. Theoretical assumptions include determinism, generality and systematicity, while methodological assumptions include empiricism, scepticism and experimentation.

Key term

Determinism: is the philosophical position that all events in the universe are caused by preceding events, and that nothing in the universe can happen without a cause. This idea is famous in metaphysics because of its implication that all events are, in principle, predictable. While this can be straightforward when considering basic physics (such as in Newtonian mechanics), it is often seen as complicated when applied to psychological or sociological phenomena such as cognition and behaviour.

CRITICAL FOCUS

Scepticism

In science, scepticism is the view that it is reasonable to question and/or investigate any assertion purporting to describe factual information. In this context, sceptics do not accept claims to knowledge on the basis of tradition, authority or the reputation of the claimant. Instead, knowledge is considered valid and reliable only when supported by verifiable evidence. Scepticism was central to the emergence of modern science because it emphasised the importance of doubting traditional (religious) explanations of nature. Today, scepticism is just as important to the critical evaluation of controversial claims. Despite its importance, the term 'scepticism' is often misunderstood (and misused) in two ways. Firstly, the term is sometimes taken to refer to any position that casts doubt on a common understanding, even when those understandings are very much based on empirical evidence. For example, commentators who dispute the fact that the Holocaust occurred during the Second World War describe themselves as 'sceptics', even though the volume of verifiable evidence for the Holocaust is overwhelming. In this case, people misuse the term 'sceptic' in order to attach unwarranted credibility to their controversial views. The second misuse of the term 'scepticism' occurs when it is treated as a synonym for 'cynicism'. A cynic is someone who takes a pessimistic or hopeless view of humanity. Despite the fact that such a view is completely unrelated to scepticism, some critics of science seek to imply that scepticism and cynicism are the same thing and that science necessitates a miserable view of the world. In this case, people misuse the term 'sceptic' in order to cast unwarranted aspersions on science and scientists.

CRITICAL FOCUS

Experiment

An experiment is a method of research that involves the comparison of different arrangements or procedures against one another in order to test a hypothesis. As well as the notion of comparing different outcomes, a critical aspect of experimentation is that the researcher is able to manipulate the relevant features of the different arrangements or procedures that are being compared. In scientific contexts, the simplest experiment involves the comparison of two groups of cases. Most typically, such a comparison is between a set of normative cases (known as a 'control group') and a set of target cases (known as an 'experimental group'), the latter of which undergoes some manipulated procedure that involves features pertinent to the hypothesis. Experimentation is often said to be a defining feature of the scientific method. However, many mainstream fields of science are not amenable to direct experimental research. Examples include astronomy, palaeontology, zoology, meteorology and climatology. As such, while experiments are certainly scientific and offer a highly authoritative type of empirical evidence, it would be incorrect to assert that a field *must* be able to support experimental research in order to be considered a science.

Other commentators argue that there is no one scientific method per se, and in fact that scientific knowledge generation is subject to the dynamics of mass delusion and other forms of groupthink, to cultural influences and to internal politics among researchers. In his 1962 book, *The structure of scientific revolutions*, Thomas Kuhn argued that scientists did not follow a strict Popperian approach of falsification, but instead worked loyally within a particular shared worldview (known as a 'paradigm') even after it had initially been falsified. Only after the weight of falsifying evidence proved unbearable would a paradigm be rejected, after which scientists would simply switch their allegiance to the new paradigm that would be founded to replace it (events that Kuhn called 'paradigm shifts'). Other critics raised similar concerns about the pragmatic nature of scientific practices, including arguments relating to the inherent subjectivity of individual researchers and the subjective nature of knowledge itself.

However, advocates of orthodox scientific methods have argued that such criticisms are usually based on naive misinterpretations of practices within science, overlook the probabilistic context of scientific analyses of evidence, and are logically inconsistent in using rationalistic arguments to argue for the rejection of rationalism.

Test your knowledge

2.7 What are the main steps of the scientific method?

2.8 What are the key philosophical assumptions of the scientific method?

Answers to these questions can be found on the companion website at:
www.pearsoned.co.uk/spsychologyexpress

? Sample question   Essay

To what extent are Kuhn's views on the progress of science valid in the case of psychology?

Chapter summary – pulling it all together

→ Can you tick all the points from the revision checklist at the beginning of this chapter?

→ Attempt the sample question from the beginning of this chapter using the answer guidelines below.

→ Go to the companion website at www.pearsoned.co.uk/psychologyexpress to access more revision support online, including interactive quizzes, flashcards, You be the marker exercises as well as answer guidance for the Test your knowledge and Sample questions from this chapter.

Further reading for Chapter 2

Topic	Key reading
Ways of knowing	Schick, T., Jr., & Vaughn, L. (2011). *How to think about weird things: Critical thinking for a new age*, (6th edition). Boston: McGraw-Hill.
Scientific method	Derry, G. N. (1999). *What science is and how it works*. Princeton: Princeton University Press.
Scepticism	Alcock, J. E. (1991). On the importance of methodological skepticism. *New Ideas in Psychology, 9*, 151–155.
Demarkation problem	Gefter, A. (2010). The fuzzy boundary between science and pseudoscience. *New Scientist, 206* (2761), 48–49.
Logical positivism	Rosenberg, A. (1999). The rise of logical positivism. In R. Klee (Ed.), *Scientific inquiry: Readings in the philosophy of science* (pp. 10–15). Oxford: Oxford University Press.
Abduction	Haig, B. D. (2005). An abductive theory of scientific method. *Psychological Methods, 10*, 371–388.
Falsification	Losee, J. (2005). *Theories on the scrap heap: Scientists and philosophers on the falsification, rejection, and replacement of theories*. Pittsburgh: University of Pittsburgh Press.
Popperism	Valentine, E. (1999). Popper's three worlds and attitudes to the explanatory gap. *New Ideas in Psychology, 17*, 31–39.

Answer guidelines

 Sample question   *Essay*

'Despite the intricacies of the scientific method, the insights gained by scientific research in psychology are ultimately no more valuable than folk wisdom handed down by human communities through the millennia.' Discuss.

Approaching the question

The essay instruction asks you to discuss the merits of an unattributed quotation. As such, you should consider carefully what the quotation states. This quotation involves a comparison between two entities: scientific knowledge and folk knowledge in psychology.

Important points to include

This question relates to a general principle, but also to any number of specific instances. A comprehensive answer should address both domains. That is to say, you should discuss in general terms why scientific reasoning is more reliable than folk reasoning. You should also offer some specific examples of this principle as it relates to psychological knowledge.

The overall narrative of the history of science offers an important point to make when comparing science to folk wisdom. Specifically, scientific methods emerged in human societies *precisely because* people observed significant limitations in the usefulness of everyday reasoning. Had science not succeeded in producing information that proved to be significantly more useful than folk wisdom, then it would hardly have lasted very long. Therefore, the cultural success of science, in terms of its rapid expansion and embeddedness throughout human society, can be taken as reasonable evidence that it is more productive than folk approaches.

Make your answer stand out

It might be useful to describe some of the famous psychological studies relating to logical reasoning, particularly research into cognitive heuristics. Such research has highlighted how humans can be poor judges of the accuracy of symbolic or quantitative information, and how we are prone to taking mental shortcuts when evaluating evidence informally. Another theme in this research relates to the many perceptual illusions and cognitive distortions that affect the way we remember and understand events in everyday life. Addressing the psychology of (scientific) reasoning will provide plenty of illustrations and evidence for your answer.

Explore the accompanying website at www.pearsoned.co.uk/psychologyexpress
→ Prepare more effectively for exams and assignments using the answer guidelines for questions from this chapter.
→ Test your knowledge using multiple choice questions and flashcards.
→ Improve your essay skills by exploring the You be the marker exercises.

Notes

Notes

3

From philosophy to laboratory: the arrival of empirical psychology

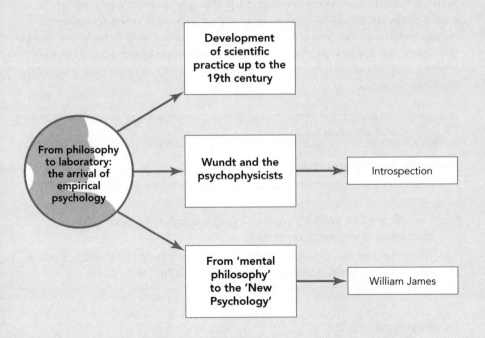

From philosophy to laboratory: the arrival of empirical psychology

Development of scientific practice up to the 19th century

Wundt and the psychophysicists → Introspection

From 'mental philosophy' to the 'New Psychology' → William James

A printable version of this topic map is available from
www.pearsoned.co.uk/psychologyexpress

Introduction

Today, psychology is highly regarded as a scientific field and as one of the most widely studied subjects in universities. However, contrary to some assumptions, psychology was not formally founded as a free-standing academic discipline at any particular time or place. Rather, the introduction of scientific approaches to the study of psychology was part of a wave of transformation that swept through academia and scholarship during the second half of the 19th century. This transformation was stimulated not only by philosophical developments relating to how knowledge was best generated and validated (leading to widespread advocacy for scientific methods), but also by social and cultural shifts, new technologies, and changes in the university system. While many historians suggest that the arrival of laboratory-based approaches to the study of psychological phenomena was a key stimulus for the emergence of psychology as an independent field, the relationship between such infrastructural developments and the status of academic psychology is essentially correlational: it can just as easily be argued that the founding of university laboratories was a consequence of the new field's emergence, rather than its cause. Either way, the use of laboratory-based scientific approaches marked a significant turning point in psychology, and fundamentally shaped the field that we know today.

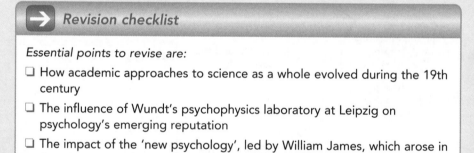

→ *Revision checklist*

Essential points to revise are:

❑ How academic approaches to science as a whole evolved during the 19th century

❑ The influence of Wundt's psychophysics laboratory at Leipzig on psychology's emerging reputation

❑ The impact of the 'new psychology', led by William James, which arose in American universities towards the end of the 19th century

Assessment advice

● Essay questions on this topic will often invite you to describe the earliest types of laboratory psychology that appeared in some European universities in the late 19th century. There may also be a requirement to describe the philosophical view of psychology that predated these developments.

● Therefore, it will be useful to be able to describe the main differences between the subject matter of psychology before and after the arrival of the laboratories.

- It is also important to remember that these changes in the behavioural sciences coincided with a period of dramatic social and cultural changes throughout the industrialised world. These changes served to transform nearly all academic disciplines, and not just psychology alone. As such, when writing about the arrival of empirical psychology, it is always desirable to contextualise it within a broader socio-cultural frame of reference.

Sample question

Could you answer this question? Below is a typical essay question that could arise on this topic.

 Sample question *Essay*

To what extent did psychophysics influence the development of modern psychology?

Guidelines on answering this question are included at the end of this chapter, whilst further guidance on tackling other exam questions can be found on the companion website at: **www.pearsoned.co.uk/psychologyexpress**

Development of scientific practice up to the 19th century

The Enlightenment had served to reinforce the notion that reason and science should supersede religion and authority as the basis for knowledge generation. Influenced by this principle, formal scholarship came to be shaped by a number of notable trends and approaches, as well as by developments in the cultural environment in which scientific work was conducted.

Theoretically, science in the 18th and 19th centuries saw an expansion of mechanistic approaches to natural phenomena. This position reflected Descartes' ideas about the physiology of humans and animals, and stated that all entities in nature followed mechanical laws by which motion was caused by physical actions and by forces such as pneumatics. This was an important alternative to animism, the view that physical entities were inherently capable of causing their own motion (perhaps with the assistance of an ethereal spirit or deity). The mechanistic approach was premised upon, and therefore fostered, an assumption that all phenomena in nature were amenable to scientific scrutiny and, indeed, some degree of measurement (i.e. the position held by empiricism). This in turn helped contribute to the expansion of computational or mathematical approaches to the study of nature, and to scientific practices of quantification. While ancient philosophers such as Aristotle had promoted the use of mathematics in order to help understand the universe, it was only after the Enlightenment that mathematical models and theories became widely used in science. The combination of computational approaches and deductive reasoning also made possible the wide use of experimentation.

Key term

Quantification: refers to the process of counting, measuring or indexing that assigns a systematic measure to an observed entity. Most often, such a measure will be expressed as a number (e.g. the number of people in a given category, or how tall a person is in centimetres). For this reason, quantitative research is often thought of as being intrinsically based on statistical evidence and analysis. However, in other situations, a quantitative measure will be presented in a non-numerical but nonetheless otherwise indexible form. For example, an entity may be assigned to one of a set of categories (e.g. whether a person is male or female). Alternatively, it may be described in terms of ordinality (e.g. whether one person is taller than another), temporality (e.g. whether one event occurred before or after another) or stability (e.g. whether a situation has changed or has remained the same). Therefore, while quantification frequently involves the use of numbers, it is untrue to state that quantitative research is reliant on numbers per se.

CRITICAL FOCUS

Socio-cultural influences on the emergence of scientific psychology

As well as developments in scholarship and academia, the arrival of an independent science of psychology was stimulated by events and conditions outside the universities in the late 19th century. Firstly, social attitudes across Europe and North America began to valorise scientific knowledge, with the scientific approach becoming recognised as the preference of educated people. Secondly, the large-scale industrialisation and urbanisation that resulted from the Industrial Revolution exposed the general population to the transformative impact of new technologies and fostered a popular view that science and technology were lucrative sources of powerful information. Thirdly, urbanisation also led to an increase in the overall secularisation of European and North American culture, and to shifts in cultural attitudes toward traditional authorities. Fourthly, some of these shifts were further influenced by catastrophic socio-political events. For example, in the United States, the devastating American Civil War (1861–1865) was followed by a notably strident social backlash in which the succeeding generation became openly critical of its predecessors. The idea of change for its own sake become fashionable among intellectuals and the general public alike, and many young American academics and scientists visited their European counterparts to see what was new in their fields.

Some historians argue that this transatlantic academic traffic helped stimulate inflation in the credentials required for credibility in university education. The fact that a PhD, or time spent at a foreign university, became the standard qualification for university professors helped accelerate the replacement of professors whose preparation for university life comprised mainly of a training for religious ministry. For psychology, this meant that professors were less likely to be biased towards religious explanations of human nature.

In terms of scientific theories, the expansion of formal scholarship during the Enlightenment generated a vast amount of new knowledge about thousands of subjects, which meant that scholars were forced to specialise their focus in order to remain at the cutting edge. This trend towards specialisation encouraged scholars to consider science not as a unitary field of knowledge, but as a collection of many different subfields, each with its own range of subject matter. Collectively, these academic trends created a fertile environment for the emergence of several scientific subdisciplines, one of which was psychology.

Test your knowledge

3.1 What major developments in scholarly thinking contributed to the emergence of empirical psychology?

3.2 How was the emergence of empirical psychology affected by world events?

Answers to these questions can be found on the companion website at: **www.pearsoned.co.uk/psychologyexpress**

? **Sample question** **Essay**

To what extent are the factors that influenced the emergence of empirical psychology in the 19th century still shaping scientific research today?

Wundt and the psychophysicists

Many historians of psychology identify Wilhelm Wundt (1832–1920) as a key figure in the development of the field, with some referring to him as the 'father of experimental psychology'. Specifically, he is often credited with establishing the first university-based psychology laboratory in Europe, at the University of Leipzig in 1879. Wundt was a medical doctor, physiologist and philosopher who studied under Hermann von Helmholtz (1821–1894) at the University of Heidelberg. Helmholtz had become famous for establishing ways of measuring the speed of signal transmission in nerves, and along with Ernst Weber (1795–1878) and Gustav Theodor Fechner (1808–1887) had developed a number of methods for quantifying various aspects of the human perceptual system. These methods, together referred to as 'psychophysics', allowed Wundt and his colleagues to design procedures for testing the limits of perception under laboratory conditions.

Key term

Psychophysics: refers to the formal study of how the physical properties of a stimulus relate to a person's psychological perception of it. Primarily, psychophysics was concerned with establishing the limits of *detection* (e.g. the quietest sound that could be heard by a human listener) and *discrimination* (e.g. the smallest difference in two sounds that would allow a listener to perceive that one was louder than the other). The psychophysicists noted that the principles by which these limits were determined were similar across different senses and different levels of sense intensity, and, significantly, that the relativities across different measurements were consistent enough to be mathematically predictable. Although such work was of limited lasting theoretical significance for psychology, the fact that it relied both on technical ingenuity and on sophisticated equipment helped it to establish psychology's reputation as a laboratory-based university discipline.

Wundt's legacy relates more to its impact on psychology's academic profile than to the findings of his research. Indeed, apart from the work on psychophysics, much of Wundt's research employed methods that were far from scientific. He was a strong advocate of introspection, a method where participants are asked to verbally report their inner thoughts and perceptions, which verged more on the ruminative approaches of philosophers than on the objectivity of the scientific method. Wundt also maintained an extensive programme of research based on the theory of recapitulation, the idea that the lifespan development of each individual human reflected the evolutionary development of the entire human species. This research involved reflecting on the history of human civilisations rather than analysing objectively gathered data.

CRITICAL FOCUS

Introspection

Introspection refers to a process of information gathering that requires people to report on their thoughts and perceptions at a given moment in time. It has been used in various scientific and therapeutic contexts as a means of gathering psychologically relevant information about people's experiences. However, it is widely acknowledged that the information gathered using introspection is highly likely to be unreliable. Firstly, many important mental processes are simply inaccessible to conscious self-observation. Secondly, it is probable that much of what people observe through introspection are the by-products and after-effects of mental processes, rather than the mental processes themselves. Thirdly, what people report as their perceptions may be distorted by sensory inaccuracy, poor memory, emotional biases or deliberate attempts to mislead. Therefore, although introspection might be used to explore ways in which people sometimes *describe* their experiences to others, it is insufficiently valid or reliable for use as primary data when attempting to research their true thoughts or emotions.

Nonetheless, Wundt's laboratory attracted a large number of international visiting scholars which ultimately helped to establish psychology's reputation across the global university system. Many of these visitors included figures who themselves made important contributions to research in psychology, including James McKeen Cattell (1860–1944), G. Stanley Hall (1844–1924), E. B. Titchener (1867–1927), Hugo Münsterberg (1863–1916) and Charles Spearman (1863–1945).

Test your knowledge

3.3 What were the strengths and weaknesses of Wundt's approach to psychology?

3.4 How did psychophysics contribute to psychology's standing as a laboratory-based university discipline?

Answers to these questions can be found on the companion website at: **www.pearsoned.co.uk/psychologyexpress**

? Sample question   Essay

How plausible is it to credit Wundt as being the 'father of experimental psychology'?

From 'mental philosophy' to the 'New Psychology'

Before the arrival of laboratory psychology, philosophy was the discipline that considered the human mind. It did so under various titles, including 'mental philosophy', 'intellectual philosophy' and 'mental science'. Such philosophy was mainly taught from a religious (Christian) perspective, which was predominant in European and North American universities up to the latter half of the 19th century. Typical university curricula of the time included subjects such as biblical studies, alongside classical languages and philosophy. Where empiricist views were presented (such as when teaching the philosophy of Francis Bacon [1561–1626]), it was usually contextualised as a way of using observations to confirm the existence of the Christian god, and to explore the laws of the universe as created by that god. A famous example was the 'natural theology' of William Paley (1743–1805), who presented the teleological argument for the existence of a deity; namely, that the intricate complexity of nature implies that it must have been designed by a supreme being. (This became better known as the 'watchmaker argument' due to Paley's comparison of the complexity of nature with that of a watch, the implication being that nature must be designed in the same way as a watchmaker designs a watch.) The mental philosophers applied a similar approach to the study of psychology. In essence, the existence of a deity was taken as an assumption, and all study was focused on explaining the godly machinations of the mind.

The laboratory-based experimental psychology that spread through universities in the late 19th century became known as the 'New Psychology'. Its starting point in the English-speaking world is often placed at the publication of *Principles of psychology* (1890) by the American psychologist and Harvard professor, William James (1842–1910). James was an enthusiastic psychologist, and offered one of the first laboratory-based experimental psychology courses in the world in 1875, some four years prior to the opening of Wundt's laboratory in Leipzig. *Principles of psychology* proved to be a highly accessible and comprehensive textbook that popularised the study of psychology for thousands of new scholars.

Example of James's teaching at Harvard

William James began teaching at Harvard University in Massachusetts in 1872, where he was originally employed as an instructor in the natural sciences. Following a period off work with illness, he introduced his first psychology class in 1875, 'The Relations between Physiology and Psychology', for which he established the world's first university-based experimental psychology laboratory. James continued to teach psychology as a formal subject at Harvard for nearly 30 years. Among his many other lecture courses were 'Physiological Psychology' (commenced in 1876), 'Psychology' (1877), 'Psychology: The Human Intellect' (1881), 'Advanced Psychology' (1881), 'Pleasure and Pain' (1890), 'Mental Pathology/Abnormal Psychology' (1893) and 'Feelings' (1895).

The new scientific approach to psychology eventually displaced the older, more theological and philosophical treatment of psychological subject matter in academia. Some early historians of psychology, such as E. G. Boring (1886–1968), reported the transition as being fraught with mutual hostility between the mental philosophers and new psychologists. However, the transition was actually far more cohesive than was first described. Contemporary records show that the older academics appreciated the merits of the new psychology, while many of the newcomers retained affection for the views of their predecessors and themselves remained quite religious.

KEY STUDY

Early scientific psychology and spiritualism

At the time that scientific psychology began to emerge in universities in the late 19th century, there was a simultaneous upsurge in public regard for phenomena and practices relating to 'spiritualism', the idea that there exists an ethereal world in which the spirits of the dead reside. Throughout the United States and Europe, thousands of people attended seances at which self-styled mediums purported to make contact with the audience's dead relatives. Such cultural spiritualism coincided with seemingly magical scientific discoveries such as the telegraph and the X-ray, which helped popularise the idea that there existed heretofore unseen realities that could be contacted using human ingenuity. It is typically assumed that university-based psychology remained aloofly distant from such cultural interests. However, it now appears that many of the first psychology departments, as well as some of the most prominent pioneer psychologists, were heavily influenced by the public's fascination with spiritualism. Coon (1992) describes historical research into American psychology between 1880 and 1920. She finds that, rather than eschewing spiritualism, American psychology actively engaged with spiritualism as a way of garnering popular interest for academic psychology. For example, William James himself developed a strong interest in the field. Coon's research found that James acquired a ouija board for the psychology laboratory at Harvard University, and that his private correspondence revealed a desire to establish a secular religion once scientific evidence for the afterlife could be established. Coon also found that the public's interest in spiritualism led to direct financial benefits for academic psychology. Several departments at prestigious universities such as Harvard, Clark and Stanford received philanthropic donations from benefactors who wrongly believed that they were supporting research into spiritual phenomena. Indeed, Coon established that in the early 20th century, the words 'psychic' and 'psychological' were considered virtually interchangeable, leading some psychologists to argue that their discipline's name should be changed altogether.

Source: Coon, D. J. (1992). Testing the limits of sense and science: American experimental psychologists combat spiritualism, 1880–1920. *American Psychologist*, 47, 143–151.

Test your knowledge

3.5 How did scholars approach psychological subject matter before the emergence of empirical psychology in the late 19th century?

3.6 How similar was the psychology of William James to that studied in universities today?

Answers to these questions can be found on the companion website at:
www.pearsoned.co.uk/psychologyexpress

 Sample question   *Essay*

To what extent were the questions of mental philosophy truly addressed by the 'New Psychology'?

Chapter summary – pulling it all together

→ Can you tick all the points from the revision checklist at the beginning of this chapter?

→ Attempt the sample question from the beginning of this chapter using the answer guidelines below.

→ Go to the companion website at www.pearsoned.co.uk/psychologyexpress to access more revision support online, including interactive quizzes, flashcards, You be the marker exercises as well as answer guidance for the Test your knowledge and Sample questions from this chapter.

Further reading for Chapter 3

Topic	Key reading
Early empirical science	King, D. B., Viney, W., & Woody, W. D. (2009). A history of psychology: Ideas and context, (4th edition). Boston: Pearson.
The 'new psychology'	Dewey, J. (1884). The new psychology. Andover Review, 2, 278–289. Uploaded to Classics in the History of Psychology by C. D. Green (2001), at http://psychclassics.yorku.ca/Dewey/newpsych.htm
William James	Coon, D. J. (2000). Salvaging the self in a world without soul: William James's The Principles of Psychology. History of Psychology, 3, 83–103.
The principles	James, W. (1890). Principles of psychology. New York: Henry Hold. Available to read online at http://www.archive.org/details/theprinciplesofp01jameuoft.
James' theory of emotion	James, W. (1894). Physical basis of emotion. Psychological Review, 1, 516–529. Republished (1994), Psychological Review, 101, 205–210.
Wundt at Leipzig	Nicolas, S., & Ferrand, L. (1999). Wundt's laboratory at Leipzig in 1891. History of Psychology, 2, 194–203.
Rejection of Wundt	Danziger, K. (1979). The positivist repudiation of Wundt. Journal of the History of the Behavioral Sciences, 15, 205–230.
Early experimenters	Stout, D. (2008). A history of modern experimental psychology: From James and Wundt to cognitive science. Canadian Psychology, 49, 179–180.

Answer guidelines

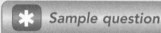

Sample question   *Essay*

To what extent did psychophysics influence the development of modern psychology?

Approaching the question

The essay title uses the format 'To what extent...' As such, you should construct your answer in a way that offers a pertinent conclusion, such as 'To a great extent', 'To a moderate extent' or 'To a small extent'. In order to achieve this, you should seek to: (a) compare the amount of modern psychology that was influenced by psychophysics with the amount that was not influenced by psychophysics; and (b) compare the contributions of psychophysics on modern psychology with those of other influences on psychology. You should finish by drawing a cogent conclusion as to the relative contribution of psychophysics.

Important points to include

When considering the first comparison, you will need to offer a broad listing of the major fields of modern psychology. These will include fields of theoretical psychology (e.g. cognitive psychology, personality theory, social psychology, developmental psychology, biological psychology, etc.) and applied psychology (clinical psychology, educational psychology, industrial psychology, etc.). You may also take the approach of describing different schools of thought within psychology (humanistic psychology, psychoanalysis, Gestalt psychology, behaviourism, etc.). Ultimately, your task will be to identify how many of these different fields were influenced by psychophysics. The second comparison will involve identifying other influences on modern psychology, such as the spread of mechanistic theories, quantification and experimentation across the sciences, the emergence of specialisation in academia, and the impact of socio-cultural events on universities.

Make your answer stand out

It might be tempting to confine your answer to a description of phenomena in psychophysics that are still studied today, along with an account of how Wundt personally tutored a large number of psychologists who went on to be internationally famous. However, on its own, such an approach will not address the 'To what extent...' element of the question. Offering a systematic analysis will present a more convincing answer. While it is important not to discount the contribution of the psychophysicists, a critical scientific approach to this question will require a balanced analysis that takes account of all the alternative perspectives.

Explore the accompanying website at www.pearsoned.co.uk/psychologyexpress

→ Prepare more effectively for exams and assignments using the answer guidelines for questions from this chapter.

→ Test your knowledge using multiple choice questions and flashcards.

→ Improve your essay skills by exploring the You be the marker exercises.

Notes

The evolution of measurement: from physiognomy to psychometrics

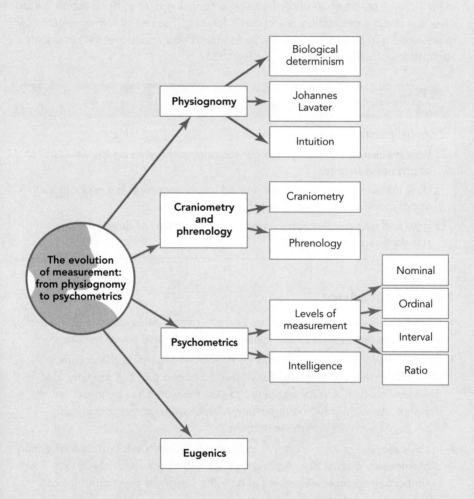

Introduction

Throughout history people have been fascinated by one another's psychological attributes and, accordingly, many artists, philosophers and other commentators have attempted to describe the human condition based on their own impressions and experiences. These sources often point to consistencies in human nature and support the view that there exists a universally observable set of human traits and characteristics. One assumption of the scientific method is that entities which are consistently observable will be amenable to some form of measurement. Simply put, the process of measurement involves estimating the magnitude or grade of an entity by using a formal system of observation, based on either direct examination or indirect inference. The use of formal systems for measurement in psychology has had a long and often controversial history, the implications of which continue to be felt today.

 Revision checklist

Essential points to revise are:
- ❏ How measurement in psychology was originally based on the assessment of physical features
- ❏ How measurement historically related to philosophical assumptions such as polygeny and biological determinism
- ❏ How and why psychometrics emerged as a system of developing standardised measurement

Assessment advice

- Essay questions on this subject are likely to relate, either directly or indirectly, to controversial aspects of the history of psychological measurement.
- Not only have there been specific controversies regarding the accuracy of measurement and the uses to which it has been put, but the very idea that human psychological attributes *can* be measures has been extensively debated. As such, it will be important to acknowledge the controversial aspects of psychological measurement.
- In this case, the study of history can be a particularly useful guide for framing contemporary discussions. Accordingly, as well as the historical details, it will be important to show awareness of how the history of psychometrics can inform current debates in useful ways.

Sample question

Could you answer this question? Below is a typical essay question that could arise on this topic.

 Sample question   *Essay*

Examine the influence of physiognomic theories on the historical development of psychology. To what extent (if any) is this influence detectable today?

Guidelines on answering this question are included at the end of this chapter, whilst further guidance on tackling other exam questions can be found on the companion website at: **www.pearsoned.co.uk/psychologyexpress**

Physiognomy

Many early attempts to apply formal measurement methods to psychological concepts relied on the principle of physiognomy. This refers to the view that a person's outward appearance reflects aspects of their inner character. Such views were recorded in some of the earliest written philosophical works, such as those by Hippocrates (460–370 BCE) and Aristotle, but it can be noted that the history of scepticism toward physiognomic claims is just as long. In essence, the idea of physiognomy rests on the theory of biological determinism, which asserts that a person's psychological make-up is dependent on various aspects of their biology.

One of the first scholars to claim there was a truly scientific basis for physiognomy was the Swiss pastor Johannes Lavater (1741–1801). Lavater wrote an extensive four-volume treatise on physiognomy focusing on how outward appearance was related to people's moral characters. He posited three aspects of human nature: the animal (indicated by features of the stomach and sexual organs); the moral (indicated by features of the upper body); and the intellect (indicated by features of the head and face). Importantly, he argued that both physical and psychological traits were passed down biologically through the generations, underlying the connection between the two. The contrary view, such as that of Georg Lichtenberg (1742–1799), was that physical traits were acquired during one's lifetime, and that the association between physical and psychological attributes resulted from the adopting of habitual expressions and postures. Lavater's work was read widely for a century after his death, but ultimately became obsolete as empirical studies consistently failed to support his ideas.

Example of the application of physiognomy

One important school of physiognomy was that of Italian criminologist Cesare Lombroso (1835–1909) who developed the field of 'anthropological criminology'. Lombroso wrote a number of manuals describing what he asserted were the physical features of different types of criminal. Scientifically, he presented explicit arguments in favour of biological determinism. He also supported the theory of atavistic criminality, which stated that criminals represented evolutionarily incomplete strains of the human species. Lombroso conducted much research in an attempt to establish empirical evidence for his views but his efforts were largely unsuccessful. In response, he resorted to adding more and more caveats to his system. His critics, such as the Briton Charles Goring (1870–1919) and the American Maurice Parmelee (1882–1969), conducted their own research and failed to find any physical differences between criminals and law-abiding citizens.

 Sample question   *Problem-based learning*

Research continues to suggest that, in general, people draw conclusions about one another's psychological attributes based on physical appearance, especially that of the face. Indeed, studies suggest that facial appearance can be a factor that influences the degree to which defendants in courts are perceived as innocent by jurors, as well as whether an individual is successful in being offered a job. Can you suggest procedures or policies that could be introduced in order to reduce the impact of such biases? Do you think it would be wise to warn assessors in advance of their likely biases in this regard, or do you think it would be preferable not to draw attention to them?

In general, respect for physiognomic theories began to evaporate once scientific research approaches were applied to their assertions. However, the work of Lavater and other physiognomists presented a strong influence on the emerging field of psychology. These writings were very widely read and proved massively popular among the general population (who were often undeterred by contradictory research). The mere idea of physiognomy became part of people's everyday approach to explaining human nature, and the device of attributing particular physical qualities to characters based on their personal attributes was regularly employed by novelists and artists. Many later psychologists, including a number of those more commonly associated with more scientific measurement approaches, would continue to recommend that important psychological information could be derived from judgements of physical appearance.

Sample question   *Problem-based learning*

The claims of physiognomy have been extensively debunked. However, many common stereotypes exist regarding the relationship between physical appearance and psychological character. Some examples include the stereotypes that suggest that overweight people are jolly and that thin people are mean. Compile a list of other modern physiognomic-type associations. Can you think of any examples of such beliefs that might actually be true, even partly? What processes might underlie such associations, and what evidence exists for them?

Test your knowledge

4.1 What are the main differences between the physiognomic approaches of Lavater and Lombroso?

4.2 How do physiognomic approaches relate to beliefs about biological determinism?

Answers to these questions can be found on the companion website at:
www.pearsoned.co.uk/psychologyexpress

 Sample question   *Essay*

Examine the influence of physiognomic theories on the historical development of psychology. To what extent (if any) is this influence detectable today?

Craniometry and phrenology

The theory of biological determinism reached something of a peak in the late 19th century for many reasons. The work of anthropologists, who had begun to travel far and wide, drew attention to the sheer variety of races and cultures that they saw in different parts of the world. The publication of Darwin's theory of evolution raised new questions about the influence of biology on behaviour. And political events, such as the emancipation of slaves in the United States, created much public concern about issues of race and ethnicity. For both political and scientific reasons, many scholars turned their attention to how the statuses of different races and classes of people might be assessed.

At Harvard University, the American scientist Samuel Morton (1799–1851) attempted to approach this issue empirically. As a devout Christian, Morton believed in the historical accuracy of the story of Noah's Ark. From this he formulated an argument that, rather than constituting a single unified species in nature, the different human races actually constituted separate unrelated species (a position known as 'polygenism'). On this basis he felt certain that some races were more valuable, and so more intelligent, than others and that this would be revealed by differences in the sizes of their brains. He used an approach known as 'craniometry' to investigate his views, involving the analysis of skulls of deceased members of different races. Morton amassed a large collection of over a thousand skulls, measured the volume of each, and then published data purporting to show ethnic differences in brain size. Perhaps unsurprisingly, he reported his own race to have the biggest brains, and the race represented by American slaves (who he felt were morally inferior) to have the smallest. However, there were at least two major problems with this work. Firstly, it has subsequently been found that Morton's published findings included a number of arithmetic miscalculations and measurement errors. Secondly, we now know that brain size is very poorly correlated with intelligence (or with any other potential indices of human worthiness).

Key term

Polygenism: refers to a controversial theory of the origins of humans, which asserts that the different human races originally emerged on separate occasions and evolved along separate lineages. The implication of polygenism is the view that each human racial group constitutes a different species. Polygenism was popularised in the 19th century by palaeontologist Louis Agassiz (1807–1873), but has since been scientifically discredited. As corroborated by modern genetics research, the more conventional biological understanding is that all humans, regardless of race, are members of the same species, a position known as 'monogenism'.

The German physician Franz Josef Gall (1758–1828) combined principles of craniometry and physiognomy to establish a related approach to psychological measurement. Gall became convinced that it was the *shape* of the brain, rather than its *size*, which held insights into a person's character. Specifically, he formulated a theory that different parts of the brain were associated with different personal attributes. From this he proposed that the relative strengths of these attributes could be established by physically examining the surface of a person's head, and inferring the sizes of each relevant brain area from the bumps detected on the corresponding section of the scalp. Gall named his system 'cranioscopy', but it later became much better known as 'phrenology' (a term coined by Gall's follower, Johann Spurzheim; 1776–1832). However, as with other physiognomic approaches, phrenology became discredited once scientific methods were used to examine its claims. For one thing, it became clear from anatomical research that the shape of the skull bore no relation to the shape of the brain underneath, meaning that the basis of Gall's system of examining people's heads was unsound. Moreover, empirical studies consistently failed to find any evidence that protuberances on the human scalp were associated with a person's psychological characteristics.

Despite losing scientific credibility in their own right, such fields did influence the way scientists approached psychological issues and left a marked impression on the wider discipline of psychology. For example, Pierre Flourens (1794–1867), who first discovered the association between different brain areas and functions such as balance and motor coordination, was originally commissioned to conduct his research in order to deal with the controversies surrounding phrenology. Similarly, researchers such as Jean-Baptiste Bouillaud (1796–1881), who was a supporter of phrenology, and Paul Broca (1824–1880), who was a committed craniometrist and a believer in polygenism, conducted research that produced important discoveries regarding the brain's language functions. Thus, while craniometry and phrenology were quite wrong about the relationship between head shape and psychological factors, their suggestions that there even *were* such relationships led a number of scientists to conduct very important research.

Test your knowledge

4.3 What is polygenism and how does it relate to craniometry?

4.4 What were the main shortcomings of phrenology?

Answers to these questions can be found on the companion website at:
www.pearsoned.co.uk/psychologyexpress

 Sample question   *Essay*

Compare and contrast the phrenologists' beliefs about the human brain with those of contemporary brain scientists.

Psychometrics

Up to the late 19th century, approaches to measure psychological characteristics involved inferring the presence or absence of attributes from the outer features of the human body. Not only were these approaches unreliable (in that they could not be supported by objective evidence), but they also lacked flexibility and precision. For one thing, they were generally nominal (or categorical), which meant they were based on labelling individuals as either being in, or not in, a given category. Based merely on judgements of equivalence, they did not assess the relative amounts of an attribute that could be present across individuals. As such, they represented what is now identified as the lowest level of measurement. Higher levels of measurement (such as ordinal, interval and/ or ratio measurement) would require quantitative indices to generate numerical scores that represent relative amounts of an attribute, ideally in a manner that was independently verifiable and replicable.

CRITICAL FOCUS

Levels of measurement

Levels of measurement refer to the four formats, or scales, by which measurement types can reasonably be described. The system was introduced by the American psychologist and statistician S. S. Stevens (1946) and aims to classify measurement types according to relative differences in sophistication and explanatory power. The four levels of measurement are: nominal measurement; ordinal measurement; interval measurement; and ratio measurement. Nominal (or categorical) measurement refers to the assigning of an entity to one of a selection of categories, thereby formally indexing its status. Ordinal measurement refers to the identification of where an entity falls when all entities in a sample are ranked according to the dimension being measured. Interval measurement refers to the use of numerical scores that represent the quantity of the feature being measured, based on a system in which the differences between consecutive numerical scores are equal across the entire range of possible scores. Ratio measurement is akin to interval measurement, except that it refers to systems in which the score of zero denotes an actual absence of the feature being measured (sometimes referred to as constituting 'a true zero-point'). Consideration of scales of measurement is helpful in determining what type of statistical summaries and analyses to use. Nominal data are best summarised using mode averages, and are best analysed using non-parametric tests. Ordinal data are best summarised using a median, and are again best analysed using non-parametric tests. Interval and ratio data are best summarised using a mean average (although modes and medians can also be used), and best analysed using parametric tests. Ratio measurement offers the most options for accurately describing the spread of the data. While these levels of measurement are widely cited and used in psychology, some statisticians question their ultimate usefulness. Some argue that there are actually far more than just four levels of measurement, while others recommend against making any distinctions at all.

The English polymath Francis Galton (1822–1911) is credited with introducing the first such standardised measurement methods, based on systematically recording participants' responses to standard questions and tests. Galton's main aim was to devise standardised procedures for measuring human intelligence, as part of a programme of research investigating whether intelligence was hereditary or the result of environment (Galton also coined the phrase 'nature or nurture'). Galton is credited with inventing the questionnaire and the survey, as well as with developing new research designs (such as twin studies) for testing pertinent hypotheses and new statistical procedures (such as the correlation) for analysing data. As well as psychology, Galton was prolific in several other scientific disciplines. However, his emphasis remained on ways of producing and analysing accurate measurements. He coined the term 'psychometrics' to describe the use of such methods to measure psychological attributes, and so is now often referred to as the 'father of psychometrics'.

Galton's intelligence tests were based on measures of behavioural and perceptual factors such as reaction time and sensory acuity, because he believed that these indices would be strongly correlated with intelligence. The American psychologist James McKeen Cattell (1860–1944) later expanded the test to include other indices such as time perception and colour naming. Still later, the French psychologists Alfred Binet (1857–1911) and Théodore Simon (1872–1961) developed a more elaborate version for measuring intelligence in children. Their test presented a general structure that continues to be used in intelligence tests today. It was converted into English by Lewis Terman (1877–1956) at Stanford University, who added further items (such as story interpretation tasks) and a method of producing a single score known as the intelligence quotient (or IQ). Later in the 20th century, this version was adapted by David Wechsler (1896–1981) and made suitable for IQ testing in adults.

CRITICAL FOCUS

Eugenics

While figures such as Binet and Simon developed their tests in order to identify the educational needs of disadvantaged groups, many others had less noble aspirations. Several prominent psychometricians wanted their tests to collect data to demonstrate that intelligence is inherited from parents, thus supporting the view that existing social hierarchies (including those based on racial and gender segregation) were fair because they reflected inherent differences in ability. Galton himself introduced the field of eugenics, which argued for selective breeding in humans in order to eliminate groups with (purportedly) lower intelligence. While Galton proposed that this could be achieved by simply encouraging less intelligent groups to have fewer children, the field of eugenics took on a more sinister tone when adopted by later proponents. Throughout the industrialised world, eugenicists introduced laws to enforce sterilisation among groups that were deemed by societal prejudices to detract from the overall welfare of the population. Even worse, groups such as the Nazis in Germany cited eugenics as their basis for instituting campaigns of genocidal extermination. Because of the worldwide revulsion that followed the Second World War, eugenics became deeply unpopular and virtually disappeared as a mainstream field of scientific consideration.

It is important to note that while its historical link with eugenics is sometimes raised as a way of criticising IQ tests, there is nothing inherent in intelligence testing (or in psychometrics in general) that promotes or even refers to eugenics. While open to criticisms relating to their breadth, precision, validity and reliability, IQ tests are essentially just agreed methods for measuring an arbitrarily defined psychological variable. Overall, intelligence testing has been extremely valuable in helping millions of people with learning difficulties to identify appropriate special educational supports that they would otherwise have to go without. It has also proved to be an effective tool for those who wish to *tackle* inter-group discrimination and prejudice, by providing objective data to *rebut* claims that there exist intrinsic racial or other group differences in intelligence.

Apart from intelligence, psychometric approaches have been applied to a wide range of psychological attributes, including attitudes (such as optimism), psychosocial factors (such as social support) and personality traits (such as extroversion). Literally thousands of psychometric instruments have now been developed, and their use is widespread in modern psychology. Of course, essential to their effective use is a considered understanding of the limits of their usefulness. As such, in describing and delimiting psychological measurement with ever increasing refinement, the field of psychometrics has spawned a number of theoretical concepts that have become fundamental to the science of psychology (and the social sciences in general). Key examples of such concepts include the notions of validity, reliability and measurement error. The field of psychometrics also frequently seeks to tackle important conceptual debates in psychology. These relate to whether psychological phenomena can be coherently defined, whether they generalise across cultures and time periods, or whether they even truly exist independently of being measured. As such, psychometrics has become one of the most philosophically charged subfields of contemporary psychology.

Key terms

With reference to psychometrics, **reliability** refers to the extent to which a measurement method succeeds in achieving consistency. This can relate to the consistency of a measurement method when used to measure the same entity on two separate occasions (referred to as 'test–retest reliability'), the consistency of a method when used by two different testers (referred to as 'inter-rater reliability'), or the consistency of the different parts of a measurement system when considered separately and compared with one another (referred to, loosely, as 'internal reliability'). Notably, reliability does not refer to whether the measurement method achieves an accurate measure of the target entity.

In the context of psychometrics, **validity** refers to the extent to which a measurement method actually succeeds in producing an accurate measure of the entity it intends to measure. Validity can be evaluated in several ways. However, the underlying principle of all approaches is to compare the particular measurement method under scrutiny with another method or index whose accuracy is known. While this can be straightforward with some variables (e.g. height, weight, reaction time), it can often prove difficult in psychology due to conceptual disagreement as to how particular constructs of interest might be defined (e.g. intelligence, optimism, extroversion).

 Sample question   *Problem-based learning*

Consider your own system of academic assessment, including recent examples of activities, such as essays, tests and written examinations. Reflect for a moment on what these assessment activities were designed to achieve. Then, consider the validity of the assessments. Did they succeed in measuring the intended outcomes? Finally, consider the reliability of the assessments. Did they measure the intended outcomes in a way that would be the same regardless of the particular situations in which the assessments were done?

Test your knowledge

4.5 How did Galton's psychometrics differ from previous measurement approaches?

4.6 In terms of psychometrics, how does reliability differ from validity?

Answers to these questions can be found on the companion website at:
www.pearsoned.co.uk/psychologyexpress

 ## Sample question   *Essay*

In terms of establishing standardised methods of psychological measurement, what are the main difficulties in attempting to measure intelligence?

Chapter summary – pulling it all together

→ Can you tick all the points from the revision checklist at the beginning of this chapter?

→ Attempt the sample question from the beginning of this chapter using the answer guidelines below.

→ Go to the companion website at www.pearsoned.co.uk/psychologyexpress to access more revision support online, including interactive quizzes, flashcards, You be the marker exercises as well as answer guidance for the Test your knowledge and Sample questions from this chapter.

Further reading for Chapter 4

Topic	Key reading
Physiognomy	Collins, A. F. (1999). The enduring appeal of physiognomy: Physical appearance as a sign of temperament, character, and intelligence. *History of Psychology*, 2, 251–276.
Lombroso's criminology	Kushner, H. I. (2011). Cesare Lombroso and the pathology of left-handedness. *The Lancet*, 377, 118–119.
History of psychometrics	Buchanan, R. D., & Finch, S. J. (2005). History of psychometrics. In B. S. Everitt & D. C. Howell (Eds.), *Encyclopedia of statistics in behavioral science*. Chichester: Wiley.
Galton's hereditary genius	Galton, F. (2009 [originally published, 1869]). *Hereditary genius: An inquiry into its laws and consequences*. Charleston, South Carolina: BiblioBazaar.

Topic	Key reading
Biases in psychology	Guthrie, R. V. (2003). *Even the rat was white: A historical view of psychology*, (2nd edition). Boston: Allyn & Bacon.
Race in psychology	Richards, G. (2007). *'Race', racism and psychology: Toward a reflexive history*. London: Routledge.
The 'Bell curve'	Rushton, J. P. (1997). Review essay: *The Bell Curve Debate* and related books. *Society, 34*, 78–82.
Psychometrics and eugenics	Gould, S. J. (1996). *The mismeasure of man*, (Revised and expanded edition). London: Penguin.

Answer guidelines

 Sample question Essay

Examine the influence of physiognomic theories on the historical development of psychology. To what extent (if any) is this influence detectable today?

Approaching the question

The question is in two parts. The first part asks you to 'evaluate' a proposition. This instruction invites you to set out the positive and negative aspects of the proposition (e.g. its strengths and weaknesses, its advantages and disadvantages, or – as in this case – reasons for supporting the proposition and reasons for rejecting it). The second part asks for a directional response (e.g. 'to a great extent' or 'to a little extent'), but also invites an explanation (e.g. 'to a great extent, because...').

Important points to include

A thorough treatment of physiognomic theories should certainly include the works (and beliefs) of Lavater, and almost certainly also Lombroso. A thorough treatment should also refer to the presence of physiognomic beliefs throughout cultural history, including in the writings of the ancient philosophers. To be especially comprehensive, it would be legitimate (and perhaps helpful) to identify fields such as craniometry and phrenology as essentially physiognomic theories. Note that the question refers to 'the historical development of psychology'. While this certainly includes the subject matter of psychology, it also includes the practice of psychology as a scientific discipline. Therefore, when considering the influence of physiognomic theories, it would be desirable to address both aspects. Firstly, it would be helpful to describe how physiognomic beliefs influenced the knowledge base of psychology (e.g., beliefs relating to specialisation of function in the brain). Secondly, it would be helpful to note how physiognomic approaches influenced the nature of research in psychology by encouraging data collection, statistical analysis, hypothesis testing, the development of formal psychometrics, and so on.

Make your answer stand out

To make your answer stand out, consider ways of explaining the psychological appeal of physiognomy (for example, evolutionary processes that might encourage people to judge others by their appearances) and how these processes might have influenced not only the public at large, but also psychometricians themselves. Many prominent psychometricians retained physiognomic-style beliefs even after having developed standardised methods of objective measurement, while others used psychometrics to further their polemical agendas regarding racial segregation. While there are reasons to have ethical reservations regarding psychometric tests, such reasons tend to relate more to the people who use psychometrics rather than to the methods themselves. As such, to make your answer stand out, try also to emphasise ethical arguments in favour *of psychometric approaches.*

Explore the accompanying website at www.pearsoned.co.uk/psychologyexpress

→ Prepare more effectively for exams and assignments using the answer guidelines for questions from this chapter.

→ Test your knowledge using multiple choice questions and flashcards.

→ Improve your essay skills by exploring the You be the marker exercises.

Notes

Notes

5

The behaviourist revolution: actions as data

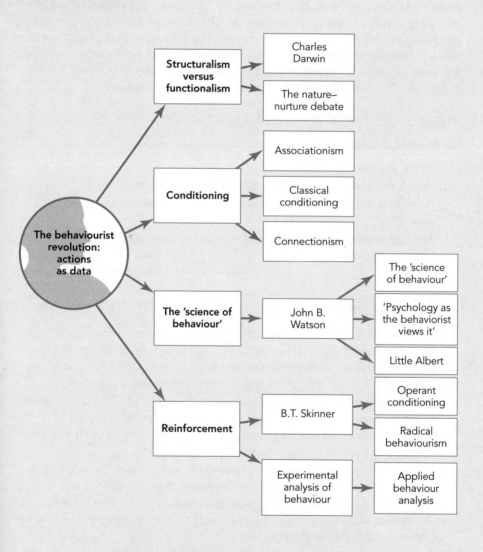

Introduction

By the late 19th century, scientific psychology had developed ways of exploring human experiences relating to perception and sensation, as well as approaches to the measurement of qualities such as intelligence and personality. However, many psychologists felt that such research addressed concepts that were abstract rather than tangible, the implications of which were philosophical rather than pragmatic. Some feared that this threatened the standing of psychology as a science. It was also noted that while these approaches helped us to describe people's feelings and attitudes, they did not help us to understand or explain why people acted in the way that they do. This was a problem because many psychologists felt that the capacity to explain (and thus predict) people's actions was a fundamental requirement for the new discipline of psychology. Therefore, it is little surprise that psychology quickly developed ways of studying human behaviour. This field of research became known as behaviourism.

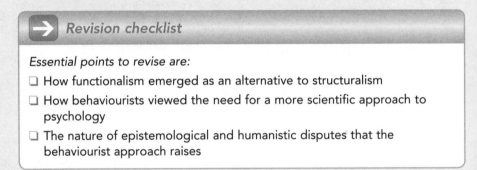

→ Revision checklist

Essential points to revise are:
- ❏ How functionalism emerged as an alternative to structuralism
- ❏ How behaviourists viewed the need for a more scientific approach to psychology
- ❏ The nature of epistemological and humanistic disputes that the behaviourist approach raises

Assessment advice

- Essay questions on this topic will often focus less on the nuts and bolts of how behaviourism seeks to explain behaviour, and more on the philosophical implications of the behaviourist worldview. Such implications relate both to the human condition and to the way science is practised in psychology.
- With regard to the human condition, behaviourism has implications regarding free will, consciousness and the nature–nurture debate. With regard to science, behaviourism argues strongly for the application of strong scientific rigour to psychology.
- In both contexts, debates are often highly charged as the relevant concerns are widely acknowledged to be finely balanced. Thus, in approaching assessments in this area, it is important to ensure that such controversies are dealt with in a balanced way, with treatments of both arguments and counter-arguments regarding each dispute.
- Of course, strong scholarship will allow (if not indeed expect) a commentator to take a particular side on these debates, assuming that arguments are supported with pertinent information and fair reasoning.

Sample question

Could you answer this question? Below is a typical essay question that could arise on this topic.

 Sample question   *Essay*

To what extent did the emergence of behaviourism represent the introduction of evolutionary theory to psychology?

Guidelines on answering this question are included at the end of this chapter, whilst further guidance on tackling other exam questions can be found on the companion website at: **www.pearsoned.co.uk/psychologyexpress**

Structuralism versus functionalism

Much of the early empirical, quantitative, laboratory-based research in psychology had been based on an agenda of setting out the dimensions and parameters of the human mind, such as its capacities for sensation and perception. The British psychologist Edward Titchener (1867–1927), who studied under Wundt in Leipzig before emigrating to the United States to establish a psychology laboratory at Cornell University, argued that all complex mental experiences could be understood in terms of combinations of small discrete perceptions and sensations. This view became known as structuralism, and is sometimes credited as being the first major school of thought in American academic psychology. However, the structuralist movement did not last long. Titchener argued that the fundamental subject matter of psychology was personal experience, and so was a strong advocate of introspection. Accordingly, structuralism attracted severe criticisms from psychologists who considered objectivity and verifiability to be essential features of scientific data. Other critics, such as Max Wertheimer (1880–1943), complained that structuralism failed to take account of how the combination of experiences can often be just as important as the individual experiences themselves, and so accused structuralists of reductionism.

CRITICAL FOCUS

Reductionism

Reductionism refers to the epistemological view that complex systems can be adequately considered in terms of the sum of their constituent parts. In other words, a reductionist view is taken when a scientist seeks to understand a multifaceted entity by studying its various facets (or subsets of them) individually. This approach is usually taken on the basis that the complexity of the whole is too great to facilitate a clear understanding, either because of the sheer number of elements involved, because the elements are truly distinct albeit interconnected, or because of the fact that some of the elements are themselves poorly understood. For example, when a biologist tries to investigate how a human hand works, a clearer explanation will be constructed if the various elements of the hand (such as the bones, muscles, ligaments, skin, nerves, veins, etc.) are considered and studied separately. Considering the hand as a whole would not lead to a particularly fine-grained explanation of its intricate functioning.

Reductionism can become controversial for at least three reasons. Firstly, it is not always possible to be sure when an entity has been reduced to the level that best facilitates understanding. While a particular biologist might consider the musculature of the hand, it is true to say that muscles themselves are made up of many components (such as fibres, spindles, connective tissue, etc.), each of which themselves could be considered separately. Determining the optimal level of reduction is a matter of judgement and, therefore frequently, of dispute. Secondly, it is not always clear that studying something in terms of its components will genuinely lead to better understanding, at least with regard to a particular field of investigation. For example, while botanists might find the cellular composition of corn to be informative in their field of study, it is not necessarily the case that such details will be as informative to the farmers who grow corn or the consumers who buy it. Finally, reductionism can be controversial if the divisions among components of an entity are themselves matters of dispute. Considering components as separate when in fact they are not could be particularly misleading.

In psychology, certain research traditions have either explicitly promoted reductionism or else been criticised for doing so implicitly. Behaviourism has tended to promote reductionism unapologetically. In behaviourism, it is argued that behaviour is best considered in terms of individual components, such as stimuli, responses and reinforcers. Criticism of behaviourism has been raised in terms of each of the three contexts mentioned above: that behaviour actually comprises many more detailed bits than behaviourists acknowledge; that information about stimuli and responses is trivial; and that the components of behaviour are too interdependently interlinked to be subdivided in this way. Behaviourists tend to defend reductionism by pointing to their impressive track record in producing replicable research findings, which succeed in accounting for highly complex behaviours and which support reliable practical applications in several contexts. They also note that an aspiration to appropriate levels of reductionism conforms to the scientific principle of parsimony, and so is necessary for scientific credibility.

Another reason why structuralism quickly became unpopular was that its emphasis deviated from the new direction of thought that was becoming popular across the biological sciences. Influenced by Darwin's theory of evolution, psychologists and biologists were more interested in the *functions* of thoughts, feelings and behaviour, than on their *forms*. Darwin's theory explained that the survival value of naturally emerging traits was not determined by their dimensions, but by the way traits interact with a species's environment. For example, Darwin noted that a particular characteristic might be useful for survival in one environment but catastrophic in another (e.g. the fur on a woolly mammoth, which allowed it to survive the cool temperatures of the Ice Age but caused its extinction when the climate warmed). Darwin observed that this principle was as true of psychological traits as it was of physical ones, and wrote extensively about evolutionary aspects of sexual communication and emotional expression.

CRITICAL FOCUS

Zeitgeist

When an idea or subject becomes prevalent across different scholarly disciplines such that it influences much of the research agenda across academia as a whole, it is often referred to representing the Zeitgeist. 'Zeitgeist' is a German term meaning 'spirit of the times', and was introduced by the philosopher Georg Hegel (1770–1831). The concept of the Zeitgeist suggests that prevailing social attitudes to particular subjects can come to influence and define the science and scholarship of a particular period more so than the contributions of individual scientists and scholars (no matter how eminent these contributors might be). It can generally be considered as the alternative to 'personalistic' views of history and science, which argue that events are influenced by the actions and contributions of key individuals. In the late 19th century, the notion of functionalism might be said to have represented the Zeitgeist of that period. Rresearchers across many disciplines became simultaneously interested in the potential purposes of phenomena in nature, rather than just their shapes or sizes. While Charles Darwin (1809–1882) is often identified as being largely responsible for the spread of functionalist thinking, it can be argued that Darwin himself was responding to a functionalist Zeitgeist when he developed his theory of evolution by natural selection. For example, Darwin's contemporary Alfred Russel Wallace (1823–1913), who was exposed to the same cultural influences and extant scholarship as Darwin, independently came to a very similar functionalist theory of evolution. Therefore, when considering the emergence of functionalism in psychology during the latter years of the 19th century, it is important to reflect on the prevailing academic influences on scientists at that time. It would be a mistake to assume that functionalist psychology emerged and prospered simply because of its own merits. It also benefited from being consistent with the prevailing Zeitgeist.

Unlike structuralism, which was associated with Titchener, functionalism in psychology was not driven by an individual psychologist but rather reflected the interests of a range of contributors to psychology during the transition from the 19th to 20th centuries. Many of these psychologists were interested in what became known as the nature–nurture debate. The basic question of this debate was: how much of behaviour can be said to be instinctive or innate, and how much is dependent on experience or learning? Traditional approaches to human nature, often informed by religious ideas about humanity as being designed and created by a deity, had tended to emphasise the extent of innate qualities, with the psychological (and physical) make-up of an individual said to be largely the result of heredity. New approaches to functionalism, together with the increasing secularisation of Western society, encouraged scholars to consider the degree to which behaviour was the result of environment. This view suggested that behavioural characteristics were not hereditary; rather, they developed gradually and were shaped by a person's experiences, in order to maximise the individual's fitness to his or her environment.

Key term

Heredity: is the sharing of characteristics by parents and offspring as a result of their biological relatedness. Because we now believe that characteristics are transmitted through genes, it is often assumed that all heredity is the result of genetic transmission. In human physiology, an example of a hereditable trait is hair colour. Many fair-haired people will produce fair-haired children. However, there are two obvious complications. Firstly, because children have two parents (only one of whom might be fair-haired), it is not straightforward to predict the characteristics of an offspring. Secondly, throughout life, offspring may experience conditions or happenings that alter the characteristic in question (for example, they may dye their hair). For this reason, it is generally acknowledged that an appropriate approach to studying such matters should investigate not just heredity on its own, but also environmental contexts and ways in which heredity and environment might affect each other. In psychology, it is believed that many traits (such as personality and intelligence) are hereditable. However, because of the complications described above, there is considerable dispute about the precise range and nature of hereditable traits. Such disputes are not only scientific, but also reflect political concerns because of the implication that people's personal attributes might vary in ways that persist within population subgroups regardless of interventions aimed at addressing associated problems.

Test your knowledge

5.1 How did functionalism differ from structuralism?

5.2 Why was functionalism proposed?

Answers to these questions can be found on the companion website at: **www.pearsoned.co.uk/psychologyexpress**

 Sample question Essay

To what extent did functionalism serve to widen the focus of psychology beyond the individual?

Conditioning

Throughout the history of philosophy, there has been a point of view stating that mental processes operate on the basis of associations; in other words, that higher order thoughts result from the combination of more elementary mental processes, which the individual learns to associate with one another based on experience. This approach, known as 'associationism', was described by Plato and Aristotle, but was particularly championed in the 17th and 18th centuries by the group of philosophers known as the British Empiricists. Figures such as John Locke (1632–1704), George Berkeley (1685–1753) and David Hume (1711–1776) were nurturists, and sought to explain how the complexity of human behaviour could be produced by environmental rather than innate influences.

With the arrival of scientific laboratories in the late 19th century, researchers began to explore associationist concepts using experimental methods. One of the most famous was the Russian physiologist Ivan Pavlov (1849–1936). Pavlov was a celebrated scientist who had won the Nobel Prize for Medicine in 1904 for work on the digestive system. Noting that the mere sight of food can initiate the physical response of salivation, Pavlov became interested in the psychological factors that stimulated different digestive processes. He famously conducted a series of experiments on animals demonstrating the phenomenon now known as classical conditioning. Pavlov showed that when a neutral event or stimulus (such as the ringing of a bell) was repeatedly presented alongside a physiologically relevant stimulus (such as the presentation of some food), animals would eventually learn to generate the natural physiological response (salivation) when presented with the neutral stimulus on its own. Many of Pavlov's first studies were on dogs; accordingly, references to 'Pavlov's dogs' are now common in contemporary culture to describe this type of association-based learning.

Pavlov introduced a number of terms and concepts that have had a lasting impact on the study of learning and that continue to be used today. The physiologically relevant stimulus and its resulting natural response were called the 'unconditioned stimulus' (UCS) and 'unconditioned response' (UCR), while the neutral stimulus and the learned response it came to invoke were called the 'conditioned stimulus' (CS) and 'conditioned response' (CR). Pavlov found that the stimulation of the CR by the CS on its own would gradually wear off over time, and referred to this effect as 'extinction'. He also noticed that when extinction occurred, the ability of the CS to elicit the CR would often re-strengthen following a brief rest, a process he called 'spontaneous recovery'. Further, Pavlov described the notion of 'stimulus generalisation', where a CR could be elicited by other (unconditioned) neutral stimuli if they bore sufficient physical resemblances to the CS. Each of these concepts are today believed to be important elements of learning (in humans as well as in animals), and are invoked to explain (and treat) problems such as phobias and challenging behaviour.

Pavlov's work inspired a large number of other researchers to develop similar theories of learning, and to gather experimental evidence to test these theories. Among this group was the American psychologist, Edward Thorndike (1874–1949). While conducting much animal research (especially on problem-solving in cats), Thorndike was particularly interested in how principles of conditioning could be employed in classroom teaching. His research helped to establish a theoretical approach known as 'connectionism' and he is often credited with providing the scientific evidence base for the later field of educational psychology.

Example of classical conditioning in fiction

The phenomenon of classical conditioning presents a powerful image to represent the susceptibility of ordinary people to external influences. As such, it has been presented in various ways in fictional works, especially in allegorical descriptions of socio-political oppression. One example is the novel *Brave New World* by English writer Aldous Huxley (1894–1963). Published in 1932, the novel depicts a dystopic future in which technological change facilitates the emergence of a caste-ridden society subservient to the needs of commerce. In this society, children are subjected to a rigorous process of conditioning in order to maximise their complicity. These sessions are conducted by physicians in 'Neo-Pavlovian Conditioning Rooms'. For example, in order to generate an instinctive fear of books, the physicians expose the children to books while sounding frighteningly loud alarm bells and administering electric shocks. Huxley was a keen reader of psychological research. He named one of his characters Helmholtz Watson, an allusion to two psychologists whose work he had become interested in: the psychophysicist Hermann von Helmholz and the behaviourist James Watson.

Test your knowledge

5.3 How does the study of conditioning improve on older theories of associationism?

5.4 In classical conditioning, how does a conditioned stimulus end up provoking a conditioned response?

Answers to these questions can be found on the companion website at: **www.pearsoned.co.uk/psychologyexpress**

 Sample question   *Essay*

Why is Pavlov's work considered to be psychology as opposed to physiology?

The 'science of behaviour'

Another leading American researcher in this area was John B. Watson (1878–1958). Watson became prominent for combining the various findings on conditioning with those of his own research in order to establish the field of behaviourism. Watson, a professor at Johns Hopkins University, had become uneasy at the widespread use of introspection in academic psychology. He felt that the psychology of James and Wundt was ultimately dependent upon subjective judgements by researchers and the people they studied, and so lacked the objective rigour required for proper science. Further, he felt that this lack of rigour detracted from the explanatory and predictive power of psychology as well as from its applicability to everyday life. In 1913, he set out his views in a landmark article called 'Psychology as the Behaviorist Views It' published in the journal *Psychological Review*, which he edited. He asserted that psychology should only use objective data (such as observable behaviours), and should avoid all forms of subjective or unverifiable data (such as self-reported perceptions or cognitions). According to Watson, the latter had no place in scientific psychology. He also argued that psychology should not only seek to explain people's behaviour, but also to establish means of predicting and influencing it. Drawing on Darwin's explanation of the evolution of species from common ancestors, he asserted that the basic principles of learning were likely to be similar across species and that animal research was therefore an important source of knowledge about human psychology. Watson's paper became known informally as the 'behaviourist manifesto'. It is also commonly referred to as the source of a popular definition of psychology itself: 'the science of behaviour'. However, while this definition of psychology was used by Watson, it was actually coined by Titchener's student, W. B. Pillsbury (1872–1960).

KEY STUDY

Little Albert

Watson famously demonstrated classical conditioning in an experiment involving an eight-month-old boy, referred to by the pseudonym Little Albert. Together with his student Rosalie Rayner (1899–1936), Watson succeeded in conditioning Albert to become fearful of a white rat by consistently presenting loud noises when the rat was present (Watson & Rayner, 1920). As the loud noises were frightening to Albert, they served as a powerful UCS. Watson also demonstrated stimulus generalisation by showing Albert to have developed negative reactions to other objects similar in appearance to the white rat, including Watson's own white hair. Although the study provided an effective demonstration of conditioning, it was also controversial. For one thing, Watson and Rayner did not seek to decondition Little Albert after the study had concluded. While extinction may well have occurred eventually, it is also possible that Albert's new phobias persisted following the experiment. By the standard of today's conventions, as formulated by professional bodies and universities, such procedures for research with a small child would be deemed unethical.

Source: Watson, J. B., & Rayner, R. (1920). Conditioned emotional reactions. *Journal of Experimental Psychology*, 3, 1–14.

Watson was a charismatic communicator who did much to popularise psychology, even after he left academia to embark on a successful career in advertising. For example, he published many magazine articles explaining how the principles of conditioning could be applied to child-rearing. While his views on these issues are often considered extreme (for example, the logic of his position implied that parents should not hug their children when they cry), many of the core elements of his approaches have been found to be very effective. Further, his promotion of scientific rigour had a long-lasting impact on how psychological research was conducted throughout the 20th century.

Test your knowledge

5.5 What were Watson's key concerns regarding the use of scientific methods in psychology?

5.6 Why is behaviourism called 'behaviourism'?

Answers to these questions can be found on the companion website at: **www.pearsoned.co.uk/psychologyexpress**

Sample question   Essay

To what extent are studies of learning in animals similar to studies of learning in small children, and to what extent are they different? Is either approach truly informative regarding the behaviour of adult humans?

Reinforcement

One psychologist who was profoundly influenced by Watson's views on behaviourism was B. F. Skinner (1904–1990). After reading works by Watson, Pavlov and the philosopher Bertrand Russell (1872–1970), Skinner enrolled at the psychology department at Harvard University to conduct research for a PhD, which he obtained in 1931. Skinner's primary contribution to psychology was his explication of the role of reinforcers in conditioning. A reinforcer is a stimulus that, when presented *after* a response, increases the probability of that response being elicited again in the future. In other words, a reinforcer acts like a reward for a particular response. Over time, if reinforcers are provided, the individual organism will learn to produce the response that elicits the reward (for example, if a dog is given a titbit of food every time it retrieves a stick thrown by its owner, then it will become more likely to retrieve the stick when it is thrown in the future; eventually, it will learn to retrieve the stick each time it is thrown). As in classical conditioning, the organism learns to associate the stimulus and the response. However, in this context, the organism is producing the response *before* the reinforcing stimulus is experienced. As such, these concepts marked a significant addition to our overall understanding of how conditioning underlies learning. Because this type of conditioning is related to an operation (i.e. a voluntary behaviour) carried out by the organism, it became known as 'operant conditioning'.

? Sample question   **Problem-based learning**

Consider a behaviour that you have acquired during your post-childhood years. Now consider the situations in which you engage in this behaviour, the benefits you perceive of doing so, and the potential costs. Write down some of the reasons that you think you engage in this behaviour. Categorise your reasons as relating to (a) inner motivations or tastes and (b) external stimuli and reinforcers. Which category do you think represents the more valid explanation for your behaviour? To what extent can you be sure that the inner motivational explanations are valid at all? Could you rule out the possibility that your behaviour is driven only by external factors? Or do you think behaviour is the product of both types of antecedent?

Skinner developed a repertoire of experimental procedures for demonstrating the scope of operant conditioning. Perhaps his most famous invention was the operant conditioning chamber, better known as the 'Skinner box'. Skinner designed this apparatus as part of his graduate studies at Harvard. It comprised a box large enough to house an experimental animal (e.g. a laboratory rat), the basic elements of which included a lever for the animal to press, a food dispenser, a light and a loudspeaker. All these elements were connected to electronic recording and control equipment. The apparatus could be used to present experimental animals with food pellets as reinforcers. The experimenter could demonstrate operant conditioning by presenting reinforcement for desired behaviours, such as lever presses, and observing whether the frequency of these behaviours increased in proportion to the amount of reinforcement offered. Further, the experimenter could attempt to use stimulus generalisation to train the animal to respond to light-blinks or loudspeaker-buzzes instead of food pellets. Over time, Skinner boxes of varying designs and configurations were developed, and were used to demonstrate a huge range of operant phenomena.

The impact of reinforcement on behaviour was found to be dramatic. This field of research, which became known as the 'experimental analysis of behaviour', grew rapidly through the first half of the 20th century and became dominant in mainstream psychology. Over the years, operant conditioning was found to influence complex behaviours in animals and in humans. Skinner expanded the conceptual basis of the work to attempt to account for highly complex operants such as cognition and language. Some of these views were considered to be controversial. His philosophy of 'radical behaviourism' implied that all behaviours were influenced by reinforcement. Critics complained that this did not allow for individual free will, and Skinner was accused of being indifferent to human emotion and dignity. His approach to language, which he referred to as 'verbal behaviour' was similarly criticised.

Nonetheless, Skinner's influence on psychology was profound, both in developing its content through the contribution of research findings, and in raising the profile of the scientific nature of psychology as a discipline. The experimental analysis of behaviour has generated many productive insights and applications in fields such as clinical and educational psychology. For example, the contemporary field of applied behaviour analysis (essentially the use of behaviourist approaches to systematically modify people's behaviour) has proved to be one of the most successful approaches to addressing the problem of challenging behaviour in populations compromised by disorders such as autism. Applied behaviour analysis has also been helpful as a means of developing interventions for persons with unusual brain injuries, and as a source of a number of effective behaviour change interventions (in areas such as health promotion) aimed at the general population. Such contemporary fields have sought to maintain the strengths of traditional behaviourism's scientific rigour, while addressing its perceived narrowness in excluding the consideration of cognitions in psychology.

Test your knowledge

5.7 What is a reinforcer and why does it affect behaviour?

5.8 How is behaviourism applied in real-life contexts?

Answers to these questions can be found on the companion website at:
www.pearsoned.co.uk/psychologyexpress

? Sample question   Essay

Does behaviourism include or exclude mental processes?

Chapter summary – pulling it all together

→ Can you tick all the points from the revision checklist at the beginning of this chapter?

→ Attempt the sample question from the beginning of this chapter using the answer guidelines below.

→ Go to the companion website at www.pearsoned.co.uk/psychologyexpress to access more revision support online, including interactive quizzes, flashcards, You be the marker exercises as well as answer guidance for the Test your knowledge and Sample questions from this chapter.

Further reading for Chapter 5	
Topic	Key reading
Thorndike	Galef, B. G. (1998). Edward Thorndike: Revolutionary psychologist, ambiguous biologist. *American Psychologist*, 53, 1128–1134.
Watson	Brewer, C. L. (1991). Perspectives on John B. Watson. In G. A. Kimble, M. Wertheimer, & C. White (Eds.), *Portraits of pioneers of psychology* (pp. 170–186). Hillsdale, New Jersey: Erlbaum.
The 'behaviourist' manifesto	Watson, J. B. (1990). Psychology as the behaviorist views it. *Psychological Review, 20*, 158–177.
'Little Albert'	Harris, B. (1979). Whatever happened to Little Albert? *American Psychologist, 34*, 151–160.
Skinner	Skinner Foundation (2010). *B. F. Skinner Foundation: Currently available videos* [webpage]. Retrieved January 10, 2010, from http://www.bfskinner.org/BFSkinner/Videos.html
Skinnerism	Skinner, B. F. (1974). *About behaviorism*. New York: Vintage.
Radical behaviourim	Skinner, B. F. (1971). *Beyond freedom and dignity*. Indianapolis: Hackett Publishing.

Answer guidelines

✳ *Sample question*   *Essay*

To what extent did the emergence of behaviourism represent the introduction of evolutionary theory to psychology?

Approaching the question

The essay title asks a question regarding the 'extent to which' the proposition is valid. As such, it will be important to address this phrasing directly, and to construct your answer so that it offers a conclusion regarding this particular point. Strategically, given the material and the general value in avoiding absolutisms, it is probably wise to acknowledge the substantial extent to which the proposition is true (or false if this is what you believe), while allowing for the alternative point of view.

Important points to include

As the essay invokes both behaviourism and evolutionary theory, it will be necessary to offer working definitions of both. In considering the influence of one on the other, it would be helpful to refer both to the theoretical overlap that might exist (for example, by explaining how the concept of functionalism is relevant to both). When considering behaviourism, it would be useful to cover the full range of activities that this represents, from early work on functionalism and conditioning, Watson's science of behaviour, to Skinner's work on reinforcement.

Make your answer stand out

As well as explaining the conceptual relevance of evolutionary theory to behaviourism, it would be effective to describe some of the practical aspects involved in corroborating the statement in the essay title. Specifically, it may be helpful to describe the socio-cultural realities of scholarship in this historical context. In other words, it will be pertinent to mention the degree to which evolutionary theory was widely understood and discussed in universities during the period when behaviourism began to emerge. This can be demonstrated by referring to the history of evolutionary theory as well as to the impact of this theory on many fields other than psychology.

Explore the accompanying website at www.pearsoned.co.uk/psychologyexpress

→ Prepare more effectively for exams and assignments using the answer guidelines for questions from this chapter.

→ Test your knowledge using multiple choice questions and flashcards.

→ Improve your essay skills by exploring the You be the marker exercises.

Notes

The cognitive revolution: the metaphor of computation

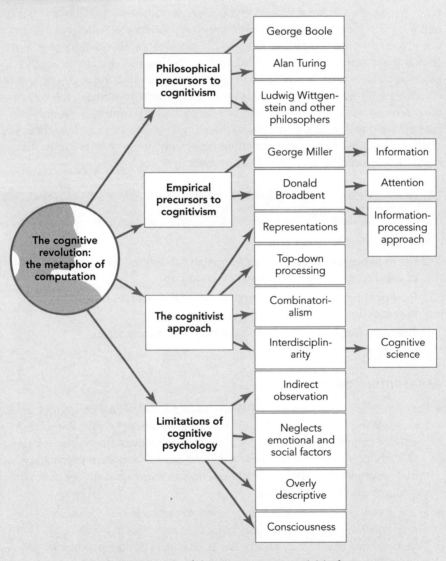

A printable version of this topic map is available from
www.pearsoned.co.uk/psychologyexpress

Introduction

In the middle of the 20th century, behaviourism had become the dominant approach to psychology in the United States, and was also very influential in other parts of the world. Behaviourism had helped psychology generate an extensive base of empirical research, a repertoire of effective interventions, and a strong scientific reputation. However, its focus on observable behaviour necessarily served to restrict its range. For example, many psychologists felt that their discipline should be free to concern itself with more invisible phenomena, such as memories, mental images and even consciousness itself. The behaviourists' view (at least as it was then widely interpreted) was that science was required to restrict itself to the study of observable phenomena only, and so that these less tangible concepts could not be examined scientifically by psychologists. Implicit in this position was the criticism that those psychologists who were interested in such matters were not properly scientific in the way they did their work. However, in the middle of the 20th century, a number of researchers developed approaches to the study of human thoughts and thinking that honoured the principles of scientific objectivity, without reverting to the introspection used by Wundt and the psychophysicists.

 Revision checklist

Essential points to revise are:

❑ How philosophical approaches to human thought began to suggest ways of conducting scientific research on cognition

❑ How post-psychophysics research on mental processes moved beyond introspection and into science

❑ The main features of the cognitivist approach to psychology

Assessment advice

● Essay questions on this topic will often involve fundamental philosophical issues relating to the nature of the human mind. Not only does the subject matter of cognitive psychology focus on the workings of the human mind and its thought processes, but the methods used in cognitive psychology raise fundamental questions about how we can know what is truly going on in somebody else's consciousness.

● In many ways, cognitive psychology offers a multitude of impressive examples of the creativity and ingenuity of researchers in psychology. That said, cognitive psychology also presents examples of how psychology can be accused of producing elaborate theoretical explanations that remain hypothetical even when the most pertinent data have been collected.

- As such, when approaching questions on the historical and conceptual dimensions of cognitive psychology, it is important to give attention to both its subject matter and its research paradigms.

Sample question

Could you answer this question? Below is a typical essay question that could arise on this topic.

 Sample question *Essay*

Evaluate the success of the metaphor of 'mind as computer'.

Guidelines on answering this question are included at the end of this chapter, whilst further guidance on tackling other exam questions can be found on the companion website at: **www.pearsoned.co.uk/psychologyexpress**

Philosophical precursors to cognitivism

The term 'cognition' has long been used to refer to mental activities such as thinking, remembering, visualising, reasoning and understanding. Unsurprisingly, the nature of cognition has been considered by philosophers for many centuries. Virtually all of the major philosophers have attempted to explain the nature of mental processes. As early as the 13th century, Thomas Aquinas (1225–1274) specified that emotional mental processes were qualitatively different from processes relating to knowledge. This identification of cognition as being dispassionately concerned with the mental processing of information proved very resilient, and continues to influence the way in which cognitive psychology is studied today.

Interest in the nature of how information was processed in the mind was not confined to philosophers. The way logic was necessary for the performance of mathematical operations led many mathematicians to argue that logical principles provided the template on which all human reasoning abilities were based. One particular example was British mathematician George Boole (1815–1864), who described 'universal laws of thought' which he felt could be modelled mathematically. Boole was innovative in using arbitrary symbols (such as letters) to represent the components of thought, in order to avoid the vagueness of natural language. He then developed systems of combining these symbols using arithmetic functions, and so provided a method of representing logical propositions using algebra. Fundamentally, he observed that such a system allowed thoughts to be reduced to a series of binary (i.e. two-valued, such as 'on/off' or 'true/false') elements. Boole's efforts to create a symbolic system for representing logical thought were considered obscure by his contemporaries, but were later to be recognised as applicable to a variety of technological contexts. For example, today his system underlies all digital electronics.

Another figure whose work greatly influenced the study of mental processes was Alan Turing (1912–1954), a British mathematician who worked as a code-breaker for the UK Government during the Second World War. Turing is credited as being the first theorist to conceive of a machine that, in theory, could perform any calculation imaginable. His theoretical device, known today as a Turing machine, comprised an infinitely long magnetic tape and tape-reading scanner that followed instructions based on a binary code. His mathematical demonstrations suggested that it was possible for such a computing machine to

CRITICAL FOCUS

The Turing test

Alan Turing made a number of important contributions to mathematics, psychology and computing. He also presented a number of highly influential concepts in the philosophy of knowledge and, in particular, the philosophy surrounding the notion of artificial intelligence. One of his most famous philosophical ideas relates to a hypothetical test that might be used to identify whether a machine has successfully demonstrated intelligence. This procedure, originally proposed in 1950, is now known as the Turing test. Put simply, the Turing test involves a machine participating in a three-way conversation involving two human contributors, one of whom is explicitly seeking to establish which of the other two is the machine. All communication is conducted remotely (for example, using the equivalent to a modern-day computer-based chat room). The test is passed if the human tester is unable to guess which of the other two conversationalists is actually the machine more frequently than would be predicted by chance. Key features of the Turing test include the requirement that the tester make explicit attempts to identify the machine (for example, by asking questions that are thought likely to expose flaws in the machine's attempts at human-like conversation) and that the procedure be run multiple times in order to establish the statistical likelihood of correct identifications of the machine by the tester. As such, while a number of computer programs have been produced that appear to convincingly reproduce human-like conversation in online contexts (even to the extent that they successfully fool casual observers), programs that meet the rigorous standards of the Turing test have not yet appeared. Consistent with Turing's own conclusions, this state of affairs is often taken to constitute evidence that true artificial intelligence has not yet been developed, thereby testifying to the unique cognitive competence of human minds. However, critics have described a number of problems with using the Turing test as an identifier of artificial intelligence. For example, animals and small children would fail the Turing test despite possessing intelligence. Similarly, even if a machine fooled all observers who tested it, it could still be the case that it has merely been *imitating* intelligence because of the proficiency of its human programmers, rather than *manifesting* true intelligence in its own right. As such, neither failing nor passing the Turing test is actually definitive. Nonetheless, the test has been very influential in contextualising debate in the philosophy of cognition and intelligence.

execute an indefinite number of operations. Together with Boole's suggestion that all thought could be expressed in terms of binary codes, Turing's work strongly implied that human thought could be modelled mechanically. As well as providing a starting point for the development of electronic computers, Boole and Turing's principles opened the door for psychologists who wished to study mental processes in scientific ways.

Among the other thinkers whose ideas contributed to the developing study of mental processes were Austrian philosopher Ludwig Wittgenstein (1889–1951), who described how language symbols relate to mental processes; British philosopher Gilbert Ryle (1900–1976), who, as a monist, argued that mental phenomena were necessarily rooted within human biology; Hungarian-American mathematician John von Neumann (1903–1957), who developed theories of computation that attempted to allow for randomness; and American polymath Noam Chomsky (b. 1928), who emphasised the centrality of mental events for explaining human learning and development.

Test your knowledge

6.1 How does Boolean logic assist the study of human thought?

6.2 Why was the Turing machine important for cognitive psychology?

Answers to these questions can be found on the companion website at: **www.pearsoned.co.uk/psychologyexpress.**

? Sample question   Essay

Do mathematical or mechanical systems of symbols serve merely as analogies for human thought processes, or do they truly inform our understanding of such processes?

Empirical precursors to cognitivism

In the 1950s, a number of psychologists conducted studies that applied scientific methods to mental phenomena. Rather than fall back on the pure introspection of the psychophysicists, these researchers sought ways of measuring objectively verifiable indices that indirectly revealed the nature of mental constructs. A number of studies were based on the principle that thought processes occurred in real-time sequences of discrete steps. They concluded that measuring the time it took people to perform cognitive tasks would shed light on the number of steps involved in the thought processes required. For example, researchers noticed that, when asked to respond as quickly as possible to reaction time tasks, participants responded fastest when the number of choices required to be made was minimised. Other researchers noted that participants were quicker at recalling details of remembered objects when they related to features located close to each other (e.g. the side-window and the door of a car) than when they related to features located far apart (e.g. the headlights and the exhaust pipe). Although the researchers could not directly examine the mental images inside the participants' minds, they could form certain conclusions about how these images were experienced from reaction time data collected in experiments.

KEY STUDY

Miller's magical number seven

A landmark paper by American psychologist George A. Miller (1956) suggested that, on average, human learners can comfortably maintain up to around seven discrete items of information in their mind at the same time. Miller presented the results of a series of studies examining different aspects of cognition, including people's perceptual judgement of differences across stimuli and their short-term memory for stimuli. He noticed an important commonality between the findings on both topics. Firstly, when participants engaged in tasks that required them to concentrate on fewer than around seven items, they usually found it quite easy and the speed and competence of their performance directly corresponded to task complexity. However, when participants engaged in levels of the task that required them to concentrate on more than seven items, they usually found it extremely difficult and the quality of their performance deteriorated. Miller then noted that experiments on memory spans seemed to match these findings perfectly, insofar as participants were regularly found to be comfortably able to maintain up to around seven items in short-term memory. When asked to maintain more than seven items, participants' memory performance became compromised. Including a margin of error to take account of individual differences, Miller identified the pertinent threshold as ranging between five and nine items, or in other words, seven plus or minus two items. He called this 'the magical number', a term that is still in use today.

Miller offered the view that the magical number represented a useful benchmark for interpreting the results of relevant research studies, rather than being particularly informative regarding fundamental functional aspects of cognition. Moreover, subsequent research has suggested that the magical number is not as widely applicable as was first believed. However, the widespread inference that Miller's synthesis revealed a genuine basic law of the human cognitive system proved to be highly influential. His paper also showed early cognition researchers how their dispersed findings might be usefully integrated into a common field of science. Accordingly, Miller's 1956 paper has become one of the most cited in cognitive psychology.

Source: Miller, G. A. (1956). The magical number seven, plus or minus two: Some limits on our capacity for processing information. *Psychological Review, 63,* 343–355.

British psychologist Donald Broadbent (1926–1993) is credited with presenting landmark research on mental attention. He conducted a programme of studies looking at the extent to which people could divide their attention between different streams of simultaneously presented information (e.g. by playing different audiotapes of digit sequences into participants' left and right ears). From his empirical work he developed an explicit model of how people screen out unnecessary information, which became known as the filter model of attention. Importantly, Broadbent integrated his model within a broader set of concepts that drew on other areas of cognitive research. He proposed an architectural model of cognition in which different elements were laid out in schematic form, rather like in a mechanical blueprint for an engine. For example, in his filter model, he located the filter as lying between the mechanisms that handled sensory input and those that handled short-term memory. While such constructs were described in terms of their spatial locations, it was not proposed that they related to actual physical entities located in different places (e.g. in the brain). Rather, Broadbent's spatial language was intended to serve as a metaphorical way of explaining the sequences of processes involved in cognition and the inter-relationships of the various underlying subsequences. Broadbent's work, which came to be referred to as the information processing approach, led to the widespread use of schematic diagrams to represent theories about cognition. It also inspired many observers to argue that human minds operate in essentially the same way as electronic microcomputers.

Key term

Information: a term that is used widely in everyday conversation and yet is one that has a very specific meaning in technical contexts. In technical contexts, information refers to a quantity of symbols that form part of an ordered system. This quantity reflects the number of choices a user has when handling the symbols. Assuming that the symbols carry significant meanings for the user, then we can use such terms to explain the complexity of decision-making involved handling them. In the field of mathematics and engineering known as 'information theory', such approaches are used as the basis of quantifying the smallest possible components (known as 'bits') that make up a piece of knowledge. Awareness of how many 'bits' of information are contained in a piece of knowledge helps engineers develop efficient ways of storing, compressing, and transmitting knowledge through electronic media. In cognitive psychology, principles of information theory are used in considering the parameters of how humans might perform the same tasks.

Miller and Broadbent were joined by several other researchers who collected empirical data in order to examine inferential theories relating to human cognition. Cumulatively, their work came to be identified as a single stream of research in psychology. In 1965, German-born American psychologist Ulrich Neisser (b. 1928) coined the term 'cognitive psychology' to refer to this new field. Its sudden blossoming and its perceived incompatibility with behaviourism led many to refer to its arrival as the 'cognitive revolution.'

Test your knowledge

6.3 What does Miller's magical number explain regarding the nature of human memory?

6.4 According to Broadbent, how does filtering affect attention?

Answers to these questions can be found on the companion website at:
www.pearsoned.co.uk/psychologyexpress.

 Sample question Essay

Which is more important to a scientific 'revolution': a radical change in how subject matter is conceived, or a radical change in how scientists perform their research? Which is more true of the 'cognitive revolution'?

The cognitivist approach

While acknowledging that the cognitivist approach has been applied to a very wide range of subject matter in psychology, it is probably reasonable to list its major areas of study as: attention and perception; memory; decision-making and reasoning; concept formation and categorisation; and language. Indeed, cognitive psychology is perhaps most often described only in terms of the areas of study covered by its research. However, perhaps a more important way of describing the field is to outline some of its main conceptual principles.

In brief, cognitive psychology seeks to use empirical methods to study the mental processes that consitute human thought. It is largely premised on the assumption that thinking occurs within an internal system of mental representations. This means that, when we think, we invoke images, ideas, concepts, memories, words and strategies that exist within our minds. These are posited to occupy an intermediate conceptual level between the actual objects in the real world and the biological or neurological systems that underlie that which we call our 'minds'.

A second major principle is the idea of top-down processing. This refers to the fact that humans regularly use prior knowledge, experience and assumptions to help organise and interpret new information. This helps us to adapt quickly to new challenges, and to learn related tasks faster. Many cognitively focused theorists, such as Noam Chomsky and Canadian-American psychologist Steven

Pinker (b. 1954), have interpreted the occurrence of top-down processing as constituting evidence for the existence of innate, and therefore genetically endowed and naturally selected, human cognitive abilities.

A further important principle of cognitive psychology is that cognitive computations can be structured in combinatorial ways. This essentially means that even small cognitive processes can be combined to produce complex mental capabilities, reflecting the original Boolean idea that all logic can ultimately be represented in terms of binary operations. Overall, the field of cognitive psychology is often described in terms of a philosophical view that likens human minds to computers, with our thought processes assumed to be very similar (if not equivalent) to the internal functions of a modern microprocessor.

Example of interdisciplinary nature of cognition

Since the 1970s, cognitive psychologists have seen their ideas and research embraced by scholars in a wide range of other academic disciplines, as well as a burgeoning of interdisciplinary research focused on cognitive phenomena. Collectively, this collection of disciplines has become known as 'cognitive science'. In brief, cognitive science can be defined as an interdisciplinary field that is focused on how thought occurs in the human brain. Although such classifications are essentially arbitrary, many observers identify the constituent subdisciplines of cognitive science as being drawn from psychology, philosophy, linguistics, anthropology, neuroscience and artificial intelligence (AI) research. While each discipline can be credited with specific contributions, especially in terms of research methodologies, it is perhaps arguable that most of the cross-cutting principles and subject matter have originated from the contributions of the psychologists.

Test your knowledge

6.5 What are the main features of the cognitivist approach?

6.6 What main disciplines comprise cognitive science?

Answers to these questions can be found on the companion website at:
www.pearsoned.co.uk/psychologyexpress.

Sample question   *Essay*

To what extent can the metaphor of the computer be applied to human cognition?

Limitations of cognitive psychology

Although cognitive psychology has been very successful, it has attracted criticisms. While its researchers valorise the scientific method, it is nonetheless the case that its core subjects (thoughts, mental images, memories, etc.) are not directly observable. Critics such as Skinner have argued that this means cognitive psychology is ultimately premised on a theoretical assumption – that of the existence of mental representations – which can never be empirically demonstrated. Researchers have resorted to measuring the indirect consequences of representations or their biological correlates, and to imitating cognition using mathematics or computer models. This is seen as a problem because conventional critiques of science have always emphasised the importance of direct observation in ensuring scientific validity. The extent to which cognitive psychology is based on indirect observation may therefore represent a weakness. It fails to exclude the possibility that researchers' own biases and limitations affect their interpretations of data (as well as the explanatory theories that these interpretations yield).

CRITICAL FOCUS

Cognitive psychology and behaviourism

At the level of scientific ethos, cognitive psychology has often presented itself as a response, if not an antidote, to behaviourism. Behaviourism, cognitivists argued, requires undue methodological and theoretical reductionism: its research is accused of focusing on (purported) trivia, such as the training of lever-pressing in laboratory rats, while its theories are said to reduce people to the status of operant organisms, thus failing to recognise the dignity of the human condition. However, it is not clear that cognitive psychology has demonstrably moved much beyond these alleged failings of behaviourism. Because of its reliance on indirect measurement, cognitive psychologists focus on a type of core data (such as recalled lists of words or reaction times) that does not seem much more profound than that gathered by behaviourists. It can also be argued that the computational metaphor in cognitive psychology is just as reductionist as the stimulus–response metaphor of behaviourism. The comparison of human minds with computers may be taken to imply that our minds are little more than information processing units housed in the neural computers that are our brains. It is also the case that in many applied areas, such as health promotion or education, interventions based on behaviourist principles regularly appear to be more successful than those informed by cognitive psychology. Indeed, many practitioners advocate the use of both cognitive and behavioural principles in order to maximise the benefits of therapy, which has led to the development of the combined therapeutic approach known as cognitive behavioural therapy (or CBT).

Other criticisms of cognitive psychology have pointed to its tendency to ignore the vagaries of emotions and the complex influence of social environments when seeking to explain human thinking. Similarly, the field is accused of being overly descriptive: in general, unlike behaviourism, cognitive psychology fails to offer an explanation as to why people are motivated to act they way they do. On a technical level, critics have also noted that much human cognition is dynamic and conducted in multiple simultaneous processes, and so is quite unlike the computation seen in human-built microcomputers.

Finally, despite their success in describing patterns of memory, language, reasoning and so on, cognitive psychologists acknowledge that they have yet to make much progress in accounting for the main difference between human brains and technological computers; namely, the presence of consciousness.

Test your knowledge

6.7 Why might the reliance on concepts such as mental representations raise concerns about the scientific rigour of cognitive psychology?

6.8 How might emotions affect cognitions?

Answers to these questions can be found on the companion website at:
www.pearsoned.co.uk/psychologyexpress.

? Sample question   Essay

Are behaviourism and cognitive psychology incompatible?

Chapter summary – pulling it all together

→ Can you tick all the points from the revision checklist at the beginning of this chapter?

→ Attempt the sample question from the beginning of this chapter using the answer guidelines below.

→ Go to the companion website at www.pearsoned.co.uk/psychologyexpress to access more revision support online, including interactive quizzes, flashcards, You be the marker exercises as well as answer guidance for the Test your knowledge and Sample questions from this chapter.

Further reading for Chapter 6

Topic	Key reading
Boole's system	Boole, G. (1853). *An investigation of the laws of thought.* Retrieved from http://www.gutenberg.org/ebooks/15114
Turing machine	Turing, A. M. (1963). Computing machinery and intelligence. In E. A. Feigenbaum & J. Feldman (Eds.), *Computers and thought.* New York: McGraw-Hill.
Miller's impact	Crowther-Heyck, H. (1999). George A. Miller, language, and the computer metaphor of mind. *History of Psychology, 2,* 37–64.
Broadbent and attention	Broadbent, D. E. (1954). The role of auditory localization in attention and memory span. *Journal of Experimental Psychology, 47,* 191–196.
The 'cocktail party affect'	Cherry, E. C. (1953). Some experiments on the recognition of speech, with one and with two ears. *Journal of the Acoustical Society of America, 25,* 975–979.
Baddeley	Baddeley, A. (2010). *Alan Baddeley: Cognitive revolution* [Video]. Retrieved from http://www.youtube.com/watch?v=wyfEETtWgCY
Information processing	Broadbent, D. E. (1980). The minimization of models. In A. J. Chapman & D. M. Jones (Eds.), *Models of man* (pp. 113–127). London: British Psychological Society.
Cognitivism	Gardner, H. (1985). *The mind's new science: A history of the cognitive revolution.* New York: Basic Books.
Cognitive science	Neisser, U. (1987). *Concepts and conceptual development.* Cambridge: Cambridge University Press.
Contemporary cognitivism	Pinker, S. (1997). *How the mind works.* New York: Norton.
Ideology of cognitivism	Sampson, E. E. (1981). Cognitive psychology as ideology. *American Psychologist, 36,* 730–743.
Critique of cognitivism	Skinner, B. F. (1990). Can psychology be a science of the mind? *American Psychologist, 45,* 1206–1210.

Answer guidelines

✻ Sample question   Essay

Evaluate the success of the metaphor of 'mind as computer'.

Approaching the question

The essay question requires an evaluation of the success of cognitivism's computational metaphor. In order to approach the question effectively, some working definition of 'success' needs to be offered. This could refer to the validity of the metaphor in aiding our understanding, or it could also refer to the utility of the metaphor in spawning lucrative avenues of research. It could even refer to the contribution of the metaphor to the positive reputation of psychology as a research science. Not all these working definitions overlap, so a choice is required.

Important points to include

Whatever approach you take to the notion of 'success', it is important to provide a balanced account of the metaphor of 'mind as computer'. This will require a consideration of how the metaphor has been widely used in cognitive psychology, but also how it has latterly been identified as limited (due to contrasts between the dynamic quasi-parallel processing seen in human minds and the essentially serial processing of computers). While the metaphor might be discussed in terms of its abstract dimensions, such as how human minds perform processes like computers, it may also be discussed in terms of its tangible dimensions, such as how computer modelling has been used as a research technique (for example, in studies of artificial intelligence).

Make your answer stand out

In discussing the role of computer metaphors during the history of cognitive psychology, it would be interesting to trace the development of actual computers in society during this time and to consider whether such technological developments influenced the ways in which computer metaphors were discussed and understood. For example, in Turing's time, computers were largely hypothetical devices, while today large numbers of people have personal computers in their own homes. As such, over time, cognitive psychologist's metaphors may have become skewed by practical developments in how publicly available computers have been designed. Try to think of examples of how modern computers differ from older ones, especially in terms of how users interact with them (for example, today's computers present information using spatially arranged and vivid graphics, while the first computers relied on uniform verbal and numerical characters presented in lines). Then see if you identify similar differences between newer and older cognitive theories of, say, memory. You could then consider whether such cultural factors might have influenced the success of the metaphor over the history of cognitive psychology.

Explore the accompanying website at www.pearsoned.co.uk/psychologyexpress
→ Prepare more effectively for exams and assignments using the answer guidelines for questions from this chapter.
→ Test your knowledge using multiple choice questions and flashcards.
→ Improve your essay skills by exploring the You be the marker exercises.

Notes

7

Neuroscience and genetics: 21st-century reductionism?

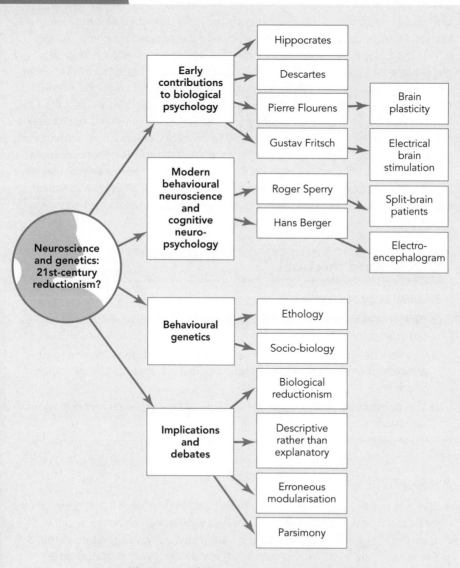

A printable version of this topic map is available from
www.pearsoned.co.uk/psychologyexpress

Introduction

The term 'neuroscience' refers to the scientific study of the nervous system, while 'genetics' refers to the study of genes, heredity and variation both across and within species. Within both fields, specialisations focusing on psychological phenomena have emerged. Behavioural neuroscience considers the role of the nervous system in psychological contexts. Put simply, the nervous system is a network of neurons spread throughout the body which co-ordinates its movements and through which its information signals are communicated. In humans (and many other animals) the nervous system is typically described as comprising two sections, the central nervous system (CNS) and the peripheral nervous system (PNS). The CNS, which primarily includes the brain and spinal cord, is largely responsible for integrating information and controlling actions; the PNS is mainly used for connecting the CNS to outlying organs. Behavioural neuroscience comprises an extensive range of biological disciplines that have studied the CNS (such as neurology, molecular biology and cellular biology), as well as disciplines concerned with how complex mechanised systems operate (such as mathematics, computer science, physics and even philosophy). Behavioural genetics focuses on how genes and heredity influence the evolution of behaviour across species. Among its contributing disciplines are genetics, ethology, zoology and statistics. Behavioural neuroscience and behavioural genetics both have long histories and important conceptual implications for psychology.

 Revision checklist

Essential points to revise are:

❑ How scholars first identified the relevance of biological influences on psychological outcomes

❑ The way behavioural neuroscience and behavioural genetics emerged as fields of study as a result of technological advances in the biological sciences

❑ The epistemological critique of behavioural neuroscience and behavioural genetics

Assessment advice

● Essay questions on this topic may tempt you to provide lengthy descriptions of the technical details of research in behavioural neuroscience and behavioural genetics. Descriptions of the historical developments of these fields are likely to be punctuated by landmark studies that feature the introduction of new technologies.

- However, just as it might be recommended that psychologists in these fields not become overly distracted by technological innovation away from the psychological implications of their research, so it will be important for you to ensure that your essays maintain a focus on the relevant conceptual implications.

- When presenting such studies in the context of historical and conceptual issues in psychology, it will be necessary to emphasise their psychological relevance. How these historical developments served to provide new insights, to create new strategies of inquiry, and to raise new questions about psychology as a whole will be more pertinent than how the studies were conducted in practical terms.

Sample question

Could you answer this question? Below is a typical essay question that could arise on this topic.

 Sample question   *Essay*

Critically evaluate the impact of technology on behavioural neuroscience and behavioural genetics.

Guidelines on answering this question are included at the end of this chapter, whilst further guidance on tackling other exam questions can be found on the companion website at: **www.pearsoned.co.uk/psychologyexpress**

Early contributions to biological psychology

Observers of nature (including human nature) have long noticed associations between biology and behaviour. Breeders of animals have noticed that behavioural traits frequently re-emerge in successive generations of offspring. Psychological characteristics, and many mental illnesses, also sometimes appear to run in families. Similar species of animals often have quite different, but species-specific, behaviour patterns: for example, different species of fish can have species-specific mating behaviours, or different species of bird can have species-specific grooming behaviours. And significant biological changes in the body, such as those caused by brain injuries or drug use, can lead to significant changes in psychological function. Accordingly, theories of how human biology determines or is otherwise involved in psychological outcomes are as old as civilisation itself. While many of the prominent ancient Greek and Roman scholars (such as Aristotle) believed the heart to be the organ with primary control over behaviour, it is also true that many historical communities correctly judged that the brain was centrally responsible. Hippocrates (460–370 BCE) argued that this was the case, and anthropological evidence shows that trepanning – the drilling of a hole through the human skull and into the brain in order to treat mental disorders – has emerged in several cultures throughout the world dating back to Neolithic times.

Perhaps the first extensive scientific study of the brain's implications for behaviour can be credited to Descartes. His 17th-century studies of physiology described a complex pneumatic system where the brain controlled behaviour by transmitting vibratory motions through filaments inside the body's nerves. In the 19th century, a number of researchers, including Pierre Flourens and Paul Broca (see Chapter 4), studied the impact of brain injuries on behaviour. The French physiologist Flourens surgically removed sections of cortex from the brains of live animals, and found that younger animals, but not older ones, were able to eventually recover aspects of the behaviour patterns they had lost following injury. This revealed the principle of brain plasticity, where surviving parts of an injured brain are capable of assuming the specialised functions that would have subsequently developed in the injured areas had typical brain development been allowed to occur. Broca, a surgeon based in Paris, presented a number of medical case histories of patients with brain injuries. His most famous case involved a man who had lost the capacity to produce speech except, oddly, when he was in a temper (a point which demonstrated that his vocal cords were working normally). Autopsies of his various patients led him to identify a particular area of the brain's left temporal lobe as its primary speech production centre.

Key term

Aphasia: a disorder of language capabilities that results from damage to the brain. The disorder can relate to the ability to produce language, to comprehend it, or both. There are several different types of aphasia, reflecting the highly complex nature of language itself. Aphasias have been of interest to behavioural neuroscience because studying the location of the damage suffered helps identify those parts of the brain that are associated with different aspects of language. Perhaps the two most commonly mentioned types of aphasia reflect this principle, as they – and the brain locations implicated in their aetiology – are named after the clinicians who first discovered them. These are Broca's aphasia (named after Paul Broca, characterised by difficulties with language expression, and associated with damage to an area of the left temporal lobe now known as Broca's area) and Wernicke's aphasia (named after German physician Carl Wernicke [1848–1905], characterised by difficulties with language comprehension, and associated with damage to a left temporal lobe area now called Wernicke's area).

The 19th century saw new breakthroughs in the study of electricity and the introduction of electrical engineering, both of which led to widespread attempts to use electricity in scientific research. The study of the brain was no exception. In

Germany, Gustav Fritsch (1838–1927) and Eduard Hitzig (1839–1907) conducted animal experiments where they applied low-level electric currents to the brains of live dogs. They discovered that electrical stimulation of different brain areas led to a corresponding range of physical movements on the opposite side of the body. Their studies further established the principle of localisation of brain function, an idea discussed in phrenology. Significantly, Fritsch and Hitzig's findings served to debunk phrenology, insofar as the localised functions they found in the brain were entirely different from those described by the phrenologists.

Test your knowledge

7.1 What observations helped people appreciate the likelihood that our psychological selves were at least partly biologically determined?

7.2 How did studies of brain damage inform our understanding of psychology in the 19th century?

Answers to these questions can be found on the companion website at: **www.pearsoned.co.uk/psychologyexpress**

 Sample question   **Essay**

How was our understanding of the human brain altered by the study of aphasic patients, and to what extent was it confirmed?

Modern behavioural neuroscience and cognitive neuropsychology

The 20th century saw the emergence of a number of research approaches that came to typify modern neuroscience. These included studies involving modifications and interventions with the live human brain, as well as ways of measuring and then visually representing brain function. Such has been the development of sophistication in this research that subfields began to emerge. Many researchers now use the term 'behavioural neuroscience' to refer to the broad application of neurophysiology to psychology, with the term 'cognitive neuropsychology' used to describe the particular implications of neuroscientific discoveries for our understanding of cognition.

Recalling Broca's earlier case studies on patients with different brain injuries, a number of 20th-century researchers sought other clinical domains in which analogous work might be conducted on larger, more homogeneous, samples. In the 1970s, American neurologist Roger Sperry (1913–1994) conducted a number of studies on patients who had received a standardised surgical treatment for epilepsy. In order to contain the impact of epileptic seizures, these patients had received a type of brain surgery that separated the left and right halves of the brain by cutting through the corpus collosum (the bundle of nerve fibres that connects the brain's two hemispheres). In Sperry's specially designed experiments, the cognitive and behavioural performance of these so-called 'split-brain' patients was found to reveal important differences in the functioning of the two hemispheres. Sperry also showed that each hemisphere was capable of functioning without affecting, or being affected by, the functions of the other. This latter finding is often described as though demonstrating that each hemisphere is capable of separate awareness, raising immediate philosophical questions about the nature of human consciousness.

KEY STUDY

Penfield's direct electrical brain stimulation

Several medical treatments that emerged in the 20th century, especially for brain-related disorders such as epilepsy, provided unique contexts for investigating direct electrical brain stimulation in humans. In the 1950s, Canadian neurosurgeon Wilder Penfield (1891–1976) devised a procedure for safely applying electrical currents to the cortexes of patients while they were under local anaesthetic. His procedure was designed to help identify those parts of an epileptic patient's brain that were responsible for the particular seizures they experienced. Following the use of the procedure on a number of patients, Penfield (1952) reported that some patients spontaneously described highly vivid memories from their personal histories when certain parts of the brains were electrically stimulated. From this he concluded that human memories were stored separately throughout different locations of the brain. However, subsequent memory research has failed to corroborate this finding. One problem with Penfield's observation was that he did not try to confirm the accuracy of his patients' reports and so we do not know whether they represented authentic memories. Also, the vast majority of his patients did not report any such memories at all. Nonetheless, the introduction of a safe procedure for electrically stimulating the live human brain marked an important breakthrough, and researchers using this method have produced a number of significant contributions.

Source: Penfield, W. (1952). Memory mechanisms. AMA Archives of Neurology and Psychiatry, 67, 178–198.

The 20th and 21st centuries also saw great strides in the way researchers have attempted to measure, and subsequently visually represent, aspects of brain function. In the 1920s, German psychiatrist Hans Berger (1873–1941) developed the electroencephalogram (EEG), a system for measuring the brain's own electrical activity using electrodes placed on the scalp. Using an EEG, Berger established that a brain's natural electrical activity fluctuates at around 10 Hz (i.e. 10 cycles per second) when an awake person rests with closed eyes, and accelerates to between 12 and 30 Hz when the person opens his or her eyes. He referred to these wave patterns, respectively, as alpha waves and beta waves. Since this work, EEG research has become decidedly more complex. For example, while Berger used just two electrodes, modern EEG research often uses a network of several separate electrodes spread over the scalp to allow for electrical activity to be mapped across the surface of the brain (a technique known as EEG topography). In addition, modern EEG research often measures changes in electrical brain activity that occur in response to a cognitive event (such as a thought or perception), which are referred to as event-related potentials (ERPs). The study of ERPs allows researchers to establish the relative similarities of different cognitive events by comparing their ERP profiles.

Example of brain imaging technology

Developed in the 1970s, magnetic resonance imaging (MRI) is a technique that allows researchers to examine pictures of the structure of a living brain. In practical terms, MRI is rather like traditional X-ray technology, except that it is fundamentally based on magnetism instead of radiation. It is used for a variety of imaging purposes in medicine, but has become prominent in psychology due to the particular clarity of the brain images it produces. One advantage of MRI is that it allows researchers to examine associations between brain injuries and cognitive symptoms while a patient is still alive, rather than having to wait for the opportunity to perform an autopsy. Since the 1990s, researchers have also been able to use a related technique known as functional MRI (fMRI), which provides images of brain blood flow. Given that blood flow correlates with neural activity in different parts of the brain, fMRI has allowed researchers to compare images taken at two time-points (for example, before and after a cognitive task) in order to infer where neural activity has occurred. Because fMRI does not expose patients to radiation, it has facilitated much more research than previous technologies used for recording images of the brain, such as computerised axial tomography (CAT) and positron emission tomography (PET).

Advances in measurement technology have influenced the focus of neuroscience over time. While originally concerned with broad aspects of cognition and behaviour such as perception, control of movement and general memory, contemporary neuroscience has come to develop a strong focus on the study of cognition. Typical subject areas include decision-making, learning, attentional control, the production and comprehension of language, and specific memory processes.

Test your knowledge

7.3 How can hypotheses relating to localisation of function in the cortex be tested?

7.4 What are the main ways for producing images of the living brain?

Answers to these questions can be found on the companion website at:
www.pearsoned.co.uk/psychologyexpress

> **? Sample question**   *Essay*
>
> Has the introduction of brain imaging technologies universally enhanced behavioural neuroscience?

Behavioural genetics

The fact that traits can appear to be transmitted to successive generations through sexual reproduction has been noted throughout history. Such a belief underlies the traditional breeding practices (for both crops and animals) that were used in agriculture for centuries. In psychology, many of the early psychometricians (such as Galton) also based their work on an assumption that psychological characteristics were hereditary. In the early 20th century, the field of academic study concerned with this principle became known as 'genetics'. These first geneticists, such as the British scholar William Bateson (1861–1926), did not use the term to refer to what biologists nowadays call genes. Instead, they used the term 'genetics' to refer to the complex patterns of inherited traits (both physical and psychological) that had been observed within species. From this information, later researchers inferred that some biological entity responsible for inheritance must exist in each individual organism. These entities were eventually identified by the American embryologist Thomas Hunt Morgan (1866–1945) as existing on chromosomes. Later researchers located genes more specifically as being segments of the deoxyribonucleic acid (or DNA) that forms part of each chromosome. Even more recently, an international team of researchers have conducted the Human Genome Project (launched in 1990), which is an attempt to identify and catalogue the range of variations and functions of all 25,000 or so individual genes that make up the human genetic blueprint.

Over the 20th century, behavioural genetics emerged as a distinct specialism, influenced in part by research in ethology (the study of animals in their natural environments) and sociobiology (the study of the evolutionary aspects of social behaviour). Such research has attempted to use genetic principles to help identify the relative contributions of heredity and environment to behaviours such as altruism, aggression, kinship and jealousy, as well as to personality traits and attitudes. Some of this research has employed approaches common in the social sciences, such as twin studies and adoption studies. In recent decades, technological methods drawn from molecular biology have been added. For example, genetic screening and manipulation techniques have enabled researchers to test whether psychological traits or behaviours can be associated with specific genes. Thus far, this research has suggested that several behaviours, such as aspects of aggression and nurturing, are indeed influenced by genetic factors.

Key term

Genome: in genetics, the term 'genome' refers to the full collection of genes in an organism. It is located in each cell (specifically, within strands of DNA comprising the chromosomes inside the cell's nucleus), and contains all the information needed to produce and develop the organism's body throughout its life. Prior to the 1990s, it was generally believed that the human genome contained up to 200,000 distinct genes. However, as new technologies have facilitated more powerful ways of studying genes in humans, we now know that the genome is encapsulated within 23 pairs of chromosomes in each cell and comprises between 20,000 and 25,000 distinct genes in total. The finding that the human genome contains much fewer genes than previously thought has generally been acknowledged as surprising. One consequence of this finding is that we now know that humans have roughly the same number of genes as ostensibly simpler organisms such as mice, and even roundworm. Similarly surprising have been findings relating to the number of genes humans have in common with other species. For example, it appears that 50% of the genes found in humans can also be found in bananas. While it may be tempting to reflect on the implications for psychology of such apparent genetic similarities between humans and other species, it should be noted that such comparisons can be quite misleading. Firstly, the impact of genes on the sophistication of an organism relates not only to their number in the genome, but also to aspects of their function (especially with regard to their production of proteins) that tend to differ substantially across species. Secondly, while many human genes have counterparts in other species, their composition (in terms of DNA sequences) is not necessarily the same. In addition, many of these genes govern universal microbiological functions such as the growth of different types of cells, and so are needed by all species of organism. This renders their presence in species other than humans unremarkable.

Key term

The idea that psychological attributes are rooted in the interactions between genetic predispositions and environmental contingencies has led to the emergence of much research in psychology focusing on how such characteristics have been influenced by the principles of natural (and sexual) selection. This field has become known as **evolutionary psychology**, or EP. Following contemporary approaches to Darwin's original theory of evolution, evolutionary psychologists consider how psychological attributes might have evolved as adaptations to changing human environments. While they are particularly interested in social behaviour (such as what determines perceptions of physical attractiveness), evolutionary psychologists are also interested in complex cognitive phenomena (such as language). Overall, the approach argues that considering the possible contribution of psychological attributes to the adaptation of persons is helpful in explaining both their purpose and their complexity.

Test your knowledge

7.5 How do genes relate to the biological development?

7.6 What are the main questions addressed in behavioural genetics?

Answers to these questions can be found on the companion website at:
www.pearsoned.co.uk/psychologyexpress

 Sample question Essay

Is it truly possible to attribute behaviour to genes?

Implications and debates

Advances in biological sciences have added a distinct technological dimension to much contemporary research in psychology. They have also allowed researchers to investigate research questions that heretofore could only be considered hypothetically. The capacity to identify how the brain functions biologically during psychological experiences is regularly described as offering profound insights, as has the ability to attribute genetic underpinnings to certain behaviours and traits. However, in terms of epistemology, critics suggest that these technologically advanced fields are actually quite limited in their explanatory power.

It can be argued that disciplines focused on producing biological explanations for behaviour offer little additive information to psychology because, owing to determinism, it can always be assumed that there exists some biological basis (or correlate) to any expressed psychological process. For example, with regard to behavioural neuroscience, unless it is argued that psychological processes can occur independently of brain activity then the only additional information generated by neuroscientific research is the identification of precisely where that brain activity occurs. As such, although the technology required to produce the relevant data might be truly awe-inspiring, it is not clear that the data themselves – in purely informational terms – are similarly profound.

CRITICAL FOCUS

Biological reductionism

One of the main criticisms of behavioural neuroscience and behavioural genetics is that they are heavily reductionist. As mentioned in Chapter 5, reductionism is the view that complex systems can be adequately considered by studying their constituent parts. Behavioural neuroscience is often considered reductionist because it explicitly seeks to study complex psychological phenomena in terms of individual neural events rather than, say, broader factors such as experience, culture, environmental impact, social influence, intellectual creativity, personal motivation or aesthetic choices. Behavioural geneticists are accused of reducing psychological phenomena to individual genes. In other words, critics of reductionism in psychology accuse neuroscientists and geneticists of failing even to seek comprehensive explanations for the complexities of the human condition. Both fields can be accused of offering ways to describe, rather than to account for, the details of human nature. While neuroscience and genetics may eventually offer complete descriptions of the neural events that correlate with psychological ones, or of the individual genes that underlie all psychological traits, such information lies essentially at the level of taxonomy. One important implication of this is that, like all taxonomies, the emphasis is on classification rather than explanation. Being able to classify behaviours, cognitions and traits will not necessarily make us able to provide explanations of why people think, act and feel the way they do, give us the ability to predict future behaviours or cognitions, or suggest to us useful ways of intervening to change behaviour. In other words, the contribution of neuroscience and genetics to psychology may be limited to an essentially methodological role.

Another concern relates to the fact that, in order to correlate psychological phenomena to discrete neural events or genes, the explanations of the phenomena themselves have to be organised into discrete elements or steps. Some commentators, such as the American cognitive neuroscientist William R. Uttal, have questioned whether it is in fact valid to define psychological processes in a way that permits them to be organised in this manner. According to Uttal, the quest to describe psychological subjects in formats that allow them to be associated with brain regions may represent a modern equivalent to phrenology, and may distort our depictions of psychology in ways that fatally limit our understanding. A further complication is that, biologically, the various regions of the brain are complexly intercorrelated rather than truly modular, meaning that, even if a thought process can be associated with a particular neural mechanism, this mechanism will itself possess thousands of connections with other neurons. The question then arises as to whether some or all of these additional connections also contribute to the thought process in question. Likewise, it is well recognised in genetics that individual genes can rarely be implicated in individual psychological outcomes, be they behaviours, traits or thought patterns. Rather, outcomes will be influenced by a combination of (often multiple) genetic predispositions and by environmental, social and cultural factors, all of which will be subject to evolution over time.

Sample question   *Problem-based learning*

Consider the question of whether personality is genetically heritable. In order to do this, write a brief summary of your own personality in terms of whether you are shy or outgoing; calm or irritable; risk-averse or a risk-taker; methodical or creative; and emotional or stable-minded (these descriptors relate to dimensions of personality that psychological research suggests are helpful in describing the majority of people). Next, write down brief summaries of the personalities of your biological parents or, if different, the people who cared for you when you were growing up. Make a decision as to whether you have a similar personality to your childhood caregivers. Do you think that degree of biological relatedness can explain the degree of similarity or difference in personality? Are there other (environmental) factors that may contribute to the explanation? What information would be necessary to *disprove* the assertion that your personality was genetically determined?

Proponents of behavioural neuroscience and behavioural genetics will often defend their disciplines either philosophically or pragmatically. In philosophical terms, a reductionist approach will generally have the strength of being parsimonious and of reducing the number of unexplained elements in a theory (however, the main problem with this philosophical argument is that it is not always clear when a proposition is truly reducible to smaller elements). Defenders of reductionism in these fields will also point out that their reductionist findings are not intended to constitute free-standing explanations for psychological events, but to form part of larger holistic-level or systems-based theoretical explanations. More pragmatically, neuroscientists and geneticists can argue that some of their findings have been tangibly beneficial in different contexts. For example some behavioural neuroscientific data have assisted the development of therapeutic interventions for conditions such as Parkinson's disease. Meanwhile, findings in behavioural genetics have helped shed light on important public interest debates, such as whether there is a genetic basis to homosexuality. However, such benefits relate more to the possible application of neuroscience and genetics to problems that lie *outside* of psychology, than to their contributions to psychology itself.

Test your knowledge

7.7 How might behavioural neuroscience be likened to phrenology?

7.8 How do behavioural neuroscientists and geneticists defend reductionism?

Answers to these questions can be found on the companion website at: **www.pearsoned.co.uk/psychologyexpress**

Sample question   *Essay*

To what extent do behavioural neuroscience and behavioural genetics offer descriptions rather than explanations?

Chapter summary – pulling it all together

→ Can you tick all the points from the revision checklist at the beginning of this chapter?

→ Attempt the sample question from the beginning of this chapter using the answer guidelines below.

→ Go to the companion website at www.pearsoned.co.uk/psychologyexpress to access more revision support online, including interactive quizzes, flashcards, You be the marker exercises as well as answer guidance for the Test your knowledge and Sample questions from this chapter.

Further reading for Chapter 7	
Topic	*Key reading*
Early biological psychology	Clarke, E., & Jacyna, L. S. (1987). *Nineteenth-century origins of neuroscientific concepts*. Berkeley: University of California Press.
History of neuroscience	Gross, C. G. (1998). *Brain, vision, memory: Tales in the history of neuroscience*. Cambridge, Massachusetts: MIT Press.
Penfield	Penfield, W. (1960). *Wilder Penfield's brain stimulation* [video]. Downloaded from http://www.youtube.com/watch?v=52bYneF6JEk.
History of EEG	Rösler, F. (2005). From single-channel recordings to brain-mapping devices: The impact of electroencephalography on experimental psychology. *History of Psychology, 8*, 95–117.
Critique of neuroimaging	Coltheart, M. (2006). What has functional neuroimaging told us about the mind (so far)? *Cortex, 42*, 323–331.
Critique of neuroscience	Uttal, W. R. (2001). *The new phrenology: The limits of localizing cognitive processes in the brain*. Cambridge, Massachusetts: MIT Press.
Evolutionary psychology	Buss, D. (2011). *Evolutionary psychology: The new science of the mind* (4th edition) London: Pearson.
Nature–nuture debate	Pinker, S. (2003). *The blank slate: The modern denial of human nature*. London: Penguin.

Answer guidelines

 Sample question Essay

> Critically evaluate the impact of technology on behavioural neuroscience and behavioural genetics.

Approaching the question

The essay question asks for a critical evaluation, which requires a consideration of both the strengths and weaknesses of the proposition. It also refers to both behavioural neuroscience and behavioural genetics, and so both fields should be discussed.

Important points to include

As a critical evaluation is called for, it will be important to include both the strengths and weaknesses associated with the contribution of technology to these fields. While the strengths are frequently discussed (tending to involve the way technology has served to increase the quantity and detail of knowledge relating to brain function and genetics), the weaknesses are less so. As such, the discussion of limitations will be particularly important in an essay such as this. Perhaps the most obvious class of limitations will relate to how the sophistication of research technologies might be seen as being disproportionate to the psychological insight that has been generated by these approaches. In other words, although the technology has advanced apace, the information generated remains descriptive rather than explanatory.

Make your answer stand out

While it will be important to discuss the details of research in both behavioural neuroscience and behavioural genetics, it might also be helpful to consider research in other areas of psychology. This would be in order to support a consideration of the relative impacts of these fields on mainstream psychology. While the findings of these fields are intricate and multitudinous, your evaluation might reveal that they have had little influence on mainstream psychology. As such, it could be argued that the greatest impact of technology has been to radically alter the way research in these particular fields has been pursued, rather than on widening our understanding (or even our descriptions) of human nature. Such a distinction between the professional practice and the scholarly products of research will help make your answer stand out.

Explore the accompanying website at www.pearsoned.co.uk/psychologyexpress
→ Prepare more effectively for exams and assignments using the answer
   guidelines for questions from this chapter.
→ Test your knowledge using multiple choice questions and flashcards.
→ Improve your essay skills by exploring the You be the marker exercises.

Notes

Notes

Can psychology be scientific?

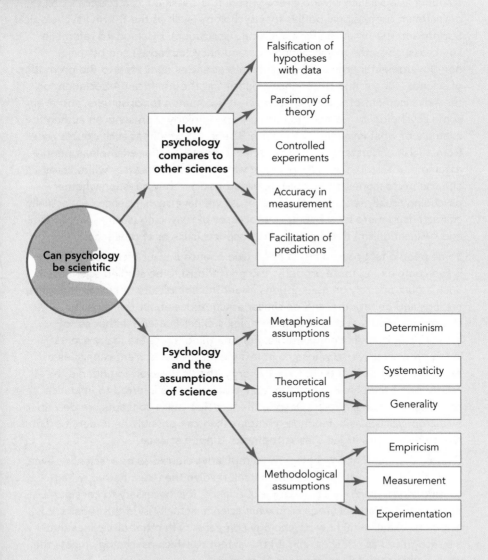

A printable version of this topic map is available from
www.pearsoned.co.uk/psychologyexpress

Introduction

The formal discipline of psychology has now become recognised in both academic and public contexts as a thriving empirical field. Much of its credibility is dependent on the fact that it has sought to embrace the scientific method as a means of corroborating its explanations of human nature. This has served to define psychology as a standard academic discipline distinct from everyday speculation concerning why people are the way they are. Psychology's standing as a science is widely recognised. It is classified as a science by all the mainstream professional bodies for psychology (such as the British Psychological Society and the American Psychological Association), by standard reference sources (such as the major dictionaries and encyclopaedias) and by major non-governmental organisations and state agencies dedicated to the promotion of science (such as the UK Science Council and the American Association for the Advancement of Science). However, it is common for observers, and even some psychologists, to question whether psychology represents an authentic example of what is meant by the term 'science'. Sometimes such doubts arise from a false understanding of what science actually is. For example, if people assume that sciences are disciplines in which practitioners wear white coats and use microscopes, then it will be unsurprising if they question whether psychology really is a science. However, as we have seen, sciences are actually characterised more by substantive processes of reasoning (such as empiricism and falsificationism) than by superficial aspects (such as appearances).

Some people feel psychology is not a true science because its subject matter is too complex (or, more properly, too mysterious) to be studied scientifically. Such arguments rely on assumptions about the complexity of human thoughts, feelings and behaviours, and on similar assumptions about the capacity of scientific methods to elucidate complex subject matter. Neither set of assumptions is easily demonstrable. For one thing, there are many events in the physical universe whose complexity exceeds our current capacities to explain. Examples include the 'dark energy' that is believed to underlie the expansion of the universe and the 'dark matter' that is inferred to influence certain gravitational effects. Despite the fact that these concepts are described by astrophysicists as being more complex than can possibly be understood, it is rare to hear critics argue that astrophysics is not a science.

Overall, the fact that psychology is so regularly referred to as a 'science', even by reputable authorities, does not in itself resolve the issue. Rather, when considering psychology's standing as a science, it is necessary to consider the substantive aspects regarding what science actually is. In this regard, it is helpful to examine (a) how psychology compares with other disciplines that are recognised as sciences, and (b) the extent to which psychology meets the various philosophical assumptions of science.

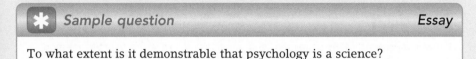

→ *Revision checklist*

Essential points to revise are:
- ❏ How psychology compares to other sciences
- ❏ The degree to which psychology meets the assumptions of science
- ❏ The degree to which the definition of science itself can be questioned

Assessment advice

- The question of whether psychology is a science is one of both principle and practicality. In terms of principle, it relates to whether or not psychology is a discipline that meets a reasonable semantic definition of the term 'science'. In terms of practicality, it relates to whether or not psychologists are considered to be and treated as scientists in the real world, and in turn whether or not psychology is seen as a credible source of scientific information about human thoughts, feelings and behaviour.

- As any attempt to argue that a particular entity meets the definition of a particular term will hinge on the degree to which the term's definition is objectively demonstrable and consensually accepted, such arguments can easily become circular. As such, it will be helpful to bear in mind the practical aspects as well.

- In other words, when contemplating whether or not psychology is a science, it will be helpful to be conversant with the philosophical issues, but also with the practical ways in which the term science is used in academic contexts.

Sample question

Could you answer this question? Below is a typical essay question that could arise on this topic.

✱ *Sample question*   *Essay*

To what extent is it demonstrable that psychology is a science?

Guidelines on answering this question are included at the end of this chapter, whilst further guidance on tackling other exam questions can be found on the companion website at: **www.pearsoned.co.uk/psychologyexpress**

How psychology compares to other sciences

One common approach to considering the issue of whether psychology is a science involves identifying the main descriptive features of established sciences and assessing whether psychology possesses these features. In such contexts, psychology is frequently compared with physics and chemistry, which are among the most commonly mentioned fields of science. In particular, physics is often held to be the archetypal science, as it is one of the oldest academic disciplines and one of the first to successfully exploit mathematics as an explanatory tool. Both physics and chemistry are considered to possess all of the major descriptive features of science. These include an emphasis on the falsification of hypotheses using empirical data, parsimony of theory, the ability to conduct controlled experiments, accuracy in measurements and the facilitation of predictions.

By comparison, while psychology certainly seeks to falsify hypotheses with data, it is unclear whether it is successful in achieving the other major features usually mentioned. Many theories in psychology appear to lack parsimony in the sense that unsupported assumptions (such as the existence of mental representations) are often tolerated, if not indeed intrinsic. It is also difficult in psychology to conduct fully controlled experiments. For example, when studying gender differences, the psychology researcher does not have control over the major grouping variable of gender (that is to say, the researcher cannot allocate cases to the comparison groups at random). Further, unlike in physics, where qualities can be measured very precisely (e.g. mass can be measured to the nearest microgram), psychological qualities (such as attitudes or personality type) are often arbitrarily defined and so difficult to quantify with any specificity. Finally, while a chemist can predict the exact composition of a compound that will be produced in a particular chemistry experiment, psychologists find it very difficult to predict the behaviour of any particular person. Viewed in this context, psychology could be said to lack the basic features of parsimony, experimental control, measurement and prediction. Some observers will argue that psychology, therefore, cannot be considered a science.

Key term

Quasi-experiment: Many philosophical discussions regarding the scientific method posit a requirement that it be possible to conduct experiments. Specifically, experiments are systematic research inquiries conducted under controlled conditions, in which the researcher manipulates a variable (or a number of variables) in order to record observed changes in an outcome. By doing so, the researcher seeks to make inferences about the relationship (causal or otherwise) between manipulated variables and outcomes. A successful experiment requires that the researcher be able to exert control over (i.e. to set the value of) all the active variables so as to eliminate the risk of outcomes being determined (in part or wholly) by extraneous factors. However, such an approach assumes the possibility of complete knowledge regarding relevant

▶

active variables, as well as the capacity to change the value of all variables if required. In reality, most experiments fall short of such assumptions. Firstly, it is impossible ever to know whether all relevant variables have been identified. For example, scientific experiments in biology were radically altered when researchers discovered the existence of micro-organisms. Secondly, full control over pertinent variables is rare in nature. For example, researchers cannot easily alter the genetic composition of biological specimens, which means that in many experiments, findings might technically be the result of genetic factors rather than manipulated variables. When such shortcomings exist, the type of research conducted is referred to as a 'quasi-experiment'. The term is often used to describe research in behavioural and social sciences, and often with the purpose of highlighting flaws in these disciplines. However, in the philosophical sense, quasi-experimentation is the norm rather than the exception across the sciences as a whole.

However, such a line of argument is premised on the assumption that physics and chemistry constitute a suitably representative basis for making these comparisons. One problem with this assumption is that physics and chemistry are just two of the several disciplines that could be used. In fact, there are very many branches of science. As well as physics and chemistry, there are major fields such as biology, astronomy and the environmental sciences. Each of these fields is composed of multiple subfields that themselves constitute separate sciences. For example, within biology there are fields such as botany, genetics, physiology, palaeontology and zoology, as well as the various biomedical sciences, such as anatomy, bacteriology, histology, immunology, virology and so on. Some bibliometric studies that seek to identify patterns in which research papers are thematically linked in the scientific literature have suggested that there may be up to 200 areas that could reasonably be counted as separate sciences in their own right.

Example of the proliferation of specific sciences

Many new sciences emerge from work conducted in existing disciplines that essentially fragment into independent fields. One example where this has occurred is chemistry. Chemistry as a whole refers to the study of the composition and properties of matter. However, the ways in which such objectives are met by scientists, and the range of contexts in which relevant work is done, can vary substantially. As a result, a plethora of chemistry-related fields now exists, and each is largely regarded as a separate science in its own right. These include such fields as organic chemistry, polymer science, crystallography, biomaterials science, physical chemistry, analytical chemistry, spectroscopy and chemical engineering. While there can be some overlap between them (as is the case across all sciences), each of these fields is generally characterised by its own particular set of topics, methods, equipment, theories and investigators.

A scientometric taxonomy of science

Attempting to count the number of different fields of science is considered difficult for many reasons. Firstly, the range of sciences evolves over time. Many thousands of scientific studies are conducted every year, each of which, while having its own disciplinary origins, is a unique piece of empirical work that may or may not be considered to reside fully within an already established discipline. Secondly, because all such fields share a common epistemological philosophy and so will appear similar in certain respects, observers will differ on the categorical boundaries (if any) that exist between closely related sciences. Many researchers have attempted to establish the number of different sciences, and the hierarchical structure of their inter-relationships, using statistical analyses of publication patterns in the research literature. This activity has become known as 'scientometrics'. Although many such efforts have been critiqued on the basis of the statistical limitations encountered when analysing such large sets of data, Leydesdorff and Rafols (2009) are credited with achieving an effective categorisation using factor analysis. These authors based their analyses on publication patterns derived from one of the most commonly used databases of research literature, the Science Citation Index published by the Institute for Scientific Information. This database, established in 1960 by American scientometrician Eugene Garfield (b. 1925), stores summaries of all papers published in 6500 peer-reviewed scholarly journals together with the full details of each paper's reference section. Researchers can use the database to find new articles related to a particular subject of interest, and can then use the reference data to locate the previous work cited by the researchers in their articles. Leydesdorff and Rafols's analyses looked at the degree to which clusters of research publications emerged from the way scientists chose to cite one another's work in their own papers. Based on the research literature published in 2006, they found that the sciences that year contained 172 separate disciplines, within 14 higher-order categories. The results of their analyses can be represented graphically as a set of maps of interrelated sciences, which are viewable in full detail on the Internet (http://www.leydesdorff.net/map06/).

Source: Leydesdorff, L., & Rafols, I. (2009). A global map of science based on the ISI subject categories. *Journal of the American Society for Information Science and Technology*, 60, 348–362.

In this context, comparisons with other sciences can often imply that psychology's claim to the status of science is in fact relatively strong. Several fields have much more difficulty than psychology in exerting control over experimental variables (for example, a meteorologist cannot randomly manipulate a tornado in order to examine its effects), and several fields are unable to avail of experimentation at all (for example, a palaeontologist cannot use experiments to directly test hypotheses regarding the breeding habits of dinosaurs). Research in botany makes far less use of prediction than psychology does. Astrophysics lacks parsimony just as much as psychology, if not more so:

its major theories incorporate a multitude of highly complex and yet unproven assumptions. Further, a great many sciences have problems with measurement accuracy. For example, in palaeontology and archaeology, there is considerable controversy regarding the accuracy of the carbon dating methods used to measure the ages of prehistoric specimens.

Overall, while psychology does not manifest the major of features of science quite as effectively as they are seen in physics and chemistry, these features are seen to a much clearer extent in psychology than they are in several other disciplines that are generally regarded, without dispute, to be sciences. In this sense it would be difficult to argue that psychology is not a science. To do so would require that it then be argued that astrophysics, botany, meteorology, palaeontology, and many more such fields, are also not sciences.

Test your knowledge

8.1 What are the main features of science as demonstrated by fields such as physics and chemistry?

8.2 How many fields are considered to be sciences?

Answers to these questions can be found on the companion website at: **www.pearsoned.co.uk/psychologyexpress.**

 Sample question   *Essay*

In terms of scientific practice, how does psychology compare with (a) physics and (b) meteorology? How does such a comparison inform our attitude toward psychology?

Psychology and the assumptions of science

Another approach to this issue is to examine the philosophical assumptions of the scientific method and to consider whether psychology meets these assumptions. Such an analysis has been presented by British psychologist Elizabeth R. Valentine. Valentine (1992) offers the view that science proceeds on the basis of three categories of assumption: metaphysical assumptions, theoretical assumptions and methodological assumptions. In each case, arguments are frequently raised that psychology fails to meet the assumptions of science. However, closer inspection suggests that such concerns are misplaced.

Key term

Metaphysics: is the branch of philosophy concerned with the study of existence, truth and knowledge, especially as is yielded by considerations that go beyond that which can be observed empirically, or analysed mechanically or physically. As well as exploring the classification of entities in the universe, metaphysics considers their inter-relationships, and the basis for drawing conclusions about such inter-relationships. For example, metaphysicists present arguments regarding what constitutes evidence of causality. Prior to the emergence of empirical science, metaphysics was the primary discipline to consider the workings of the universe and its inhabitants. Now that empirical science exists, the contribution of metaphysics relates mainly to non-empirical (but nonetheless essential) issues, such as the logical requirements for making valid inferences from empirical data.

? *Sample question*   *Problem-based learning*

Consider a well-known scientifically established principle, such as the fact that the Earth orbits the sun. What is the evidence for this principle? Can the principle be tested experimentally? What data would falsify it? Is the principle reliant on an assumption of determinism? Next consider a principle of human behaviour that you feel is well established. (An example might be the assertion that adults possess superior moral reasoning skills to children.) Again, consider the questions presented above. In what way, if any, do the questions require re-interpretation in order to be applicable to human behaviour?

Metaphysical assumptions include beliefs about determinism (the idea that all events in the universe have causes and that nothing happens without a cause) and its implications (such as predictability and the applicability of mechanical models). Many people intuitively feel that humans possess independent free will, which essentially makes it impossible to ascribe our thoughts or behaviours to objectively identifiable causes. It also makes much (if not all) behaviour unpredictable. As such, critics have argued that psychology cannot truly make an assumption of determinism. Concerns have also been raised about the implications of determinism for moral responsibility. If determinism is assumed, then immoral acts must be viewed as the predictable results of causal conditions. This could imply that individual actors ought not be held personally responsible for their immoral behaviours.

Proponents of scientific psychology suggest that such criticisms miss the point of psychology's assumption of determinism. Firstly, the fact that most people intuitively *feel* they have free will does not necessarily mean that they actually *have* free will. Furthermore, human behaviour can only be truly unpredictable if it is truly random; but people who argue for free will rarely suggest that human behaviour is random. So long as behaviour is non-random, then it is reasonable for psychology to assume it can be predicted. Secondly, determinism's implications for moral responsibility are peripheral. Many findings in science carry disturbing implications (such as some studies in genetic engineering). However, although such research might make us uncomfortable, this does not mean that the theoretical assumptions underlying the research are unsound. In fact, we could only really be uncomfortable if we perceived the assumptions underlying the research to be, in fact, sound. Therefore, overall, psychology's assumption of determinism (at least in general) is valid. While people's behaviour can often appear unpredictable, this is probably due more to the multiplicity and complexity of the causal factors involved than to exceptions to deterministic principles.

Theoretical assumptions in science include the expectation that science will produce a body of knowledge that demonstrates both systematicity (whereby knowledge can be organised within a coherent and knowable system) and generality (whereby laws and principles can be applied in different contexts of space and time). Critics who argue that psychology cannot meet these assumptions tend to refer to the complexity and interdependence of its relevant variables, and to the fact that findings in psychology are rarely fully generalisable from one context to all others. It is also frequently noted that, unlike in other sciences, researchers in psychology have to deal with problems relating to reflexivity. In broader contexts, reflexivity refers to the confounding of cause and effect. In psychology, reflexivity is mentioned because research generally involves the study of human behaviours by human observers. The resulting argument is as follows: given that psychology constitutes the study of behaviour, and that the conducting of psychological research itself constitutes a behaviour, then this means that the very act of conducting psychological research becomes part of its own subject matter. It is implied that such self-referencing constitutes a type of reflexivity that is absent in other sciences, and that obstructs the meeting of theoretical assumptions in psychology. Valentine points out that complexity in and of itself does not undermine the principle of systematicity. In fact, most sciences are characterised by a high degree of complexity and of interdependence among relevant variables. In addition, difficulty in generalising psychological research findings is merely a function of this complexity. Further, while the generalisability of findings in psychology is not perfect, it is certainly untrue to say that psychological findings are *never* generalisable. It can also be noted that the self-referencing nature of psychological research does not constitute reflexivity per se. While it is true that people may alter their behaviour when participating in psychological research (thereby responding to the fact that the researcher is a member of their own species), this itself is just an additional type of complexity. Therefore, in summary, it is reasonable for psychology to operate on the theoretical assumptions of science.

Free will and determinism

Philosophers have debated the nature of free will for centuries. Free will is the ability of people to make volitional choices independently of coercion or constraint. This is often said to be incompatible with the scientific (and otherwise rational) assumption of determinism. The concept of free will is not just of interest to scholars who wish to offer explanations for human thoughts and behaviours, it also underlies many of the assumptions of politics, law and religion. In political terms, principles of democracy are based on the assumption that citizens can express independent personal choices in elections. In legal contexts, people are considered to be entirely responsible for their own actions (unless facing rare conditions of diminished responsibility resulting from, for example, an intellectual disability). In religious contexts, many formal religions posit free will as a sacred component of the human condition (although many also imply a diminution of free will in the sense that there is said to exist an omnipotent deity who can intervene to alter human affairs). Notwithstanding these applications of the concept, it can be noted that philosophical positions regarding free will are divided, with many philosophers arguing that free will does not exist at all (a position known as 'hard determinism'). In philosophy, the so-called 'standard argument against free will' is that *indeterminism* would imply a randomness to human behaviour that is not apparent from our observations. This argument appears to be supported by psychology, insofar as psychological research seems to confirm that behaviour is non-random. In addition, many phenomena in psychology appear to imply that people do not always exert explicit volitional control over their behaviour. For example, cognitive psychologists point to the fact that many of our behaviours are automatic (such as the way we learn to drive cars without having to concentrate on the individual elements of doing so). Behaviourists such as Skinner have argued that as behaviour is determined by environmental contingencies, free will is essentially an illusion. Other theorists have argued that behaviour is the result of unconscious drives, biological variables or innate dispositions subject to evolution by natural selection.

In a different stream of research, psychologists have demonstrated that people tend to perceive free will in their own behaviour in situations where it is not truly warranted. For example, research suggests that people tend to attribute causality to events differently based on whether the event is positive or negative. We are inclined to perceive negative events (such as poor grades) as being the result of external factors (such as an unfairly difficult examination), while perceiving positive events (such as good grades) as resulting from internal factors (such as our ability or hard work). Such perceptions can be shown to fluctuate across events even when the events concerned are essentially equivalent. This pattern of attributions is akin to what Skinner identified as the use of the notion of free will as an 'explanatory fiction'. Similarly, other research suggests that humans tend to possess an exaggerated sense of control over events, at least in terms of the degree to which their perceptions of control over outcomes deviate from the statistical probabilities of such outcomes. One example of this is the tendency for people to consistently bet more money than is statistically justified when gambling, an illusion of personal control that has supported the gambling industry for hundreds of years. Nonetheless, a number of philosophers and scientists have presented theories that posit the existence of human free will in a universe that is otherwise deterministic. However, it is not always clear whether such theories arise from empirical observation or from a sentimental view of humanity. Overall, free will is a notion that is intuitively seductive but empirically questionable.

Key term

Generalisability: refers to the extent to which a finding can be considered valid in conditions other than those under which it was made. In scientific research, this mainly refers to the idea that a finding can be considered informative with regard to phenomena other than those specifically studied in the research. Typically, the generalisability of findings in psychological research is worth considering in terms of whether the findings can be applied to persons other than those who participated in the research, in situations other than those prevailing in the research, and at times other than that during which the research was done (this latter example relates primarily to the issue of whether a finding is replicable). Observers of psychology often raise two types of concerns regarding generalisability of research findings. Firstly, concerns can be raised about the basic generalisability of findings beyond the immediate research context. For example, people who participate in a psychology study may not be representative of their peers in the wider population, and the circumstances of the research might be highly artificial and so most unlike real-world situations. The second category of concerns relate to the extent to which human psychology is universally experienced. For example, on many issues it is questionable whether research on the attitudes or perceptions of men can be generalised to inform us about those of women. Similar questions relate to attempts to generalise findings from one culture to another, or from one historical period to another. The quality of being widely generalisable is referred to as 'external validity', while the process of generalisation is an example of inductive reasoning.

Finally, among the methodological assumptions of science are expectations relating to empiricism (namely, that phenomena can be observed), measurement (namely, that pertinent variables can be measured precisely) and experimentation (namely, that researchers can conduct studies in which variables are manipulated under controlled conditions). Critics occasionally question whether psychology meets these assumptions. For example, the mental representations studied in cognitive psychology cannot be directly observed, concepts such as intelligence are difficult to measure precisely, and experimental control is difficult to exert over variables such as gender or personality. However, as mentioned earlier, such methodological assumptions are not universally met by all sciences (for example, phenomena in astrophysics, such as black holes, cannot be directly observed, measured or experimented upon), while they are at least partly (if not substantially) met by psychology.

When considering the scientific standing of psychology, one common misconception is that such metaphysical, theoretical and methodological assumptions are absolute requirements for a field to be considered a science. However, in reality, such assumptions are rarely fully met by any science. The standing of a particular field is better judged not in terms of *whether* such assumptions are met, but rather in terms of the *degree* to which they are met. As argued by Valentine, such limitations as have been identified in psychology are greatly outweighed by the *degree* to which psychology meets these assumptions of science. As such, an analysis of its assumptions serves to corroborate the view that psychology is indeed a science.

Test your knowledge

8.3 What are the main philosophical assumptions of science?

8.4 Are the assumptions of science absolute or aspirational?

Answers to these questions can be found on the companion website at:
www.pearsoned.co.uk/psychologyexpress.

 Sample question   **Essay**

Critically evaluate the view that far from being unscientific, psychology is in fact a leader in the promotion of scientific values.

Chapter summary – pulling it all together

→ Can you tick all the points from the revision checklist at the beginning of this chapter?

→ Attempt the sample question from the beginning of this chapter using the answer guidelines below.

→ Go to the companion website at www.pearsoned.co.uk/psychologyexpress to access more revision support online, including interactive quizzes, flashcards, You be the marker exercises as well as answer guidance for the Test your knowledge and Sample questions from this chapter.

Further reading for Chapter 8	
Topic	*Key reading*
Philosophical aspects	Valentine, E. R. (1992). *Conceptual issues in psychology*, (2nd edition). London: Routledge.
Free will and determinism	Bertelsen, P. (1999). Free will in psychology: In search of genuine compatibilism. *Journal of Theoretical and Philosophical Psychology, 19,* 41–77.
Critique of psychology	Lilienfeld, S. O. (2010). Can psychology become a science? *Personality and Individual Differences, 49,* 281–288.
Scientometrics	Boyack, K. W., Klavans, R., & Börner, K. (2005). Mapping the backbone of science. *Scientometrics, 64,* 351–374.
Methods of science	Wolpert, L. (2000). *The unnatural nature of science.* London: Faber.
Science and psychology	Dilman, I. (1996). Science and psychology. *Royal Institute of Philosophy Supplement, 41,* 145–164.

Topic	Key reading
Psychology as a science	Drenth, P. J. D. (1996). Psychology as a science: Truthful or useful? *European Psychologist, 1*, 3–13.
Misconceptions	Uttal, W. R. (2003). *Psychomythics: Sources of artifacts and misconceptions in scientific psychology*. Mahwah, New Jersey: Erlbaum.

Answer guidelines

 Sample question   *Essay*

To what extent is it demonstrable that psychology is a science?

Approaching the question

This essay asks about the extent to which it is demonstrable that psychology is a science. Although the question appears similar to the common simpler question, 'Is psychology a science?', it is important to note that the question as phrased here assumes the determination to be one of degree rather than of absolute classification. In other words, the question invites a response as to the *degree* to which the proposition is true, rather than *whether* the proposition is true (i.e., rather than being phrased as a yes/no question). This should inform the approach taken in response to this question. In considering the degree to which the definition is met, it will be important to address each defining characteristic of science in terms of how it applies to psychology; the issue of degree might then be articulated in terms of the number of characteristics of science that psychology possesses. The question also specifically asks about the *demonstrability* of the proposition. This might offer an opportunity to distinguish between theoretical and practical aspects (on the basis that the latter are likely to be more demonstrable, at least in superficial terms).

Important points to include

As the question concerns a definitional determination, it will be important to offer a working definition of the target term ('science'). As mentioned earlier, this might well include pragmatic professional issues (such as whether psychology is generally regarded as a science) as well as the theoretical ones (such as whether psychology conforms to the scientific method). In light of the tendency for debates on this point to rely on stereotypes of science (such as the use of physics and chemistry as representative examples of science), it will be important to include points relating to the breadth of science, the overall number of sciences, and psychology's relative place among them.

Make your answer stand out

When reading articles about whether psychology is a science, it can often seem as though the reader is being invited to be sceptical about the scientific standing of psychology. This might reflect a general caution among psychologists, or it might reflect the extent to which psychologists think more about epistemological issues than other scientists do. It may even reflect a general trend among psychologists to react against established hierarchies, such as the perceived hierarchy of disciplines in universities that appears to privilege the traditional sciences with extra resources, prestige and influence. Whatever the reason, it is probably true that the clichéd position to take on this essay would be to focus on the shortcomings of psychology and to question its scientific standing. Therefore, one way to make your answer stand out would be to take a more balanced position that acknowledges the scientific strengths of psychology as much as its weaknesses, as well as the weaknesses of other sciences as much as their strengths. Another way to make your answer stand out would be to include commentary on this very matter, that is to say, the tendency for psychology, unlike other disciplines, to question its own scientific standing.

Explore the accompanying website at www.pearsoned.co.uk/psychologyexpress

→ Prepare more effectively for exams and assignments using the answer guidelines for questions from this chapter.

→ Test your knowledge using multiple choice questions and flashcards.

→ Improve your essay skills by exploring the You be the marker exercises.

Notes

9

Subjectivist approaches to psychology

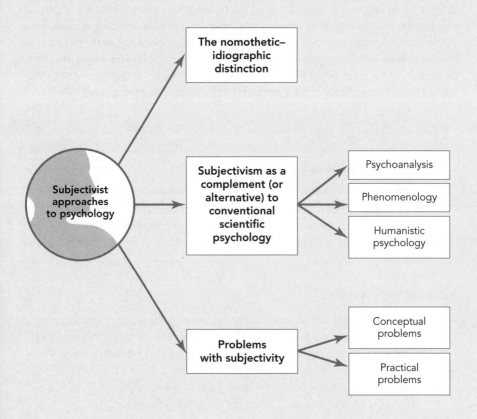

A printable version of this topic map is available from
www.pearsoned.co.uk/psychologyexpress

Introduction

Approaches such as behaviourism, cognitivism, neuroscience and genetics adhere to the principle of objectivity. In other words, they seek to deal in information that is verifiable by third-party observation and that is independent of observer judgement. They do this in order to maximise the validity of psychological research. Adhering to the principle of objectivity served psychology well in its endeavours to be recognised as a truly scientific discipline, and the widespread recognition of psychology's standing as a science owes much to its emphasis on objective knowledge-making. In some ways, the focus on objectivity in psychology is quite different from the personal curiosity that many people feel about the human condition. Indeed, it may be that such personal curiosity is what stimulates most psychologists to become interested in their discipline in the first place. As such, a number of movements within psychology have aspired to give more consideration to subjective experiences. While such approaches to psychology can be very appealing (perhaps because they resonate with the approaches taken by non-psychologists when attempting to explain other people's behaviour), their flirtation with anti-objectivity can make them conceptually challenging and scientifically controversial.

 Revision checklist

Essential points to revise are:

❑ The nature of the nomothetic–idiographic distinction in psychology

❑ The contribution of subjectivist fields to psychology, including psychoanalysis, phenomenology and humanistic psychology

❑ The limitations of the subjectivist approach

Assessment advice

● The subjectivist areas of psychology are by their nature controversial, and so require fair and balanced consideration. While it can be tempting to attach value-judgements to fields such as psychoanalysis and phenomenology (by either dismissing them as 'bad' or championing them as 'good'), it is important that academic rigour be applied to their assessment. This means that strengths as well as shortcomings should be acknowledged.

● Also, ideally their merits should be described in terms of validity and utility, rather than in terms that imply an emotional or moralistic determination.

● Perhaps the biggest problem in discussing subjectivism relates to the fact that most people's initial approach to all information is somewhat subjective. Thinking objectively does not come naturally to people. As such, critiquing the nature of subjectivism in psychology can sometimes appear as an attempt to 'de-humanise' the discipline. This type of impression should be avoided as it detracts from the more central point that the validity and reliability of data, reasonably achievable only from a position of objectivism, are useful attributes in any knowledge system.

Sample question

Could you answer this question? Below is a typical essay question that could arise on this topic.

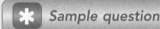

✱ *Sample question*	*Essay*
Is subjectivism the answer to psychology's neglect of the individual?	

Guidelines on answering this question are included at the end of this chapter, whilst further guidance on tackling other exam questions can be found on the companion website at: **www.pearsoned.co.uk/psychologyexpress**

The nomothetic–idiographic distinction

While psychology's development as a science over the past 150 years has certainly been dramatic, it would be untrue to say that its contemporary focus is satisfactory to everyone. One area of concern relates to the way scientific approaches rely on the demonstration or detection of basic principles in nature that can be applied universally. For example, when investigating gravity, physicists attempt to develop explanations that can be used to account for the way gravity works in all circumstances. Likewise, a chemist will assume that a chemical reaction observed in a laboratory will represent the way all such reactions occur when the same chemicals are mixed in other settings. In psychology, researchers may similarly wish to develop explanations of cognition, behaviour or emotions that are intended to be relevant to people in general. Indeed, the discipline of psychology might appear very limited if psychologists did not seek to do this (for example, if they claimed that psychological research examining subjects such as child development, racial prejudice or addictions had *no* relevance to cases other than those included in the individual studies). However, some critics have suggested that focusing on generalisable human characteristics has led psychology to exaggerate the commonality of human beings and to overlook (if not indeed to devalue) the uniqueness of individual life histories and perceptions.

In several contexts, psychology is very clear in its attempts to incorporate individual variation into its explanations of human nature. For example, psychologists offer theories relating to personality that suggest a plethora of ways in which people differ from one another. The very principle of psychometric assessment intrinsically acknowledges that people are not all the same. However, it is nonetheless true that such explanations posit a finite structure on which human variability is based, and so describe human nature in ways that balance differences with similarities. For example, particular personality theories will imply not only that introverts are *different from* extroverts, but also that introverts are *similar to* one another. As such, psychology's typical approach can be seen in terms of the development of generalisable principles. This epistemological approach is referred to as 'nomothetic', which means it assumes that such knowledge can be constructed in terms of a finite number of explanatory laws.

Key term

Personality: is a term that is used widely in psychology (and in general society) without having a clear definition. It broadly relates to those psychological characteristics of an individual that make up his or her distinctiveness. It is ordinarily a descriptive term (in that it relates to information about individuals) rather than a normative one (in that it does not involve a prescription of what constitutes a 'good' or 'bad' personality); nonetheless, there is a tradition of describing some unusual and maladaptive behaviours as constituting a 'disordered' personality. Personality is essentially a subject matter within psychology, and the study of it can be approached with just about any of psychology's paradigms. Therefore, there are distinct traditions of personality theory that emanate from cognitive psychology and behaviourism, as well as from fields such as psychoanalysis, humanism and social psychology. However, perhaps the dominant approach to the study of personality is that represented by the psychometrically devised trait theories, which are usually linked (at least metaphorically) to principles of biological psychology (such as genetic determinism).

In contrast, the 'idiographic' approach considers a person's experience as being unique in all important respects. In methodological terms, an idiographic approach rests on a promotion of subjectivism, the epistemological assumption that the most important (if not the only) source of knowledge is personal experience. As such, while particular researchers might be considered idiographic, their methods will be classified as subjectivist (most typically, the soliciting of experiential testimony directly from individual research participants, for use as the raw material from which to formulate new theories and conclusions). While the nomothetic approach has become dominant in psychology (as it is in all the natural sciences), the idiographic approach has been advocated by a number of theorists throughout the history of the discipline and is still promoted by many psychologists today. Perhaps the person most commonly described as using this term in psychology was American theorist

Gordon Allport (1897–1967), although even his model of personality was based on a finite number of traits said to be present to varying degrees in all humans. As such, it can be noted that the distinction between nomothetic and idiographic approaches in psychology is rarely exclusive, with few idiographically oriented psychologists truly questioning the value of nomothetic explanations. Rather, debates in this area tend to concern not the contrast between the two approaches, but instead the degree to which truly idiographic approaches are of genuine usefulness.

Test your knowledge

9.1 How does psychology approach the notion of generalisability?

9.2 What is meant by the term 'idiographic research'?

Answers to these questions can be found on the companion website at: **www.pearsoned.co.uk/psychologyexpress**

 Sample question   *Essay*

Is it possible for research to be characterised by both nomothetic and idiographic aspects?

Subjectivism as a complement (or alternative) to conventional scientific psychology

A number of subfields in psychology have taken an idiographic approach and have promoted subjectivism as a basis for gathering key psychological data. To varying degrees, these subfields have continued to advocate their worldviews as presenting a useful complement to conventional scientific psychology, if not indeed a desirable alternative to it. Three of the main subfields to have promoted idiographic approaches are psychoanalysis, phenomenology and the related area of humanistic (or existentialist) psychology.

Psychoanalysis is the term used to describe the theory of psychology proposed by Austrian neurologist Sigmund Freud (1859–1939). While scientifically controversial, Freudian ideas have proved culturally enduring, and have provided the basis for a form of psychotherapy that has become highly popular around the world. Freud's original development of psychoanalytic theory was archetypally idiographic, as it was based on some 40 years of experience listening to the testimonies of clients presenting at his clinical practice for psychotherapy. Nonetheless, psychoanalytic theory posits a continuity of psychological function across persons. Key elements of psychoanalysis include the assumption that all human behaviour is significantly influenced by unconscious processes (and indeed that such unconscious influences regularly dominate), that early-life experiences greatly influence later-life behaviours (by interfering with the optimal emergence of key developmental stages), that human behaviour is a function of biological antecedents (and so can be compared to that of animals), and that intellectual dimensions of human experience are often subject to such biological influences (such as innate drives relating to sexuality or aggression). When considered in this broad manner, each of these psychoanalytic ideas can be seen as having been validated by subsequent developments in scientific psychology. Indeed, it can be argued that psychoanalysis deserves some credit for introducing these ideas to psychology in the first place. In addition, psychoanalytic psychotherapy, as developed by Freud, was responsible for pioneering a number of practices that have become standard in contemporary clinical psychology.

Key terms

It is probably accurate to state that there is widespread public confusion (if not some within the relevant professions themselves) regarding the specific names given to different occupations that are involved in mental health treatment. Typically, such confusion leads to conflation of the various terms involved. Put simply, the main ones are as follows.

Psychoanalyst: a person who practises psychoanalysis (i.e. the advanced therapeutic activity related to the Freudian theory of the mind), and who has received the required psychoanalytic training to do so. Technically, psychoanalysts can be from any profession, although they are usually medical doctors or psychologists.

Psychotherapist: a person who practises psychotherapy more broadly, which is taken to include therapies of all theoretical orientations. Again, a psychotherapist can be from any profession but is likely to have a background in health, social care or psychology.

Psychiatrist: a person who has received medical training and who has gone on to specialise in mental health care. Because of this medical background, psychiatrists will be licensed to prescribe psychoactive medication.

Psychologist: a person who has been trained in the academic discipline of psychology (i.e. the empirical science that considers the nature of human thought, behaviour and emotion). Many psychologists will receive further training that will help them specialise in careers relating to teaching, research, consultancy and/or care. Only a subset will receive training to practise therapeutically in mental health care. Of these terms, 'psychologist' is by far the broadest.

However, despite such achievements, Freudian psychoanalysis, as well as the post-Freudian forms inspired by such figures as Alfred Adler (1870–1937), Carl Jung (1875–1961), Karen Horney (1885–1952) and Jacques Lacan (1901–1981), has proved very controversial. Primarily, psychoanalysis has been criticised for being scientifically unsound, and as a result, for presenting explanations of human behaviour that are invalid, misleading and thus potentially damaging. One regular criticism of psychoanalysis is that it conspicuously disregards the standard epistemological requirement that scientific theories be falsifiable. In other words, psychoanalytic theories present open-ended predictions that can be supported whatever situations arise. A good example is the typically psychoanalytic assertion that a traumatic experience will result in *either* the presence *or* the absence of emotional symptoms. Obviously it will always be true that symptoms are *either* present *or* absent, and therefore no scenario can emerge that would suggest such a prediction to be false. This is why the prediction is said to be unfalsifiable. Theories that produce unfalsifiable predictions lack usefulness because they cannot guide our understanding of future events, or, as a consequence, past ones. In the case of psychoanalysis, the unfalsifiability issue means there is little basis to be confident that psychoanalytic explanations of behaviour can be generalised from one person to another, or that psychoanalytic therapy will be effective in any particular individual case. In summary, the criticism in this regard is that psychoanalysis is a scientifically pointless endeavour.

Some writers on the philosophy of science, such as Karl Popper and Peter Medawar (1915–1987), have used psychoanalysis as a case study to explain the nature of pseudoscience. Indeed, other commentators, such as the science writer Lewis Wolpert (b. 1929), use psychoanalytic examples to argue that psychology *as a whole* is unscientific (even though psychoanalysis is not at all representative of psychology as a whole). Given that psychoanalytic commentators rarely accept the validity of scientific criticisms, psychoanalysts are often accused not just of being unscientific, but of being essentially *anti*-scientific. For such reasons, many psychologists consider psychoanalysis to be an unwelcome distraction from psychology's scientific mainstream, and a somewhat obsolete branch of modern psychology. Nonetheless, many psychoanalytic psychologists (as well as psychoanalytically influenced therapists in other professions) continue to practise clinically and to produce scholarly writings in relatively large numbers today. Further, many academics in the humanities and social sciences cite psychoanalysis as their primary scholarly philosophy, essentially employing psychoanalytic theory as a form of hermeneutics.

Example of psychoanalysis as hermeneutics

One way in which psychoanalysis has been applied in the humanities and social sciences is in the use of psychoanalytic ideas to inform evaluations of artistic work. A particular example is the work of British film theorist Laura Mulvey (b. 1951) who has sought to critique a number of Hollywood movies from a psychoanalytic perspective. She argues that the structure of storytelling and production in film is unintentionally influenced by tastes and desires in film-makers and audiences that reflect Freudian explanations of the human psyche. Specifically, Mulvey uses psychoanalytic ideas about the nature of unconscious sexual desires to help explain how meaning is conveyed in cinema, as well as how work is received by viewers.

Phenomenology in psychology refers to the view that the best way to study the human condition is to examine immediate perceptual experiences, either of research participants or of researchers themselves. It is based on the premise that an objective knowledge about the world is impossible to achieve because knowledge formation for each individual will be influenced by the way human consciousness itself operates. As such, conventional scientific studies of experience are viewed as intrinsically limited by their assumption of an objectively knowable reality. The phenomenological approach was introduced to psychology by the German philosopher Edmund Husserl (1859–1938) and extended by French philosopher Maurice Merleau-Ponty (1908–1961). Methodologically, phenomenology requires individuals to provide verbal descriptions of their own perceptions after having sought to eliminate all presuppositions from consideration. As an approach, phenomenology attaches no priority to the objective verification of testimonies, but rather attaches value to the personal meaning of experiences for those testifying to them. One criticism of phenomenology is that it relies on people's ability to provide theoretically neutral interpretations of their own experiences. While an aspiration to base psychology on unadulterated descriptions of human thoughts (and, hence, analyses that are uncontaminated by people's preconceptions) is certainly laudable, it also seems unachievable. For one thing, the capacity to communicate personal experiences relies on the existence of a shared vocabulary, and hence on a consensually agreed lexicon of concepts, symbols and relationships among them. In other words, the recording of phenomenological experiences will never be uniquely personalised, but instead will always be a function of communally understood notions.

Phenomenological principles are most often encountered in the context of psychotherapeutic methods such as the person-centred therapy developed by American therapist Carl Rogers (1902–1987). Rogers was a proponent of humanistic psychology, which is often described as comprising elements of both phenomenology and the philosophical field of existentialism (and so is occasionally referred to as existentialist psychology). Originally proposed by American psychologist Abraham Maslow (1908–1970), humanistic psychology focuses on aspects of human nature that are said to be distinctively human, including such higher motivations as aesthetics, morality, dignity, choice, meaning and self-worth. As a method, the field relies heavily on assessments of personal testimony by individuals, most often in the context of client–therapist relationships. Humanistic psychology does not pursue ordinary scientific goals such as establishing objective evidence to support generalisable explanatory principles, and Maslow (1969) himself noted that humanistic psychologists 'hover on the edge of antiscience'. Instead, like the phenomenologists, humanistic psychology sought to consider all people's testimonies as providing equally valid accounts of reality. The principle was that all views should be treated non-judgementally, and that all persons should be accepted with unconditional positive regard.

CRITICAL FOCUS

Socio-cultural influence on humanistic psychology

While humanism can be seen as an intellectual response to perceived shortcomings in the psychology of the late 1950s and early 1960s, it can also be seen as being influenced by socio-cultural trends of the time. Throughout Western societies, the period in question witnessed a strident emergence of non-conservative social movements, many of which sought to leave behind the rigidities of convention and to instead embrace a spirit of universal love and common humanity. The hippie movement, the beat generation and other offshoots of 1960s counterculture that were originally popularised by trends in fashion, music and literature quickly permeated society as a whole and led many to question the traditional assumptions of politics, economics and science. Against such a backdrop, humanistic psychology became widely discussed as providing an alternative to the mainstream, one which was characterised by fashionable notions. For example, the Rogerian view that therapists should approach clients with unconditional positive regard resonated strongly with the non-judgemental philosophy of the contemporaneous hippie subculture.

KEY STUDY

Maslow's hierarchy of needs

Despite the fact that humanistic psychology was strongly influenced by phenomenology, it nonetheless sought to propose theories that explained human behaviour in general terms. The most prominent such theory was proposed by Maslow (1954), who derived a generic hierarchy of human needs said to underlie all human motivation. The theory argued that people were ultimately motivated to achieve *self-actualisation* or, in other words, to fulfil their own personal potential after having satisfied lower-order needs. These lower-order needs, which each required successive fulfilment in their own right, related to issues of *physiology*, *safety*, *belongingness*, *esteem*, *cognition* and *aesthetics*. Maslow's hierarchy of needs has provided a useful basis for discussing human motivation across a variety of contexts, including as part of person-centred psychotherapy. However, the theory has also proved controversial. Ironically, given the fact that the humanists sought to acknowledge the uniqueness of each individual person, the theory has been criticised for assuming all persons to be motivated by the same objectives, regardless of age, gender or cultural background. While this would be a shortcoming of any psychological theory, it is particularly acute in this case given that Maslow developed his ideas on the basis of studying a very narrow sample of North American college students. Another irony is that, despite humanistic psychology's focus on the value of human welfare, the idea that self-actualisation represents the highest form of fulfilment could be seen as a defence of egocentrism, selfishness or even narcissism. The standard hierarchy of needs fails to acknowledge that many people are motivated to serve other people's needs rather than their own, or that some societies are collectivist rather than individualist. The theory has also been criticised for its empirical shortcomings. Firstly, the component terms (including the concept of self-actualisation) are poorly defined, leading to inconsistencies in the way they are discussed, measured or factored into therapeutic interventions. Secondly, a number of empirical studies have suggested that the ranking of needs in the hierarchy is very inconsistent across individuals, while other studies have questioned whether the relationships among needs can really be considered as comprising a hierarchy at all.

Source: Maslow, A. H. (1954). *Motivation and personality*. New York: Harper & Row.

Sample question   *Essay*

In what way could psychoanalysis be said to be scientific?

Problems with subjectivity

Almost by definition, the notion of subjectivity implies a degree of unreliability. Accounts of events that are described as subjective are acknowledged as being susceptible to bias, whereas accounts that are described as objective are considered to be bias-free. Whether or not evidence in psychology can be considered to be truly objective can certainly be questioned in many cases. However, for scientific psychology, the aspiration to maximise objectivity is fundamental, even if it is difficult to achieve. Therefore, the explicit promotion of *subjectivity* instead of objectivity presents some conceptual and practical problems.

Among the conceptual problems with subjectivity is the question of whether a truly subjective experience can ever be communicated accurately. Descriptions that invoke shared concepts and languages assume that an audience will already understand what the particular experience involves. As such, we remain unsure of how a person could successfully communicate the occurrence of a truly novel experience, one that nobody else has ever had. The idea that personal experiences represent private mental events, but that descriptions of them necessarily require a public frame of reference, was originally discussed by the German philosopher Ludwig Wittgenstein (1889–1951) who argued against the notion of private languages (i.e. languages that, hypothetically, can be understood by only a single person). The implication for psychology is that data derived from subjectivist or introspective methods are unavoidably distinct from the underlying entities being reported on. As such, these methods might not offer reliable ways of conducting research on such subjects.

Wittgenstein's argument is that it is impossible for private languages to exist. This is often described in terms of there being no sensations or experiences possible for which we do not already possess the capacity to generate a linguistic description. In other contexts, linguists describe a phenomenon known as 'loanwords', which are words from one language that are used by speakers of another. Sometimes the emergence of loanwords is interpreted as implying that speakers lack the capacity to describe a concept and so must use a different language in order to do so. It is in turn argued that the speaker's community lacks the required language because it lacks an understanding of the concept involved. Consider the word *schadenfreude*, which is a loanword from German used by English-speakers. What does this word mean? Is it true that English-speakers lack the capacity to describe this concept using their own language? Is it true that they lack the capacity to understand the concept? Make a list of other loanwords used by English-speakers. How many of these words relate to psychology? How true is it that the concepts cannot be described using the English language, or understood by English speakers? Can you think of any other reasons for the emergence of loanwords? Can you think of any sensation that cannot be described?

As regards practical limitations associated with subjectivism, the testimony of participants in idiographic research might be inaccurate or misleading in a number of ways of which a researcher will be unaware. There are at least three types of practical limitation in this regard. Firstly, informants may not have access to the information pertinent to a specific issue. For example, it may be impossible for people to describe the basis of their thinking if their thoughts are arrived at automatically. Many studies in cognitive psychology suggest that people often come to conclusions on the basis of decision-making processes or cognitive cues that exist outside conscious awareness. In many situations (such as when engaging in highly practised tasks), we respond to complex sensory information by initiating systematic response decisions that we do not consciously focus on. Examples of such tasks include explicitly learned routine-based behaviours (such as driving), as well as routine-based behaviours that are less obviously 'learned' (such as choosing one's words during a sensitive conversation). When asked to describe our experience of such behaviours, it is not clear that we will have conscious awareness of the precise factors that influenced our decisions.

Secondly, an informant may make logical errors when formulating conclusions to report to a researcher. Again, psychologists have produced substantial research to suggest that much human reasoning is based on cognitive shortcuts that are characterised by systematic errors of judgement. Such shortcuts are referred to as cognitive heuristics. Among the most commonly researched heuristics are confirmation bias (the tendency to interpret ambiguous information in a way that conforms with our preconceptions), the availability heuristic (the belief that easily remembered entities are more common than ones less easily remembered), and the representativeness heuristic (the basing of likelihood judgements on resemblance to prior experience rather than on relevant statistical factors). Overall, researchers have identified dozens, if not hundreds, of such heuristics. Similar investigations have revealed corresponding limitations on the way we remember our experiences: rather than mentally replaying our experiences as if we had recorded events with a video camera, instead we retrospectively reconstruct our memories from fragments of remembered information. Cognitive shortcuts help people to make quick decisions, and so are efficient in the majority of cases where decisions are trivial. However, the fact that they are endemic to everyday thinking means that the accuracy of subjective reports of personal experiences is likely to be highly compromised by the potential for error.

Key term

Anecdotal evidence: the term used to describe purportedly corroborative information that has been relayed through word-of-mouth channels. Most typically it refers to an event or other information that was originally observed casually (rather than, for example, to the anecdotal transmission of information about the findings of empirical research studies). Because neither the reliability of the source concerned nor that of the persons who have transmitted it is known, anecdotal evidence cannot be considered reliable. As such, it could be argued that it hardly constitutes 'evidence' per se. In science, the term is typically reserved for criticising assertions that are supported only by personal testimonials; in law, the term is used to describe hearsay testimony, which is nearly always considered to be inadmissible in court proceedings. Perhaps the main difficulty for subjectivist approaches in psychology is precisely the fact that that they are based, by definition, on the use of anecdotal evidence as data. Not only are such data of poor reliability, but the very fact that they are considered untrustworthy in several other contexts (including contexts familiar with the public) means that their use in psychology could eventually threaten the credibility of the discipline.

The third practical problem with subjective reports is that informants' descriptions of experiences may be influenced by social psychological factors. Rather than committing errors of logical computation, informants may instead distort their self-reports in ways that prevent embarrassment (to themselves or others) or that otherwise place them in a positive (or less negative) light. Such socially mediated biases can operate intentionally or unintentionally. Commonly researched examples include social desirability bias (the tendency to describe oneself in a way that will be viewed favourably by others), illusory superiority (the tendency to overestimate one's own positive qualities, and to underestimate one's negative qualities), and the subject-expectancy effect (the tendency to respond to researchers' requests for information in ways that are believed to meet the researcher's expectations).

In summary, while the idea that subjective reports of personal experiences can yield important information about the human condition is certainly intuitively appealing, it is also clear that such information is likely to be highly imperfect. Such imperfections limit the extent to which subjectivist approaches to research can contribute to our understanding of psychology. The information produced in the personal testimonies of individuals will be difficult to validate, interpret or generalise. Accordingly, although idiographic approaches may offer additional perspectives with which to supplement the theories and findings of psychology, it is difficult to envisage a situation where they will truly displace the more conventional nomothetic approaches that continue to dominate the field.

Test your knowledge

9.5 How do cognitive heuristics affect subjectivism?

9.6 Why is anecdotal evidence unreliable?

Answers to these questions can be found on the companion website at:
www.pearsoned.co.uk/psychologyexpress

? Sample question   Essay

Critically evaluate the view that the aim of nomothetic science is prediction and control.

Chapter summary – pulling it all together

 Can you tick all the points from the revision checklist at the beginning of this chapter?

 Attempt the sample question from the beginning of this chapter using the answer guidelines below.

 Go to the companion website at www.pearsoned.co.uk/psychologyexpress to access more revision support online, including interactive quizzes, flashcards, You be the marker exercises as well as answer guidance for the Test your knowledge and Sample questions from this chapter.

Further reading for Chapter 9

Topic	Key reading
Evidence and psychoanalysis	Chiesa, M. (2010). Research and psychoanalysis: Still time to bridge the great divide? *Psychoanalytic Psychology, 27,* 99–114.
Psychoanalysis and the arts	Mulvey, L. (1975). Visual pleasure and narrative cinema. *Screen, 16,* 6–18.
Criticism of psychoanalysis	Eysenck, H. J. (1985). *Decline and fall of the Freudian empire.* London: Viking.
Defence of psychoanalysis	Eagle, M. N. (2007). Psychoanalysis and its critics. *Psychoanalytic Psychology, 24,* 10–24.
Phenomenology	Kendler, H. H. (2005). Psychology and phenomenology: A clarification. *American Psychologist, 60,* 318–324.
Humanism	Maslow, A. H. (1969). Toward a humanistic biology. *American Psychologist, 24,* 724–735.
Biases of thought	Kahneman, D., & Tversky, A. (1996). On the reality of cognitive illusions. *Psychological Review, 103,* 582–591.

Answer guidelines

✱ Sample question   *Essay*

Is subjectivism the answer to psychology's neglect of the individual?

Approaching the question

This essay presents a closed-ended question that invites a response of either 'yes' or 'no'. However, as this question is asked in an academic context, you are required to offer a justification for your response, supported by logical argument and relevant evidence.

Important points to include

In dealing with this question, it will be important to present a comprehensive treatment of the notion 'subjectivism'. As such, you should present several examples of areas in psychology that represent it. Secondly, it will be insufficient merely to argue that subjectivism is not 'the answer' simply because the various subjectivist fields are themselves somehow flawed. It will be important to include points that explain precisely *why* they are flawed.

Make your answer stand out

One thing to note is that, by using the phrase 'psychology's neglect of the individual', the question is based on the assumption that psychology has indeed been guilty of such neglect. As such you can approach this question in a number of ways. Firstly, you can accept the unstated assumption and offer a response based on whether you feel subjectivism is 'the answer'; secondly, to make your answer stand out, you can try to challenge the assumption (which would in turn lead you to challenge the notion that subjectivism is the answer).

Explore the accompanying website at www.pearsoned.co.uk/psychologyexpress
→ Prepare more effectively for exams and assignments using the answer guidelines for questions from this chapter.
→ Test your knowledge using multiple choice questions and flashcards.
→ Improve your essay skills by exploring the You be the marker exercises.

Notes

Notes

The problem of consciousness

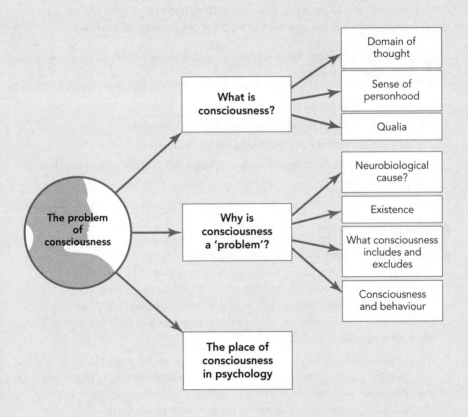

A printable version of this topic map is available from
www.pearsoned.co.uk/psychologyexpress

Introduction

It is clear that much of the history of psychology has been concerned with the subjective experience of human existence. Indeed, with the possible exception of the behaviourists, it could be said that psychology as a field has amounted to the scientific study of consciousness. However, as might be inferred from the views of subjectivism, it may also be stated that psychology has not always fully acknowledged the complete nature of consciousness per se, but has instead been involved in the reductionist study of some of its elements. For example, psychology does not operate with an agreed definition of consciousness; in fact, the core question of what consciousness actually is has been the subject of much debate. As such, the concept of consciousness poses many challenges for psychology, both in terms of the way psychologists approach the study of consciousness, and in terms of how our assumptions regarding the nature of consciousness affects our assumptions about psychology as a whole.

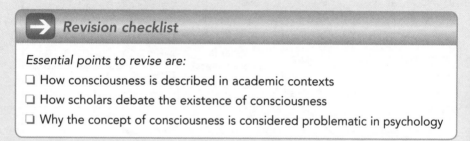

→ Revision checklist

Essential points to revise are:

❑ How consciousness is described in academic contexts

❑ How scholars debate the existence of consciousness

❑ Why the concept of consciousness is considered problematic in psychology

Assessment advice

- The concept of consciousness has attracted a great deal of complex philosophical consideration, and is generally regarded to be difficult to discuss. One of the reasons for this is that the debates around consciousness nearly all come down to a question of whether it exists in the form in which we intuitively feel it does, or, alternatively, whether it is little more than a side effect of natural brain activity.

- When approaching assessments on this topic, it will be useful to give due attention to the importance of the fundamental questions regarding the independent existence of consciousness, and on how scholars have attempted to explain its relationship (or not) with physiology.

Sample question

Could you answer this question? See opposite for a typical essay question that could arise on this topic.

Sample question *Essay*

To what extent has psychology 'regained consciousness' since the rise of behaviourism?

Guidelines on answering this question are included at the end of this chapter, whilst further guidance on tackling other exam questions can be found on the companion website at: **www.pearsoned.co.uk/psychologyexpress**

What is consciousness?

Consciousness is something we are immersed in every day, and yet it is extremely difficult for us to define. In simple terms, it refers to the state of being conscious, which itself refers to our sense of being alert and aware of our thoughts and surroundings. However, consciousness comprises more than just a set of perceptions and cognitions. When asked to describe consciousness, most people refer to some kind of personal domain of thought, which includes our awareness of immediate events and memories of past ones, as well as our sense of identity and personhood. It exists as a continuous experience across time, even though it is interruptible: consciousness appears to diminish when we sleep and vanishes altogether when we are sufficiently anaesthetised, but when we re-awaken it emerges again to continue from where it left off. As such, consciousness constitutes an integrated whole that amounts to something more than the sum of our individual perceptions and thoughts. One example of the latter point is that consciousness can, in a sense, process *itself* – it is possible for us to think *about* the fact that we are conscious (as well as to think about *the fact that we are thinking about* the fact that we are conscious, and so on) – which is one of the reasons it is difficult to imagine consciousness being located within a finite set of neurons in the brain. Perhaps the most challenging aspect of describing consciousness is that it is entirely subjective; nobody else can feel or experience yours, and you cannot feel or experience theirs. This then raises some difficult questions, such as how consciousness can be studied effectively, what drives its functions (for example, what, if anything, are its biological bases) and whether it even truly exists.

Although discussions about the nature of consciousness can appear to be almost purely philosophical, there are practical implications too. For example, if an ill person enters a coma, it becomes extremely difficult to detect whether or not their consciousness remains intact. Similarly, it is very unclear precisely when consciousness first appears in a foetus. In most communities such issues are recognised as being hugely controversial, as they can involve the making of life-and-death decisions on the basis of whether consciousness is or isn't believed to be present. As such, these issues help draw attention to the desirability of defining consciousness in a way that both is agreeable to consensus and, importantly, is accurate. However, it is generally acknowledged that scientific approaches have yet to yield definitions and understandings of consciousness that could be said to meet these aspirations.

One important aspect of consciousness is that it is said to be composed of rudimentary experiential elements known as qualia (the singular of which is quale). This term is used in philosophy to denote the elements that make up subjective conscious experience, such as those involved in seeing a particular colour. For example, it is possible to describe the colour *red* in terms of a particular wavelength of light. It is also possible to describe the sensation and perception of *red* in terms of the nerve cells in our eyes and brain that become active when we see it. However, the idea that the object we are looking at appears to possess 'redness' in a way that we feel and understand is an example of a quale. One feature of qualia is that they are wholly subjective and are thus entirely reliant on being experienced; it would be impossible to explain a quale to somebody who has not experienced it (for example, it would be impossible to explain 'redness' to somebody who is congenitally blind). Another important feature of qualia is that they encapsulate all types of subjective experiences, and not just those relating to sensations and perceptions. For example, emotional experiences will also be composed of qualia (including the qualia of being 'enjoyable', 'boring', 'intriguing', 'exciting' and so on). While we may attempt to explain such concepts objectively, they have to be experienced personally in order to be fully understood.

Key term

Gestalt psychology: a theory of psychology that emerged in the early 20th century, which questioned whether the psychophysical approach of examining perception and cognition in terms of their atomised elements was sufficient to capture the essence of human thought. Instead, the Gestaltists argued that human thought could be understood only in terms of the interaction among perceptual phenomena, in the sense that the impact of the sum of these perceptions would exceed that of its individual parts. For example, in visual perception, our experience of seeing a swarm of bees includes our impression that the swarm constitutes a single entity with its own trajectory of movement, as well as the superficial fact that we see individual bees within the swarm. The Gestaltist idea that our subjective experience of a stimulus exceeds its structural elements greatly informed the way consciousness researchers considered notions such as qualia. The leading Gestaltists all worked in Germany (the German word *Gestalt* translates roughly into English as 'essence' or 'form'), and included the Czech psychologist Max Wertheimer (1880–1943), and the German psychologists Wolfgang Köhler (1887–1967) and Kurt Koffka (1886–1941).

Even though people generally recognise particular qualia when they are referred to, the fact that qualia are wholly subjective raises the question of whether or not they truly exist as discrete entities. Several arguments have been advanced to support the assertion that qualia exist in this way. One famous argument, presented by American philosopher Thomas Nagel (b. 1937), suggests that because we can use our imaginations to distinguish between the experiences of different organisms (Nagel's illustrative question was 'What is it like to be a bat?'), we can conceive of the fact that each animal constructs an appreciation of the world that makes subjective psychological sense out of the peculiar sensory experiences available to them. According to Nagel, because different animals have different experiences of the same sensory inputs (for example, the bat's use of echolocation means that its experience of sound is profoundly different from that of humans), we humans cannot truly imagine what it is like to be one of these other animals; which in turn demonstrates how qualia exist separately from sensations, perceptions or cognitions. A second argument in favour of the existence of qualia was presented by Australian philosopher Frank Jackson (b. 1943). Jackson posited a thought experiment in which a scientist, Mary, has lived her entire life in a black and white room. While she understands all scientific information that is known about colour, including all the descriptions of colours that people have reported, she personally has never experienced anything except black and white. Jackson asks us to consider what Mary would feel if she were released from the room and exposed to objects of other colours. He says that, when Mary first sees the colour red, she will learn something new and significant about redness that she could not learn any other way, namely, what it *feels like* to experience it. According to Jackson, this again demonstrates the way that qualia exist as discrete experiential entities separate to physical realities. Philosophers such as Nagel and Jackson argue that because qualia are distinct from rudimentary aspects of sensory and perceptual events, they cannot be studied in terms of such events. In other words, when it comes to psychological experiences, the subjective cannot be explained in terms of the objective.

Example of zombies in psychology

Many philosophers have composed thought experiments in an attempt to support arguments relating to consciousness. One such traditional thought experiment involves considering whether or not it is possible for zombies to exist. In this context, zombies are seen as beings that are identical to humans in all respects except that they do not possess a consciousness. Such zombies would behave exactly the same as humans, but would not be consciously aware of their surroundings or, indeed, of their own behaviour. A conventional point that is made is that if such zombies were subjected to a stimulus that would be painful for an ordinary human, they would cry out the same as any human would but – crucially – they would not *feel* any pain. One variation of the zombie argument is to posit the possibility that everyone alive right now is, in fact, such a zombie (raising the question of how we really know that other people are conscious). Philosophers who propose zombie arguments claim that such a scenario is logically possible, in the sense that it is possible for us to conceive of it. They present

▶

this as standing in favour of the assertion that biological existence is independent of consciousness, thereby refuting the view that consciousness is dependent on neurophysiological events. However, other philosophers argue that this argument is inconclusive. Firstly, they question whether logical possibility represents a sufficient standard for judging such proposals, preferring instead a standard of metaphysical possibility. While the existence of zombies is logically possible (in that there is no inherent contradiction in believing them it be true), it is not clearly metaphysically possible (in that it contradicts what we understand to be the way that the world actually works). Secondly, critics of zombie arguments accuse them of being circular. In order for us to conceive of zombies, we must imagine that it is possible for a biological being to exist without consciousness; however, it is precisely this point that zombie arguments are intended to demonstrate. In other words, the conclusion of the argument overlaps with (and so is predetermined by) its assumptions.

Test your knowledge

10.1 What is meant by the term 'consciousness'?

10.2 What is meant by the term 'qualia'?

Answers to these questions can be found on the companion website at: **www.pearsoned.co.uk/psychologyexpress.**

Sample question   Essay

Explain Jackson's thought experiment involving Mary the scientist. To what extent does this thought experiment succeed in demonstrating the independence of qualia?

Why is consciousness a 'problem'?

Consciousness is frequently described as being a problem for psychology (and for philosophy). According to American philosopher John Searle (b. 1932) and the Australian philosopher David Chalmers (b. 1966), this problem relates primarily to the difficulty we have in explaining how something like consciousness can be caused by neurobiological processes in the brain. The reasons why this is so difficult are themselves hard to crystallise. For example, it might be difficult because we don't fully understand the way complex neurobiological mechanisms operate, because we don't fully understand the way consciousness itself operates, or because of both reasons. Secondly, it might be difficult because we are approaching the entire proposition incorrectly by, for example, assuming consciousness exists when in fact it does not.

Notwithstanding the arguments presented by philosophers like Nagel and Jackson, not all commentators agree with the idea that consciousness actually exists, at least in the way it is generally described as doing so. For example, American cognitive scientist Daniel C. Dennett (b. 1942) argues that claims about qualia are misplaced and that the arguments of Nagel, Jackson and others are flawed. He says that Nagel's bat example fails to demonstrate the crucial point that qualia are truly separate from sensory inputs. Instead, Dennett argues that while the differences between bat and human experiences of (say) sound are extreme, they amount to differences of degree rather than kind. In other words, Nagel is wrong to suppose that it is *impossible* for humans to know what it is like to be a bat; rather, it is just *extremely difficult* for us to do so. Similarly, Dennett criticises Jackson's thought experiment about Mary's room as being based on unsustainable assumptions. If Mary is said to 'know everything' that is known about colour, then she should not be truly surprised when she leaves the room. The fact that we expect her to learn more about redness when outside relates more to our difficulty in conceptualising the implausible notion that Mary 'knows everything' beforehand, than it does to the nature of qualia. Critics such as Dennett note that a major problem with thought experiments is that they cannot ever be conducted. As such, while they might be intuitively convincing, this is not sufficient to demonstrate their correctness. As the experiments cannot ever be conducted, it is impossible for us to know whether we are mistaken in our conclusions.

Key term

Thought experiment: an exercise where an investigator mentally considers the possible outcomes of an actual experiment, but without actually conducting the experiment in question. A thought experiment might be proposed if the actual experiment was ethically problematic (such as involving harm or maltreatment to humans), metaphysically impossible (such as requiring the ability to see through walls, to talk to animals, or to engage in time travel), or in some other way impractical (such as involving prohibitive costs). Thought experiments have been contemplated by scholars throughout the history of philosophy, and have been employed widely in other fields where hypothetical scenarios are of particular concern (such as jurisprudence, medical ethics, quantum physics and economics).

Other problems relating to consciousness concern the fact that it is unclear what it includes and excludes. For example, a number of authorities have sought to distinguish between primary consciousness and self-consciousness. Primary consciousness refers to one's awareness about the world in general (which results from the processing of information mediated by the senses). Self-consciousness refers to one's awareness of one's own being and identity, which will include reflections regarding one's own thoughts (and as such, is not reliant on information received through the senses). This is an important distinction because while the former can be seen as akin to the theories of information processing studied by cognitive scientists, the latter appears to be more in the domain of phenomenological psychology. Chalmers uses this distinction to separate the 'easy problems' of consciousness (explaining how human attention works) from the 'hard problem' of consciousness (explaining how personal consciousness exists). However, others, including Dennett, question the distinction between primary consciousness and self-consciousness.

A third set of problems relating to consciousness concerns the association between consciousness and behaviour. The most common view of people in general is that consciousness is a precursor to behaviour; in order to act, we must first have thoughts that stimulate our actions. One problem with this view is that much behaviour is automatic and so occurs without our having to first have specific thoughts. This problem might be resolved by acknowledging that such behaviour is indeed preceded by some cognitive activity (such as sensation, perception or decision-making) even if this activity does not occupy our attention. A second view on consciousness and behaviour is that behaviour is actually a precursor to consciousness. In this view, our biological selves are capable of responding independently to environmental cues, and what passes for consciousness amounts to some kind of after-the-fact cognitive interpretation of affairs. One example of this principle is encapsulated by the James–Lange theory of emotion, established by William James and Danish psychologist Carl Lange (1834–1900), which states that emotions occur when we cognitively (and retrospectively) interpret our automatic physiological reactions. Several studies have borne out this aspect of emotional responding. This view, that consciousness is a secondary by-product of physiologically driven behaviour, was originally promoted by a number of 19th-century scientists, including English biologist Thomas Huxley (1825–1895), who classified consciousness as an epiphenomenon (i.e. an event that occurs as the consequence of another). It was also later advocated by behaviourists such as Skinner, and continues to be

Key term

Folk psychology: As people have direct experience of their own consciousness, it is no surprise that people in general have views about the nature of human psychology. These commonsense beliefs about what influences humans' thoughts, feelings and behaviour constitute folk psychology. More specifically, folk psychology refers to the beliefs about psychological subjects that emerge within general society in the absence of specific strategic or scientific attempts to establish relevant information or evidence. Typical examples include beliefs about the causes of crime, the best way to bring up children, how men and women differ emotionally, and what constitutes intelligence. The notion that humans possess a consciousness that is independent of corporeal reality is an example of folk psychology, because people generally believe it automatically, without seeking to consider the evidence for or against it. It should be noted that folk psychology beliefs are not by necessity inaccurate. However, because their accuracy is not investigated, it is unsafe to assume that folk psychology beliefs will be reliable. Indeed, given the existence of various cognitive biases (such as the bias for people to overestimate their own good qualities, as well as those of their kin), there are reasons to expect that some folk psychology beliefs will be distinctly unreliable.

KEY STUDY

The social determination of emotion

Schachter and Singer (1962) conducted an intriguing experiment illustrating how people's subjective experiences of emotions can be secondary to objective influences, consistent with the James–Lange theory. They administered a group of participants with the drug adrenaline, which has the effect of greatly increasing overall physiological arousal. While some of the participants were correctly informed that they had received a stimulant, some of them were falsely informed that the drug would have a numbing (rather than arousing) effect. All participants were then allocated to one of two experimental conditions. Each member of the first group (the 'euphoria' group) was asked to sit in a waiting room along with another person who had been instructed to create a positive social mood. The other person did this by talking in a friendly manner and initiating an informal game of basketball with a rolled up piece of paper and a wastepaper basket. Each member of the second group (the 'anger' group) was also asked to sit in a waiting room with another person. However, for these participants, the other person had been instructed to create a *negative* social mood, by complaining strongly about the research procedures and the questionnaires that the experimenter had asked them to complete. Afterwards, all participants were asked to complete rating scales to record their emotional states after their time in the waiting room. The results suggested that all participants correctly detected that they had experienced a marked increase in physiological arousal. However, the way participants explained this arousal differed across the various experimental contexts. Participants who were correctly aware that they had received a stimulant drug reported no particular emotional state subsequent to their time in the waiting room (as, presumably, they attributed their arousal to the drug). In contrast, participants who were misinformed that they had received a *sedative* drug reported intense emotional states (as, presumably, they interpreted their arousal to have been caused emotionally). Moreover, the nature of these reported emotional states was determined by prior experience of the waiting room situation. Participants in the euphoria group reported strong positive emotions, while those in the anger group reported strong negative emotions.

Overall, the results suggested that participants retrospectively interpreted their physiological arousal states in terms of external factors. When aware of the true impact of the drug, participants reported no particular emotions (even though their physiological arousal and awareness of the social context was the same as for other participants); while participants who were misled about the drug reported emotions that were consistent with their appraisal of the social context of the waiting room. (To complete the picture, the researchers ran all the procedures with different participants using a placebo drug. These participants, who did not experience physiological arousal, did not report emotional responses to the waiting room situations.) In essence, Schachter and Singer found that physiological arousal determined emotional responses, and did so in a way that was dependent on experimental manipulations. This stands in direct contrast to the common beliefs that (a) emotional responses are based on personal judgements of events and contexts, and that (b) emotional reactions stimulate physiological responses (rather than the other way around). Schachter and Singer's findings helped to highlight how conscious experience is intertwined with physiological functioning, as well as the way common beliefs about the subjectivity of emotions can be unreliable.

Source: Schachter, S., & Singer, J. E. (1962). Cognitive, social, and physiological determinants of emotional state. *Psychological Review, 69,* 379–399.

promoted by contemporary philosophers who believe that the traditional view amounts essentially to dualism. Because it is intuitively appealing without being necessarily true, the generally held belief that consciousness exists separately to physical events is often considered as representing an example of a 'just so' story (i.e. a commonly believed explanation that is transmitted anecdotally but which cannot be verified retrospectively through direct observation).

Test your knowledge

10.3 What is the difference between the 'easy' and 'hard' problems of consciousness?

10.4 What are the various relationships that have been proposed to exist between consciousness and behaviour?

Answers to these questions can be found on the companion website at: **www.pearsoned.co.uk/psychologyexpress**

 Sample question   *Essay*

To what extent is a thought experiment actually an 'experiment'?

The place of consciousness in psychology

In the early days of scientific psychology, consciousness was considered to be its main subject matter. For example, William James promoted the view that psychology could essentially be defined as the study of consciousness (although he tended to use the term 'mental life'). However, over the succeeding decades, acknowledgement of the problematic conceptual nature of consciousness has seen this situation change. Today, the status of consciousness as a subject matter in mainstream psychology is actually quite unclear. Because consciousness is wholly subjective, it is considered by some scholars to lie outside the realm of scientific psychology. It is often noted that behaviourists, such as Watson, strongly advocated the view that psychology could not concern itself with subjective concepts such as private mental events, and so should eschew the study of consciousness. This is sometimes interpreted as a claim by behaviourists that there is no such thing as consciousness, and therefore that there are no such things as private mental events. Famously, in 1960, the British psychologist Cyril Burt (1883–1971) wrote describing the way he felt psychology had evolved (referring first to psychology's rejection of theology and psychoanalysis, and then to the arrival of behaviourism): '…psychology, having first bargained away its soul and then gone out of its mind, seems now, as it faces an untimely end, to have lost all consciousness.' In this quotation, Burt was taking the view that subscribing to behaviourism meant that psychologists could no longer consider the existence of consciousness.

However, such a depiction of the behaviourist position is somewhat misleading. Even those scholars most committed to behaviourism, such as Skinner, have noted that private mental events do indeed exist – in fact, in Skinnerian terms, such mental events are themselves classifiable as behaviours. The main concerns of behaviourism are (a) that the nature or occurrence of such private mental events cannot be objectively verified and (b) that there is no compelling argument that these private experiences collectively comprise a single entity known as 'consciousness'. Essentially, the behaviourist view is that 'consciousness' is not a useful concept.

One dividing line in the study of consciousness concerns the distinction between dualism and monism. The philosophical view that consciousness exists as a discrete entity that is separate from such physical events as neurobiological activity, is often interpreted as an argument based on dualism (i.e. that the mind and body are two separate entities), whereas the view that consciousness is a consequence of physical events is based on monism (i.e. the view that the existence and function of the mind is dependent on the existence and function of the body). Critics of dualism argue that the dualist position is inconsistent with scientific assumptions relating to materialism and determinism, and, as such, is ultimately unscientific (if not indeed illogical). Some commentators have sought to resolve the problem of consciousness by avoiding dualism and instead invoking its sheer complexity as an explanation for its mysterious qualities. For example, American cognitive scientist Marvin Minsky (b. 1927) has argued that consciousness is essentially a form of high-level abstract thinking that can be duplicated by appropriately sophisticated machines.

CRITICAL FOCUS

The evolution of consciousness

A number of psychologists have sought to explain the emergent complexity of consciousness in terms of its adaptive value, and thus its evolutionary significance. For one thing, consciousness is considered likely to be subject to evolutionary influence because of this complexity. Typically, such depictions highlight the role of consciousness (and associated notions such as qualia and self-awareness) in helping organisms to protect themselves and their kin, to interact with others, to make complex plans for the future, to handle complex information about one's environment and relationships, and so on. Many commentators, such as Stephen Pinker, British psychologist Nicholas Humphrey (b. 1943) and British neuroscientist Howard Barlow (b. 1921), have suggested that the evolution of consciousness was particularly boosted by the advantages it confers with regard to complex social behaviour. However, critics of evolutionary explanations of consciousness raise questions about whether complex psychological traits can evolve incrementally, and where the biological advantage precisely lies.

In summary, the study of consciousness in psychology is not a unified endeavour. It emerges in fields as disparate as cognitive, behaviourist, phenomenological, biological and evolutionary psychology. While many philosophers have presented views that imply a dualistic explanation of consciousness, psychology appears to lean toward the idea that consciousness is ultimately intertwined with physical (i.e. neurobiological) realities. Despite this, there is a lack of consensus as to whether the entity commonly referred to as consciousness is the root of our behaviour or one of its offshoots.

Test your knowledge

10.5 How do behaviourists approach consciousness?

10.6 How do debates on consciousness related to the monism–dualism distinction?

Answers to these questions can be found on the companion website at: **www.pearsoned.co.uk/psychologyexpress**

 Sample question   **Essay**

What should be the place of consciousness in psychology?

Chapter summary – pulling it all together

→ Can you tick all the points from the revision checklist at the beginning of this chapter?

→ Attempt the sample question from the beginning of this chapter using the answer guidelines below.

→ Go to the companion website at www.pearsoned.co.uk/psychologyexpress to access more revision support online, including interactive quizzes, flashcards, You be the marker exercises as well as answer guidance for the Test your knowledge and Sample questions from this chapter.

Further reading for Chapter 10

Topic	Key reading
Philosophy	Banks, W. P. (2009). *Encyclopedia of consciousness.* New York: Academic Press.
Multidisciplinary views	Blackmore, S. (2005). *Conversations on consciousness.* Oxford: Oxford University Press.
Consciousness explained	Dennett, D. C. (1991). *Consciousness explained.* London: Penguin.
Burt on consciousness	Burt, C. (1962). The concept of consciousness. *British Journal of Psychology, 53,* 229–242.
Chalmers	Chalmers, D. J. (2010). *The character of consciousness.* Oxford: Oxford University Press.
Dennett	Dennett, D. (2003). *Dan Dennett on our consciousness* [Video]. Retrieved from http://www.ted.com/talks/dan_dennett_on_our_consciousness.html
Consciousness and thought	Forti, B. (2009). How could phenomenal consciousness be involved in mental function? *New Ideas in Psychology, 27,* 312–325.
Subjective consciousness	Revonsuo, A. (2009). *Consciousness: The science of subjectivity.* Hove, UK: Psychology Press.
Qualia	Jackson, F. (1982). Epiphenomenal qualia. *Philosophical Quarterly, 32,* 127–136.
Nagel's bat	Nagel, T. (1974). What is it like to be a bat? *Philosophical Review, 83,* 435–450.

Answer guidelines

Sample question   Essay

To what extent has psychology 'regained consciousness' since the rise of behaviourism?

Approaching the question

As this question includes the phrase, 'to what extent', it needs to be approached as requiring an answer such as 'to a great extent' or 'to a little extent'. This means that the question is calling for some kind of conclusion as to the amount of attention it has given to the study of consciousness. Secondly, the reference to 'regaining consciousness' is a clear allusion to Burt's famous quotation regarding psychology having 'lost all consciousness' upon the arrival of behaviourism. As such, the question is essentially asking you to evaluate whether Burt's quotation has stood the test of time.

Important points to include

Firstly, as the phrasing of the question contains a clear allusion to a famous quotation, it would be desirable to acknowledge this explicitly in your answer. Secondly, as well as describing some of the theoretical treatment given to the concept of consciousness since the 1960s, it would be advisable to describe specific empirical literatures and fields of psychology (such as cognitive psychology) that have produced scholarship on consciousness-related topics. The growth of these fields demonstrates the 'regaining of consciousness' by psychology.

Make your answer stand out

Essentially, this question presents an implicit hypothesis, namely, that psychology has indeed 'regained consciousness'. While it would be useful to provide information that supports this hypothesis (such as descriptions of the growth of research on consciousness-related concepts), it would also be useful to provide information that attempts to falsify it. In other words, a strong answer would consider whether in fact psychology has failed to 'regain consciousness' after all. This would require some kind of case to the effect that what is studied by psychologists today is not really consciousness. This approach would allow you to consider in more depth some of the themes raised in this chapter concerning the definition, description and existence of consciousness. For example, if qualia truly constitute something more than individual perceptual experiences, then psychology could be said not to be studying consciousness when it studies perception. Considering the arguments for and against the existence of qualia would allow you to consider different types of psychological research in terms of how they represent the regaining of consciousness.

Explore the accompanying website at www.pearsoned.co.uk/psychologyexpress

→ Prepare more effectively for exams and assignments using the answer guidelines for questions from this chapter.

→ Test your knowledge using multiple choice questions and flashcards.

→ Improve your essay skills by exploring the You be the marker exercises.

Notes

Notes

Notes

Science since the 20th century: postpositivism and postmodernism

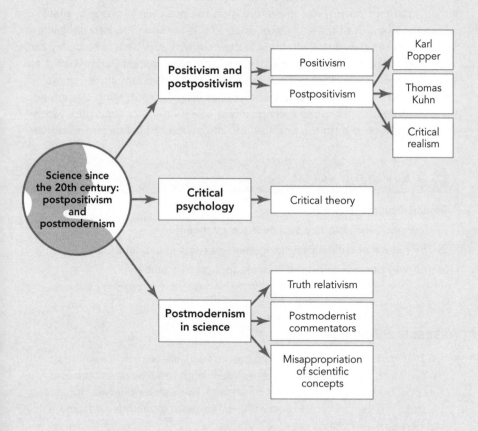

A printable version of this topic map is available from
www.pearsoned.co.uk/psychologyexpress

Introduction

The impact of modern science on the world during the 20th century was wide-ranging and multifaceted. It helped stimulate radically new understandings of natural phenomena, and spawned an overwhelming suite of new technologies that revolutionised the way daily life was lived. In turn, these developments had a fundamental influence on world events, often in ways that prompted social and political tension. New knowledge brought new perspectives on the value of resources, on political entitlements and on how easy (or difficult) some problems were to solve; while new technologies created new commodities and property, as well as new means by which countries could wage war on their enemies. The growth of science also affected intellectual culture, by producing a plethora of new subject disciplines, scholarly literature and perspectives on intellectual life. It is perhaps no surprise, therefore, that the positivist philosophy that underpinned much of the early expansion of science soon ran into difficulties. Some of these related to limitations in the positivist approach (which only came to light after the first flurry of modern scientific achievement had revealed its shortcomings), while other difficulties related to a scepticism among some scholars who felt that the perceived merits of science were being overstated. Various counterpoints to the early positivist scientific stance emerged, which served to influence both the practice and discussion of science and scientists.

> **→ Revision checklist**
>
> *Essential points to revise are:*
> ❑ How positivism has evolved over the past century
> ❑ The nature of critical psychology and its roots in critical theory
> ❑ The way postmodernism has been applied to science

Assessment advice

- Essay questions on how positivism has fared in science and psychology will invite you to maintain a healthy scepticism both towards positivism and towards the standard critique of positivism. This can be difficult, not least because the various terms used have rather loose meanings and can be defined differently in different literatures.

- As such, when discussing such notions as positivism, postpositivism, critical theory and postmodernism, it would be useful to offer a working definition of each term at the outset, while acknowledging that the terms are subject to different usage across contexts.

- In addition, the issues emerging in this area can lead to some intense conflicts of ideas. As with any controversial issue, it will be important to consider both the strengths and limitations of the competing arguments. The issues tend to relate to standards of quality in academic argumentation, so it will be especially important not to dismiss positions lightly.

Sample question

Could you answer this question? Below is a typical essay question that could arise on this topic.

 Sample question | Essay

Explain the term 'critical psychology', providing and discussing two examples.

Guidelines on answering this question are included at the end of this chapter, whilst further guidance on tackling other exam questions can be found on the companion website at: **www.pearsoned.co.uk/psychologyexpress**

Positivism and postpositivism

As noted in Chapter 2, the early 20th century saw the emergence of a philosophical approach to science known as logical positivism. According to this approach, only propositions that could be verified by observation could be considered scientifically valid. You will remember that the main flaw in this position, as noted primarily by Popper, was that verification could never be conclusive over time because there would always be the possibility of future exceptions. Moreover, as exceptions *would* be conclusive, an emphasis on *falsification* would actually be more useful. Subsequently, Kuhn noted how practising scientists are often more influenced by prevailing consensuses than by epistemological doctrines. This led him to argue that scientific progress does not evolve gradually (as was suggested by the logical positivists), but instead is punctuated by sudden revolutions of thought that occur when existing explanatory paradigms are found to be false.

It is correct to say that critics like Popper and Kuhn demonstrated weaknesses in the logical positivist position. However, it is useful to bear in mind that the logical positivists had wide-ranging views, not all of which were debunked. In fact, in many crucial respects, Popper and Kuhn agreed with the major fundamental premises of logical positivism. One such premise relates to the nature of reality. Like the logical positivists, Popper and Kuhn subscribed to the position of realism (namely, the assumption that the universe has an independent existence separate from our consciousness). Alternatives to realism include idealism (the view that reality is ultimately psychological because our experiences are founded on mental events) and subjectivism (the view that knowledge emerges from personal experience, as discussed in Chapter 9). Prior to the rise of modern science, social beliefs and practices were often quite anti-realist: many were based on the existence of magical influences, while others were derived solely from authority or tradition (rather than evidence). Thus, by advocating realism, the logical positivists placed a primary emphasis on the importance of empiricism, an emphasis that was not in any way criticised by

CRITICAL FOCUS

Criticisms of Popper and Kuhn

Popper and Kuhn's critiques of science are related, but are not completely overlapping. However, both philosophers sought to question the reasonableness of logical positivism by emphasising the provisional nature of knowledge. Popper introduced the focus on falsificationism, while Kuhn argued that all science was subject to shifting social consensuses among scientists. Their positions have been criticised on at least three grounds. Firstly, Popper and Kuhn's explanations are often faulted for being too embedded in the history of science, especially in its sociological history, and for being insufficiently grounded in philosophical analysis. As a result, they attempt to answer questions of logical import by citing historical facts instead of reasoned argument. For this reason, Popper and Kuhn are frequently described as operating separately from the mainstream of philosophy of science. Secondly, while Popper and Kuhn seek to explain what is required for theories to work in science, it can be questioned whether their own *theories of philosophy of science* meet these exacting standards. For example, it is not immediately clear whether Popper's explanation of how science works is itself falsifiable; or why we shouldn't dismiss Kuhn's explanation on the basis that it is (presumably) conjectural. The third criticism is that Popper and Kuhn's approaches do not clearly take account of the ways that the actual merits of a scientific theory might contribute to its success. Popper argues that verification is a misleading enterprise, while Kuhn argues that scientific theories prosper only because of conformity with consensus (and so can be readily discarded if the social context changes). Both of these perspectives ignore the fact that scientific theories often prosper because their predictions are so consistently corroborated by experiences in the real world. One example is the theory of gravitation as it applies to large objects in our everyday environments, such as buildings. According to Popper and Kuhn, the fact that buildings remain standing is of no relevance to the currency of the theory of gravity. For Popper, the stability of buildings is an example of verification and so contributes nothing to our understanding of gravity; for Kuhn, the theory of gravity remains conjectural despite the stability of buildings, and what really matters is the eventual consensus among scientists. In other words, neither Popper nor Kuhn accommodates the fact that theories may prosper because of, in the main, *their ability to make accurate predictions about the world*. Accordingly, Popper and Kuhn's positions have been dismissed as unreasonable by several theorists on science, such as the German philosopher Rudolf Carnap (1891–1970), the Australian philosopher David Stove (1927–1994), the American science writer Martin Gardner (1914–2010) and the British philosopher David Papineau (b. 1947).

Popper or Kuhn. Popper and Kuhn also shared the logical positivists' belief in the feasibility of objective truth, and their view that experimentation is a powerful approach to generating knowledge. These points of agreement are worth isolating because Popper and Kuhn's positions are often erroneously presented as constituting an argument against *all* positivist principles (including realism, objectivity and experimentation).

CRITICAL FOCUS

The problems with logical positivism

Logical positivism was criticised in a number of respects, all of which influenced the emergence of postpositivism. As well as the basic criticism of the verification-based approach, there were five other major criticisms. The first two relate to the way opinions differ across scientists. Firstly, logical positivism relied upon the capacity of scientists to form valid *judgements as to the meaning of evidence*. Secondly, it relied on scientists' capacity for *inductive reasoning*, which in turn required a capacity to extrapolate information from one context to another. Both these requirements involve judgement-calls by individual scientists. However, as there is no standardised way of determining the 'meaning' of evidence or the range of allowable extrapolations, it is likely that different scientists faced with the same evidence will come to different scientific conclusions. Accordingly, the overall problem for logical positivism is that *it fails to account for differences in judgement across scientists* (whereas, in contrast, postpositivism emphasises the likelihood of such disagreement). The next main criticism of logical positivism relates to the way scientists' views are distorted by their prior understanding of the world. This means that their observations will be *theory-laden* (i.e. framed by theoretical assumptions about how the world works). These theories can result from scientists' personal experiences, their prior training, the beliefs of the society in which they live, or other contextual influences. As such, the overall problem for logical positivism is that *it falsely assumes that scientific observations will be neutral* (whereas, in contrast, postpositivism acknowledges that contextual influences need to be recognised and acknowledged).

The fourth and fifth main criticisms of logical positivism relate to the way scientists react when faced with unexpected observations. The fourth criticism is that, in contrast to the recommendations of logical positivism, real scientists rarely discard their overall theories when faced with observations that contradict a particular prediction. Instead, they develop auxiliary hypotheses that accommodate the new observation in a way that retains the original theoretical worldview from which the first prediction was made. This rational use of auxiliary hypotheses was described by Hungarian philosopher Imré Lakatos (1922–1974); while the idea that individual hypotheses cannot be judged in isolation from the broader network of theories from which they are derived is known as the *Duhem–Quine problem*, named after French scientist Pierre Duhem (1861–1916) and American philosopher Willard Van Orman Quine (1908–2000). The fifth and final criticism relating to unexpected observations is that they can be particularly difficult to interpret, because each outcome can be rationalised in several different ways (assuming that no limits, such as parsimony, are imposed on the elaborateness of the explanations). In other words, theories can always be said to be *underdetermined by evidence*. As such, empirical observation alone does not generate knowledge. Instead, knowledge-generation requires additional inputs from the researcher, such as judgement and opinion. Overall, the resulting problem for logical positivism is that *it falsely assumes that empirical observations can be unproblematically translated into knowledge* (whereas, in contrast, postpositivism acknowledges that the researcher will greatly influence such translation).

Rather than concluding that Popper and Kuhn's critiques led to the extinction of logical positivism, it might be fairer to say that they led to its evolution. This evolution was accelerated by the emergence of critical realism, which led ultimately to postpositivism. Critical realism, which can be traced back to the 18th-century philosophy of Kant, was applied to 20th-century science by American philosophers Kuhn, N. R. Hanson (1924–1967) and Hilary Putnam (b. 1926). Critical realists believe that, while reality certainly exists independently of our perceptions, our capacity to record it accurately is limited. As such, our approaches to science should try to avoid these limitations, which include our mental biases, our proneness to reasoning errors, and the fact that we each view the world from a unique perspective. Postpositivism is the theoretical position that applies critical realism to logical positivism (both Popper and Kuhn can be said to be postpositivists). While logical positivists viewed observation as a direct means of both gathering information and generating theories, postpositivists recognise that all observation is fallible and all theories revisable. Instead of implying that science yields 'perfect' facts that are 'proven' by evidence, the postpositivist view is that science produces 'conjectures' that are 'warranted' by currently documented observations. Postpositivism retains the idea that there exists an objective reality that can be elucidated through empirical observation (and especially through experimentation). In contemporary psychological research (and in other sciences), postpositivism is most apparent in the form of methodological controls used to enhance construct, internal and external validity. These include the employment of sampling procedures and replication (on the basis that single observations will be fallible), triangulation and psychometric standardisation (on the basis that single measures will be context-bound), as well as blinding and control groups (on the basis that the neutrality of individual researchers' observations will be questionable).

Test your knowledge

11.1 What were the weaknesses of logical positivism?

11.2 What were the strengths of logical positivism?

Answers to these questions can be found on the companion website at:
www.pearsoned.co.uk/psychologyexpress

 Sample question   **Essay**

Compare and contrast logical positivism with postpositivism.

Critical psychology

The view that researchers' personal perspectives will impede them from producing neutral scholarship, and as a consequence that all scholarship needs to be interpreted with such potential distortions in mind, is broadly referred to using the umbrella term 'critical theory'. It is usually argued that the social and behavioural sciences are particularly affected by such distortions. Furthermore, it is often assumed that these biases result from community-level or socio-political contexts. Early critical theorists included German social scientist Max Weber (1864–1920) as well as scholars from the so-called Frankfurt School, such as German sociologist Max Horkheimer (1895–1973) and German philosopher Herbert Marcuse (1898–1979). Many of these figures were strongly influenced by the political philosophy of Karl Marx (1818–1883), the German founder of communism. In summary, in their approach to the behavioural and social sciences, critical theorists go beyond critical realism and explicitly reject the possibility of objective truth, the value of experimentation and the overall validity of positivism (including that of postpositivism).

As well as sociologists, economists and philosophers, some of the earliest critical theorists were psychologists. For example, German social psychologist Erich Fromm (1900–1980) combined Marxist ideas with psychoanalysis to describe human personality in terms of innate desires for personal freedom (which may be suppressed not only by psychodynamic forces, but also by capitalist ones). In the latter half of the 20th century, the application of such perspectives to psychology led to the emergence of a formal subfield called critical psychology. The introduction of this term is often attributed to German psychologist Klaus Holzkamp (1927–1995). He argued that mainstream psychology was incorrigibly biased by capitalist influences. In particular, he accused psychology of promoting theories that disregarded the potential for (proletariat) humans to shape their own lives. In the 1970s and 1980s, such analyses of power-based hierarchies were extended to include theories about psychiatry and mental illness. Figures such as British psychiatrist R. D. Laing (1927–1989), Hungarian psychiatrist Thomas Szasz (b. 1920), and French philosopher Michel Foucault (1926–1984) argued that conventional depictions of mental illness are based on false distinctions between 'normal' and 'abnormal' behaviour. Such distinctions, it was argued, do not reflect actual differences between healthy and unhealthy mental states, but instead serve to protect the interests of privileged groups in society. These groups include the medical profession and pharmaceutical industry (who gain financially from the administration of psychiatric treatment), as well as autocratic governments and power elites (who label people as mentally ill in order to exert social control). More recently, similar arguments have been applied in relation to physical health, bringing forth the emergence of critical health psychology.

How people view 'normality'

One aspect of critical psychology relates to the way notions of normality are defined and discussed. Psychological normality is a controversial notion that can be defined in at least three different ways. The first can be called 'normality-as-average', and refers to the state of having psychological attributes similar to those of the statistically average person (e.g. being as happy as the person with the average score for happiness). The second can be called 'normality-as-mental-health', and refers to the state of having psychological attributes that lie anywhere above a threshold that marks the boundary between abnormal and normal (e.g. having a happiness score above the cut-off for depression). The third can be called 'normality-as-ideal', and refers to the presence of positive psychological attributes coupled with the complete absence of negative ones (e.g. having the maximum possible happiness score). These options are typically presented as competing approaches in clinical and academic considerations of normality. Wood, Gosling and Potter (2007) sought to identify how these principles informed evaluations of normality among the general population. The researchers collected psychometric data from over 19,000 residents of the United States regarding both (a) their personality traits and (b) whether or not they rated themselves as normal. The researchers then examined the statistical association between these concepts in order to see which of the three definitions of normality was most closely resembled. Contrary to prior expectations, the researchers found that participants considered themselves most normal when they possessed personality traits at the extreme end of the range of possible scores. In other words, persons who rated themselves as normal were more likely to give themselves extreme scores for psychological attributes such as conscientiousness and agreeableness. The researchers concluded that, for the general population, the concept of psychological normality is not represented by statistical typicality ('normality-as-average') or by mere psychological well-being ('normality-as-mental-health'). Rather, the majority of the general population actually perceive themselves not to be normal, and instead perceive normality to be associated with levels of psychological attributes that lie at the extreme positive end of the range ('normality-as-ideal').

Source: Wood, D., Gosling, S. D., & Potter, J. (2007). Normality evaluations and their relation to personality traits and well-being. *Journal of Personality and Social Psychology, 93*, 861–879.

Example of critical health psychology

Critical health psychology focuses on how social power relationships, including those relating to economics, affect issues discussed in health psychology. One example of how these concepts are applied is when critical health psychologists argue for the quality of research to be judged not on the basis of ordinary standards of methodological validity (such as internal validity or construct validity) but also on the basis of 'psychopolitical validity', as introduced by Argentine critical psychologist Isaac Prilleltensky (2003). This refers to the extent to which a piece of research examines and accounts for the role of political and economic power differentials as they determine the wellness, oppression, and liberation of persons and communities in terms of health. The critical health psychology perspective argues that research (and subsequent applications) should not be considered as representing valid accounts of the world unless they meet these standards of psychopolitical validity.

While many disciplines in the behavioural and social sciences have spawned subfields informed by critical theory, the trend has attracted its own criticisms. One general criticism of critical psychology is that it does not seek to validate its own theories by developing hypotheses that can be tested through falsification. As critical psychology does not easily lend itself to empirical testing, it cannot facilitate the development of practical applications. Indeed, in suggesting that all our explanations of behaviour are biased in ways to which we are blind, critical psychology verges on nihilism; in other words, it appears to argue that all attempts to understand behaviour will be futile. It can be questioned whether such a depiction of human understanding corresponds with most people's shared experiences (at least insofar as can be corroborated by our interactions with others). In reality, most people (including most behavioural and social scientists) appear reasonably comfortable with the proposition that humans behave in generally coherent ways that can be observed, interpreted and understood. We can also note that critical psychologists (and critical theorists in general) do not argue that objectivity is a bad thing; instead they argue that objectivity is *impossible*. However, they appear to claim that they themselves are being objective in presenting this view. In essence, their argument – that it is impossible to produce accurate depictions of affairs in the real world – is contradicted by the very fact that they are presenting it *as a depiction of affairs in the real world*. Thus, unless critical psychologists are claiming to have a monopoly on objectivity (which would require them to explain precisely why they are more objective than other psychologists), we have to conclude that their position is self-refuting.

Key term

Positive psychology: a relatively new subfield of psychology that focuses on the study of positive human functioning. It was explicitly introduced as a mainstream concept in 1998 by the then President of the American Psychological Association, Martin Seligman (b. 1942). Positive psychologists study such notions as achievement, optimism, happiness, and their resultant benefits, rather than such traditional negative concepts as anxiety and depression. However, positive psychology is defined not just by the topics it studies, but also by its philosophy. As with the critical psychology movement, positive psychologists argue that mainstream psychology is subject to unwarranted cultural influences. These influences maintain a focus on adverse mental health states, and on research methodologies that are biased toward medicalised concepts, such as diagnoses and symptoms. However, unlike critical psychology, positive psychology seeks to supplement, rather than displace, mainstream psychology. Critics of positive psychology question its sophistication (in terms of how well defined the various positively oriented concepts actually are, and whether they are anything more than the inverse form of already well-understood negatively oriented concepts), and suggest that its major predictions are generally tautologous (in that they tend to involve one positive emotional state leading to another, which raises the question of whether they are truly separate or just differently measured aspects of the same underlying construct).

Sample question **Essay**

Critique the notion of 'normality' as used in the context of psychological and behavioural well-being.

Postmodernism in science

In the history of culture, the term 'modernism' is most often used to describe the break from tradition that affected the arts, literature, philosophy and social thought in the late 19th and early 20th centuries. One example is the emergence of abstract art, in which painters dispensed with the traditional realist styles of their predecessors in order to produce images with great visual impact but little or no correspondence to objects seen in the real world. These cultural shifts are typically attributed (at least partly) to the widespread scientific and technological modernisation seen during this period. The eventual emergence of critical ideas (which were seen as being sceptical of standard forms of knowledge) marked another transitional movement, which has become known as 'postmodernism'.

It is generally agreed that postmodernism does not represent a single field of endeavour or philosophical theory. Instead, it essentially represents any approach to an academic discipline that is based on questioning, or challenging, the preceding modernist approach in a way that is consistent with critical theory. As such, postmodernism typically advocates scepticism towards received knowledge, as well as towards more mainstream principles of epistemology (such as objectivity). In the sciences, including the behavioural and social sciences, postmodernism typically aims to critique the ways in which scientific knowledge is produced. Postmodernists discuss the influences that shape the perceptions of both scientists and readers of science, as well as their perceptions of notions such as 'truth' and 'evidence'. In general, postmodernists subscribe to the idea of truth relativism. This is the view that assertions cannot be considered as being true or valid, but instead can only ever be seen as having ephemeral (and unreliable) subjective value based on each particular individual's perspective. As a result, a fundamental postmodernist assumption is that there can be no such thing as an absolute truth. Instead, postmodernists claim that so-called truths are merely assertions that have been *classified* as true by a particular community that shares a common frame of reference.

Metanarrative (or grand narrative): an explanatory schema that seeks to provide a unifying account for all historical, social and cultural events. One example is Marxism, which seeks to explain all such events in terms of their evolution from simplicity, through capitalism, and ultimately to socialism. A second example is the idea that there exists an ongoing battle between forces of good and forces of evil, which either is permanent (perhaps cyclical) or else culminating towards an apocalypse (as in many religious accounts of humanity). A third example is the idea that human history is, and will continue to be, characterised by the spread of civilisation or democracy. Metanarratives can be identified explicitly as part of a stated theoretical position, or they can be assumed unwittingly. Many scholars have criticised the use of metanarratives in disciplines such as history and sociology. In addition, postmodernist philosophers have extended the notion of metanarratives to add to their critique of science. They argue that conventional explanations of science are restricted by an arbitrary metanarrative that requires all new scientific developments to be interpreted positively (for example, as representing human ingenuity and as exerting a positive impact on society). The problem with such a metanarrative is that non-conforming interpretations of new developments are then automatically dismissed as being irregular. Some postmodernist critics argue that the laws of physics, and even those of mathematics, are also subject to arbitrary metanarratives. The corollary of such positions is that conventional descriptions of scientific findings and principles should be regarded as oversimplified, biased and unreliable. However, it is unclear precisely when metanarratives are merely arbitrary and when they are justified by consistency across perspectives. It may well be that some explanatory accounts of the universe, such as those represented by mathematical principles (or even science), are in fact unified.

Among the most notable postmodernist commentators on science were the French philosophers Foucault, Jacques Derrida (1930–2004) and Jean-François Lyotard (1924–1998). As truth relativists, these figures claimed that, because knowledge-formation is arbitrary and personalised, scientific depictions of nature are necessarily unreliable. Foucault and Derrida focused on the way scientific knowledge is described in language. They argued that because we each use language in different ways, our scientific descriptions cannot constitute valid accounts of entities in the real world. Instead, such descriptions amount to an 'agreed discourse' shared within our 'narrative community'. According to Lyotard, such dynamics lead scientific knowledge to be treated as a commodity. Overall, these postmodernist thinkers asserted that, contrary to general belief, orthodox science is solely driven by the vested interests of industrialised Western societies and is no more likely to reveal 'truth' than any alternative (i.e. non-scientific) approach to information.

The postmodernist view of science has been criticised by both scientists and philosophers alike. Many simply find the postmodernist position to lack credibility. The idea that scientific approaches are no more reliable than, say, guess-work or magic appears inconsistent with the way science supports the development of technology. For example, the knowledge about physics that enables aeronautical engineers to design aircraft that can fly smoothly in the sky seems to be much more than just a set of arbitrary beliefs shared within a narrative community. By extension, it seems difficult to believe that (scientific) principles such as those

CRITICAL FOCUS

Postmodernist misappropriations of science

Even though postmodernist critics claim that science is an unreliable enterprise, many have sought to invoke scientific concepts in order to support their arguments. The most common examples relate to new areas of research that emerged in the late 19th and early 20th centuries and which appeared to alter fundamentally the scientific understanding of particular topics. By referring to such concepts, postmodernists seek to argue that scientific explanations of nature are highly context-dependent and revisable at any time. Because such examples appear to show how scientific evidence can be used to undermine science itself, they are frequently cited by critics of science of all hues (such as providers of scientifically dubious therapies and products), and not just by postmodernists. The most common examples include the 'uncertainty principle' in quantum mechanics (proposed by German physicist Werner Heisenberg [1901–1976]), 'chaos theory' in applied mathematics (as described by French mathematician Henri Poincaré [1854–1912]) and the 'incompleteness theorem' of mathematical logic (as described by Austrian mathematician Kurt Gödel [1906–1978]). The uncertainty principle is cited to argue that quantum physics has *proven* that random events occur in the universe and that science's assumption of determinism is unfounded. Similar conclusions are drawn from chaos theory, which is described as implying that all science is subject to chaos and so is questionable. The incompleteness theorem is taken to demonstrate that information in nature cannot be fully explained using language, and so cannot be explained by science.

However, defenders of science point out that these concepts are being misapplied when they are used by postmodernists in such contexts (which often coincides with their first having been incorrectly described). The uncertainty principle relates only to difficulties of measuring position and momentum in subatomic particles, and has nothing to do with 'uncertainty' in semantic knowledge, scientific or otherwise. Similarly, chaos theory describes the long-term responses of complex systems (such as meteorological environments) that are highly sensitive to initial conditions, and does not refer to 'chaos' in scientific research. Finally, Gödel's theorem relates only to mathematical symbols, and not to the 'incompleteness' of scientific language. At best, these three scientific concepts could be presented as metaphors of possible scenarios within science. However, the phenomena concerned do not bear upon scientific practice and so have no substantive relevance to critiques of science. Despite the fact that this has been pointed out numerous times in the academic literature, it is still common to see these concepts cited in postmodernist critiques of science, including within psychology (where, for example, quantum phenomena are occasionally cited to 'explain' the occurrence of telepathy or clairvoyance, as well as the inability of mainstream psychology to detect such effects).

that underlie the production of aeronautical knowledge are also merely arbitrary. Critics have noted that postmodernist writings on science are often extremely convoluted, and many have accused postmodernists of obscurantism. Others have drawn attention to cases where postmodernists have made obvious mistakes in their descriptions of scientific subjects. Prominent critics of the postmodernist approach to science include psychologist Noam Chomsky, American biologist Paul R. Gross, American mathematician Norman Levitt (1943–2009), Belgian physicist Jean Bricmont (b. 1952) and American mathematical physicist Alan Sokal (b. 1955). Famously, in 1996, Sokal submitted a hoax manuscript to one of the most renowned postmodernist academic journals. He wrote the manuscript as a parody of postmodernist critiques of science, ensuring that it included a range of nonsensical assertions about physics. Because the paper was quickly accepted for publication by the editors of this major journal, Sokal claimed this demonstrated the overall weakness of the postmodernist critique of science as presented in academic contexts.

Test your knowledge

11.5 What is the postmodernist critique of science?

11.6 How might postmodernism affect psychology?

Answers to these questions can be found on the companion website at:
www.pearsoned.co.uk/psychologyexpress

? Sample question   Essay

Is it ever reasonable to critique science from an aesthetic perspective?

Chapter summary – pulling it all together

→ Can you tick all the points from the revision checklist at the beginning of this chapter?

→ Attempt the sample question from the beginning of this chapter using the answer guidelines below.

→ Go to the companion website at www.pearsoned.co.uk/psychologyexpress to access more revision support online, including interactive quizzes, flashcards, You be the marker exercises as well as answer guidance for the Test your knowledge and Sample questions from this chapter.

> **Further reading for Chapter 11**
>
> | Topic | Key reading |
> | --- | --- |
> | Popperism | Losee, J. (2005). *Theories on the scrap heap: Scientists and philosophers on the falsification, rejection, and replacement of theories.* Pittsburgh: University of Pittsburgh Press. |
> | Critique of Popperism | Stove, D. (1991). *The Plato cult and other philosophical follies.* Oxford: Blackwell. |
> | Postpositivism | Phillips, D. C. & Burbules, N. C. (2000). *Postpositivism and educational research.* Lanham, Maryland: Rowman & Littlefield. |
> | Critical health psychology | Prilleltensky, I. (2003). Critical health psychology needs psychopolitical validity. *Health Psychology Update, 12,* 2–11. |
> | Positive psychology | Seligman, M. E. P. & Csikszentmihalyi, M. (2000). Positive psychology: An introduction. *American Psychologist, 55,* 5–14. |
> | Postmodernism | Gergen, K. J. (2001). Psychological science in a postmodern context. *American Psychologist, 56,* 803–813. |
> | Response to Gergen | Locke, E. A. (2002). The dead end of postmodernism [Response to Gergen (2001)]. *American Psychologist, 57,* 458. |
> | The Sokal hoax | Sokal, A. (1996). A physicist experiments with cultural studies. *Lingua Franca,* 62–64. |
> | Critique of postmodernism | Dawkins, R. (1998). Postmodernism disrobed [Review of the book *Intellectual Impostures*]. *Nature, 394,* 141–143. |
> | Misappropriation of science | Stenger, V. J. (1992). The myth of quantum consciousness. *Humanist, 53,* 13–15. |

Answer guidelines

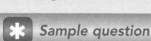

Sample question   **Essay**

Explain the term 'critical psychology', providing and discussing two examples.

Approaching the question

This question is phrased as a relatively straightforward instruction to provide an explanation and some examples. However, such questions are usually phrased in a straightforward manner because the content they refer to is itself far from straightforward. Typically there are in fact multiple possible explanations for the target concept, and you are required to describe the various options and to present the one you believe to be most suitable. In addition, when asked to provide multiple examples, you should ensure you offer examples that are clearly distinct from one another, rather than ones that overlap to the extent that a reader might perceive them to be variations of the same thing.

Important points to include

You should be careful to note that the question asks you to 'explain' critical psychology, rather than to 'describe' or to 'define' it. This means you will need to elaborate not just on what critical psychology is, or what it contains, but also why it has emerged, how it operates, and what its strengths and weaknesses are. In offering a consideration of the ways 'critical psychology' can be best explained, you could attempt to provide a list of criteria for judging the quality of an explanation. Such criteria could include principles such as specificity, concreteness, coherence with related concepts and parsimony. You can then invoke these concepts when explaining the refinements in your explanation, and when rejecting alternative explanations.

Make your answer stand out

Critical psychology can be described in terms of what it itself involves. However, a fuller explanation will refer to its relationship to the broader context, including its origins as a response to positivism (and postpositivism), the nature of critical theory in general and the postmodernist critique of science. Critical psychology is part of a larger movement within academia and so being able to elaborate on this wider picture will make your answer stand out.

Explore the accompanying website at www.pearsoned.co.uk/psychologyexpress
→ Prepare more effectively for exams and assignments using the answer guidelines for questions from this chapter.
→ Test your knowledge using multiple choice questions and flashcards.
→ Improve your essay skills by exploring the You be the marker exercises.

Notes

Notes

Relativism, constructivism and their implications for psychology

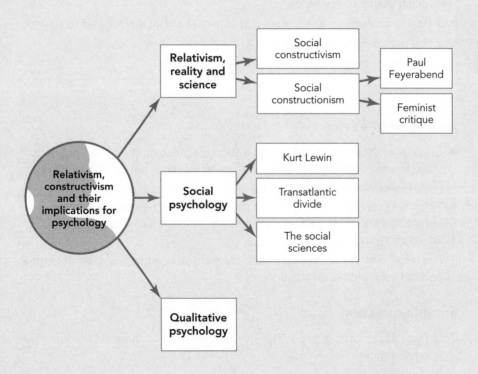

A printable version of this topic map is available from
www.pearsoned.co.uk/psychologyexpress

Introduction

Currently, one of the key conceptual ideas in scientific psychology relates to the very notion of understanding and human experience. Specifically, the idea that each person will experience life differently – and, so, that each researcher will view data differently – creates obvious complications for psychology as a scientific study of people's thoughts, feelings and behaviour. Accordingly, the rootedness of people's perspectives in social and cultural contexts has been widely discussed in psychology, in terms of its impact on epistemology, its relevance as a subject matter, and its implications for methodologies of inquiry.

> **→** *Revision checklist*
>
> *Essential points to revise are:*
> ❏ How relativism, constructivism and constructionism are applied to science
> ❏ The nature of social psychology
> ❏ The nature of qualitative psychology

Assessment advice

- Essay questions on this topic can be very searching, and may tempt you to offer personal opinions and judgements. However, it will be important not to become polemical in your thinking.
- When anticipating controversies in psychology, it is normally advisable to ensure that you have a strong grasp of the relevant factual elements of the arguments you wish to present.
- Assuming that this is the case, then you can – and possibly should – adopt a partisan view on the controversy.

Sample question

Could you answer this question? Below is a typical essay question that could arise on this topic.

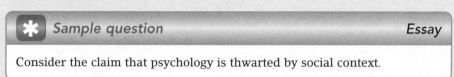

> **✱** *Sample question*   *Essay*
>
> Consider the claim that psychology is thwarted by social context.

Guidelines on answering this question are included at the end of this chapter, whilst further guidance on tackling other exam questions can be found on the companion website at: **www.pearsoned.co.uk/psychologyexpress**

Relativism, reality and science

Relativism, the broad-ranging idea that truth is a function of perception and dependent on perspective, has been a consistent theme throughout the history of psychology. Its most extreme form is solipsism, in which it is argued that there is no basis to believe in the existence of anything other than our own immediate conscious experiences. Indeed, according to solipsism, there is no basis to assume that our experiences have any external causes at all. This is because, by definition, we cannot step outside our own subjectivity in order to establish the existence of such externalities. In reality, there have been very few committed solipsists in scientific psychology (we can note that a true solipsist would have to believe themselves to be the only being in the universe). However, the related position of subjective idealism has been more influential. Subjective idealism holds that material entities exist only insofar as they are perceived by minds. The idea was famously promoted in the 18th century by Irish philosopher George Berkeley (1685–1753), who developed the arguments of Descartes (who a century before had linked cognition to personal existence). These ideas eventually formed the basis for subjectivist approaches to psychology (see Chapter 9) as well as informing theoretical considerations of consciousness (see Chapter 10). They also contributed to the emergence of critiques of logical positivism, and to the postmodernist view of science (see Chapter 11). Two aspects of relativism are of particular conceptual importance. The first is its implications for our explanations of how individuals gather knowledge from their own perspectives. The second is its implications for our explanations of how knowledge itself is garnered and shared by groups of individuals such as communities and societies. Respectively, these two concepts are referred to using the similar terms social constructivism and social constructionism.

Put simply, social *constructivism* is the view that each individual constructs a personal understanding of the world through interacting with social environments. The idea is often used to explain concepts in cognitive development or child education. For example, both Swiss developmental psychologist Jean Piaget (1896–1980) and Russian psychologist Lev Vygotsky (1896–1934) formulated theories of individual learning that were based on constructivism. Given their reliance on social feedback, it is unlikely that social constructivist processes would lead to true solipsism. Nor is there anything inherent in social constructivism that casts doubt on the existence of external realities. However, the principle of social constructivism does draw our attention to the way personal understandings of the world can be shaped, and therefore biased, if unreliable information is promulgated within society.

Example of constructivism in education

Constructivism posits a means by which knowledge is acquired by human learners. As such, as well as theories of scientific epistemology, it has informed theories of education and developmental psychology. In turn, this has led to the use of constructivist ideas to formulate theory-based approaches to teaching. In general, constructivist approaches to teaching aim to help learners assemble knowledge by presenting opportunities for dynamic engagement with concepts, in social settings where learners interact with one another. Examples of such opportunities include practical exercises, discussion groups, project work, group presentations and the keeping of class journals. These methods can be employed at all levels of education. They have largely superseded previous approaches, which had relied on students working on superficial cognitive subtasks (such as memorisation through repetition) and usually alone.

Social *constructionism* is a related but different worldview, which attempts to describe the nature of knowledge in general. According to social constructionism, all so-called objective knowledge (including all scientific knowledge) is constructed by humans, rather than discovered by them. In other words, what we believe to be the details of everyday reality are not a set of objectively verifiable truths. Instead, they are actually perceptions that are negotiated and agreed by the members of one's particular society. Such shared perceptions are referred to as 'social constructions'. Many concepts in everyday life can be seen as socially constructed, in that they would not exist if society had not agreed them. Examples of these include money, marriage, sport and the law. However, other concepts that are sometimes considered to be social constructions are not so straightforward, but may still lack true correspondence to entities in the real world. Examples include several concepts studied in the social sciences, including 'communities', 'the economy' and 'the body politic'. As they are socially constructed, it can be argued that these entities do not truly exist (but are actually accumulations or variations of other entities that do), and that considering them to exist amounts to a collective error of reasoning. A further concern is that socially constructed concepts can create unwarranted expectations of what constitutes normality. Aspiring to meet these unwarranted expectations may then produce undesirable outcomes (for example, when countries aspire to 'economic development' or individuals aspire to 'mental health').

Key term

Essentialism: Social constructionism is often contrasted with 'essentialism'. While social constructionism represents the idea that concepts exist only insofar as their meanings have been produced and agreed by common audiences, essentialism relates to the idea that concepts have single, unique and intrinsic definitions. The essentialist approach argues that every concept has an 'essence', amounting to the set of properties that it possesses. As such, the task of observation is purely objective: to recognise correctly the essence (or 'essential nature') of a concept so that it be properly identified. In this context, there is no such thing as a subjective or socially constructed concept. However, essentialism is not antonymic to constructionism. Essentialism also contrasts with empiricism, the view that the nature of entities will be derived from ongoing observation. For example, an essentialist approach to gender would presuppose that men possess essential natures that differ from those of women, and would declare observable differences to be related to these essences. An empirical approach would allow for the possibility that what appear to be differences on the surface might actually be artefacts of particular cultural situations. In the empirical view, differences in the characteristics of men and women can be detected through observation, but cannot be said to exist unless they are observed.

Many scientists openly acknowledge that their work is frequently shaped by social interests. For example, many scientists focus on identifying environmentally sound energy sources precisely because of the relevance of such research to public concerns. In this sense, scientific *practice* can be loosely described as being socially constructed. However, social constructionism is most controversial when applied to epistemology rather than practice. For example, by arguing that science is an agreed discourse shared within a narrative community, most postmodernists take the view that all scientific *knowledge* is socially constructed. According to this analysis, scientific knowledge is generated by social forces (alone), and so cannot be assumed to correspond with reality. The Austrian philosopher Paul Feyerabend (1924–1994) was perhaps the most prominent scientific social constructionist. Feyerabend argued that, because all knowledge is socially constructed, there was no difference in validity between scientific knowledge and non-scientific knowledge. By implication, he argued that activities such as witchcraft, astrology and alternative medicine made claims about nature that were just as legitimate as those of scientists. Ultimately, Feyerabend rejected all suggestions that some methodologies were better than others. In doing so, he dismissed *both* the positivist emphasis on verification *and* the Popperian emphasis on falsification. His philosophy, which became known as 'epistemological anarchism', was neatly encapsulated in the title of his most famous book, *Against method* (1975).

KEY STUDY

The social construction of laboratory life

The French philosopher and anthropologist Bruno Latour (b. 1947) together with British sociologist Steve Woolgar (b. 1950) have each developed many theories regarding the way science is produced in contemporary society. In 1979, they published *Laboratory life: The construction of scientific facts*, a book describing practices at an endocrinology laboratory at the Salk Institute for Biological Studies in California. Latour and Woolgar produced their findings by using methodologies of field-based ethnographic research, observing activities in the laboratory in the same way as anthropologists observe the cultural practices of remote communities. Their book, which is written in a semi-fictionalised style, records their observations of the work of scientists and technicians as they gathered and scrutinised data, conducted meetings, wrote papers and carried out all the tasks involved in a complex scientific research programme. They concluded that scientists rarely address research questions simply by gathering and analysing data in a systematic and objective manner. Instead, Latour and Woolgar argue that scientists come to conclusions through diplomatic manoeuvring, assertions of political influence and exchanges of favours among each another (aimed primarily at maximising the status of protagonists). Latour and Woolgar's descriptions have been criticised by a number of philosophers and scientists, who argue, among other things, that the work fails to accurately describe the content of the endocrinological research taking place at the Salk Institute, and that Latour and Woolgar's sociological analyses are tainted by a political bias. The book also falls foul of a common criticism of constructionist works, namely, that Latour and Woolgar do not specify why the interpretations of their own research are immune from the biasing factors that so distort the work of the scientific researchers they are studying. If the Salk researchers were unable to draw valid conclusions from their observations in an objective and neutral manner (because of being embroiled in unseemly processes of bartering and political competition), then how is it that Latour and Woolgar were able to do draw valid conclusions from theirs?

Source: Latour, B., & Woolgar, S. (1979). *Laboratory life: The construction of scientific facts*. Beverly Hills: Sage

Feyerabend's flamboyant lifestyle and entertaining polemics contributed to his fame, but his philosophy of science ultimately failed to gain widespread acceptance. The chief problem related to his claim that the conclusions of pseudoscience were just as valid as those of science. Most observers felt this claim was conspicuously contradicted by the relative track-records of pseudoscience and science. In addition, Feyerabend's writings were infused with political argumentation and moral reasoning, which detracted from his philosophical position. Part of his case for epistemological anarchism was his belief that scientific progress served the interests of Western imperialism and, as such, was morally objectionable. However, even if this were true, it would not render scientific *epistemology* (with its emphasis on determination, empiricism and experimentation) invalid. Even Feyerabend himself eventually acknowledged that the successes of technology cast doubt on the social constructionist view of science.

CRITICAL FOCUS

The feminist critique of science

In the context of philosophy, feminist theory is the term typically used to describe the establishment and promotion of female perspectives on knowledge and culture, as well as critiquing the social construction of concepts such as sex and gender. Succinctly put, the feminist critique of science argues that both the principles and findings of mainstream science are socially constructed in ways that reflect a masculinist bias, and as a result are rendered arbitrary and unreliable. Major feminist critics of science include American physicist Evelyn Fox Keller (b. 1936), Belgian cultural theorist Luce Irigaray (b. 1932), and American philosopher Sandra Harding (b. 1935). For example, Keller has argued that a masculinist bias impeded cellular biologists from being able to account for the aggregation of cells of the amoeba *Dictyostelium discoideum*. According to Keller (1978), the belief of cellular biologists that living cells should follow the control of specialised leader cells resulted from a (purportedly) male belief in the importance of leadership. Only when biologists considered the (purportedly) female idea that such cells could work collaboratively together was the correct explanation discovered. Similarly, Irigaray famously questioned the accuracy of Einstein's mass–energy equivalence formula ($E = mc^2$), on the grounds that its squaring of c was based more on a male fascination with speed than on its arithmetic utility. The feminist critique also suggests that scientific epistemology as a whole is constructed along male-biased lines. Harding (1986) asserts that mainstream science's prioritisations of reason over emotion, objectivity over subjectivity, and abstraction over concreteness each reflect this bias; and that the practice of science would be improved by incorporating feminist cognitive styles, such as those involving emotion, reflexivity and social values. However, not all feminist theorists accept this social constructionist approach to the consideration of science. For example, American philosopher Cassandra Pinnick (1994) has dismissed the idea that there are different 'masculine' and 'feminine' approaches to scientific reasoning, and has noted that the claim that science is socially constructed from a masculinist perspective lacks any supporting evidence.

Test your knowledge

12.1 How does social constructivism differ from social constructionism?

12.2 What did Feyerabend mean by 'epistemological anarchism'?

Answers to these questions can be found on the companion website at:
www.pearsoned.co.uk/psychologyexpress

 Sample question   *Essay*

How true is the claim that science is just one valid way of knowing among many?

Social psychology

The phenomenon whereby perceptions and understanding can be influenced by social factors not only affects the way research in psychology is done, but also is part of the subject matter of psychology itself. One of the first psychologists to study the effects of social contact on behaviour was American psychologist Norman Triplett (1861–1931). Triplett studied the way audiences stimulate people to perform tasks more quickly than they would do alone. Later researchers, such as German-American psychologist Kurt Lewin (1890–1947) and American psychologist Leon Festinger (1919–1989) investigated how social contexts affect emotions and cognition, as well as behaviour. By being among the first to call on psychologists to study the influence of social variables, Lewin became regarded as the founder of the subdiscipline now known as social psychology. Since the mid-20th century, social psychology has grown in scope and depth. It has produced some of the most famous studies in psychology, such as the conformity research conducted by Solomon Asch (1907–1996) and the obedience experiments of Stanley Milgram (1933–1984). Furthermore, its researchers study some of the topics that non-psychologists find most fascinating about psychology, including persuasion, sexuality, inter-group conflict, aggression, prejudice and romantic love.

CRITICAL FOCUS

The transatlantic divide in social psychology

One important historical trend in social psychology has been the emergence of different emphases in North America and Europe. North American social psychologists are generally more interested in individual-level phenomena (i.e. the psychology of the individual within the group), while European social psychologists focus more on group-level phenomena (i.e. the psychology of the group as a whole). Accordingly, North American social psychologists often study topics such as attitudes, social cognition and aggression, whereas European social psychologists often study topics such as social identity, group dynamics and organisations. While it would be easy to exaggerate the extent of this divergence, it can be noted that social psychology is one of the few specialisms in psychology to differ geographically in this way.

Despite its successes, social psychology is frequently identified as lying on the fringes of psychology, rather than at its core. Some of the reasons for this include the fact that, as most social variables are meaningful only when considered in their natural context, some psychologists feel they are more properly seen as the subject matter of other academic disciplines, such as sociology (the study of society), anthropology (the study of humanity) and political science (the study of political systems and behaviour). Secondly, because they pertain to social relationships, many topics in social psychology can appear to be politically loaded. Some psychologists feel that psychology should aspire to be a dispassionate apolitical discipline, and that such topics are therefore unsuitable for psychological research. Thirdly, some psychologists worry that studying social variables will diminish the capacity of psychology to perform research that can be described as truly scientific (at least in superficial terms). This is because social variables are grounded in real-life contexts and so tend to be difficult to examine using experimental or laboratory-based methods.

As a result of this interconnectedness with real-life cultural contexts, social psychologists often employ research methods and data analysis techniques that have been adapted from other social science disciplines. For example, social psychologists make much use of survey, observation and interview methodologies, as well as statistical approaches designed for large cross-sectional, self-report datasets, such as factor analysis. Because these approaches are very commonly used in sociology, anthropology and related fields, this can in turn serve to reinforce the notion that social psychology lies outside the mainstream of psychology. One further reason why social psychology can be viewed as peripheral is that many social psychologists place strong emphasis on the relativistic nature of concepts in their research. This is not generally the case in other domains of psychology.

Key term

Social sciences: a group of academic disciplines that examine different aspects of the contexts in which humans live. The archetypal social science discipline is sociology, which is devoted to the study of human social activity and of society itself. Social sciences can also involve direct examination of humans in their environments, such as in psychology and anthropology, or they can involve examination of macro-level systems of human activity, such as in geography and economics. Often, the social sciences are taken to include fields that study specific systems within which human life is lived, such as political science, education, law and business studies. Descriptions of the place of psychology in the social sciences are sometimes qualified by references to the fact that some psychological subfields, such as the study of brain physiology, appear only distantly relevant to the notion of human living contexts. However, in fact very few areas of psychology are unrelated to the way people interact with their social environments. Further, psychology is not unique in this respect; several social science disciplines have similar sub-areas that focus on issues other than the context of human living. For example, large elements of geography involve the study of the physical landscape, while large elements of economics involve the computational analysis of financial systems (such as currency exchange rates). Likewise, much research in law, education and business studies focuses on technical aspects (such as the regulations arising from relevant legislation) rather than on the scientific examination of humans in context. For similar reasons, attempting to define the social sciences in terms of a shared methodological approach is equally limited. In summary, the social sciences are a broad and heterogeneous collection of disciplines, which share overlapping interests but have very disparate philosophical and practical approaches.

Sample question   **Essay**

Where should social psychology be located in relation to the mainstream?

Qualitative psychology

One of the consequences of the interest in the relativistic nature of observations has been the development of research methods that seek to focus on qualia (the elements of subjective conscious experience, as described in Chapter 10), rather than quanta (indexable constructs whose nature can be established objectively). This approach has become known as 'qualitative research'. Qualitative methods are widely used in some social science disciplines, such as sociology and anthropology. Given the inter-disciplinary proximity of these disciplines to social psychology, these methods have become used in psychology also, especially when studying aspects of human behaviour that are related to its social and cultural contexts. Typical qualitative approaches include observation, ethnography, interviews, focus groups and discourse analysis. Essentially, qualitative research seeks to emphasise the subjective experiences of individual research participants, in recognition of the assumption that each individual constructs an understanding of the world that is uniquely theirs. As a result, the information gathered using qualitative methods will relate primarily to those participants studied, and may not generalise to other persons in the population. However, despite this restriction, qualitative information is likely to be very rich and detailed. Many psychologists who feel sympathy with relativist positions such as social constructionism feel that qualitative methods offer a better way of capturing the essence of human thoughts, feelings and behaviour than those research methods traditionally employed in mainstream psychology.

The traditional methods are usually referred to as being 'quantitative', partly in recognition of their use of numerical data, but also partly because they focus on quanta rather than qualia. While many people suggest that quantitative research is based solely on numerical data, it is more accurate to say that it is based on objectively verifiable data. As such, quantitative methods look at concepts not only in terms of how large or numerous they are, but also in terms of whether they are present or absent, whether they are complex or simple, whether they repeat themselves or change over time, whether they are similar to other concepts or are unique, and so on. Arising from such ideas, quantitative research tends to involve comparisons, as well as the gathering of data samples from multiple cases or on multiple occasions. It is true that such research is greatly assisted by the use of statistical analysis techniques, laboratory experiments and even computer software. However, it is not strictly true to say that these tools are necessary for research to be quantitative.

CRITICAL FOCUS

The qualitative–quantitative divide

It is undoubtedly the case that the distinction between quantitative and qualitative research is a source of tension in psychology. While it is common to see recommendations that the two approaches be used together, it is important to remember that they each have quite different, and contradictory, philosophical origins. Quantitative methods descended from the positivist and postpositivist traditions of epistemology (which embody a belief in empirical realism), while qualitative methods descended from the relativist and constructionist traditions (which reject the notion of empirical realism). As such, while quantitative researchers assume that their observations can (and should) be extrapolated beyond the particular sample, qualitative researchers usually assert that their observations are not generalisable at all (and, indeed, are not intended to be). Likewise, while quantitative approaches are premised on an aspiration to achieve reliability and validity, qualitative approaches are premised on the belief that such aspirations are futile and therefore naïve. Qualitative researchers argue that their methods provide a richer and more descriptive account of their participants' experiences than would be possible using numerically focused methods. Indeed, as a result of its relativist stance, qualitative researchers often take the view that quantitative methods are in fact fundamentally unsuited to the study of human experience because of the way (it is suggested) that human experience is socially constructed. In addition, they often argue that quantitative approaches are unable to deal with the sheer complexity of human experience and its interrelatedness with social contexts. In response, quantitative researchers tend to question the degree to which human experience is in fact socially constructed. Further, because of its non-relativist stance, quantitative researchers assert that their methods produce a more representative understanding of people, and a better capacity to test the accuracy of psychological theories and predictions.

Quantitative research remains by far the more common approach in psychology. One reason for this is psychology's scientific tradition. While qualitative research can provide thought-provoking perspectives and ideas, it is difficult to say that it is 'scientific' in the conventional sense of the term. For example, in order to minimise the biasing effects of researchers' own opinions, it is an assumption of the scientific method that only objectively verifiable data can be used to test a prediction. However, because of its relativist ethos, the qualitative approach is sceptical of the notion of objectivity and relies instead on interpretivism. In addition, the tensions between quantitative and qualitative approaches can be pragmatic as well as philosophical. In critiquing qualitative psychology, some commentators have expressed concerns that its expansion could undermine the scientific reputation that psychology has built up over the past century, and thus threaten its prestige and even its resources in institutional settings. Qualitative methods are intuitively appealing and are widely employed in sociology and anthropology, although such disciplines are less committed to maintaining a purely scientific orientation. Thus, while qualitative methods are certainly academically creditable, they remain conceptually distinct, on several levels, from the mainstream of psychology.

Key term

Interpretivism: the position that scientific observations are required to be interpreted as well as recorded, and that merely recording them will not yield complete insight as to their meaning. In addition, an assumption of interpretivism is that concepts make sense only in the wider context in which they are situated, and that understanding can only occur when the whole entity is considered. As such, interpretivism is disapproving of positivism (which stresses objectivity) and reductionism (which allows for the study of elements extracted from the whole). The interpretivist perspective is possibly best exemplified by an approach to research known as interpretative phenomenological analysis (IPA). This idiographic method of qualitative data analysis seeks to emphasise the phenomenological aspects of human experience. In this sense, IPA is based on the premise that the testimony of an informant will reflect a constructivist form of knowledge, and so requires the researcher to isolate the informant's understanding by tracing the structure of concepts used, without being influenced by prior assumptions.

Test your knowledge

12.5 What are the main differences between quantitative and qualitative approaches?

12.6 What are the strengths and weaknesses of qualitative psychology?

Answers to these questions can be found on the companion website at: **www.pearsoned.co.uk/psychologyexpress**

 Sample question   *Essay*

To what extent is combining quantitative and qualitative methods philosophically feasible?

Chapter summary – pulling it all together

➜ Can you tick all the points from the revision checklist at the beginning of this chapter?

➜ Attempt the sample question from the beginning of this chapter using the answer guidelines below.

➜ Go to the companion website at www.pearsoned.co.uk/psychologyexpress to access more revision support online, including interactive quizzes, flashcards, You be the marker exercises as well as answer guidance for the Test your knowledge and Sample questions from this chapter.

Further reading for Chapter 12	
Topic	Key reading
Science and reality	Brown, J. R. (1994). *Smoke and mirrors: How science reflects reality*. London: Routledge.
Constructionism	Jost, J. T., & Kruglanski, A. W. (2002). Constructionism and experimental social psychology: History of the rift and prospects for reconciliation. *Personality and Social Psychology Review, 6*, 168–187.
Feminist epistemology	Pinnick, C. (1994). Feminist epistemology: Implications for philosophy of science. *Philosophy of Science, 61*, 646–657.
Feminism and science	Harding, S. (1986). *The science question in feminism*. Ithaca, New York: Cornell University Press.
Feminist critique of science	Irigaray, L. (1985). Is the subject of science sexed? *Cultural Critique, 1*, 73–88. [Originally published as: Irigaray, L. (1982). Le sujet de la science est-il sexué? *Les Temps Modernes, 39*, 960–974.]
Gender and psychoanalysis	Keller, E. F. (1978). Gender and science. *Psychoanalysis and Contemporary Thought, 1*, 409–433.
Critique of relativism	Sokal, A., & Bricmont, J. (2003). *Intellectual impostures: Postmodern philosophers' abuse of science* (revised edition). London: Profile Books.
The science wars	Gross, P. R., & Levitt, N. (1998). *Higher superstition: The academic left and its quarrels with science*. Baltimore: Johns Hopkins University Press.
Qualitative psychology	Morgan, M. (1998). Qualitative research: Science or pseudo-science? *Psychologist, 11*, 481–483.

Answer guidelines

 Sample question **Essay**

Consider the claim that psychology is thwarted by social context.

Approaching the question

This question sets out a proposition for you to support or reject. As such, your approach to the question should be to examine the cases for and against, to present a comparison of the strengths of the cases, and to offer a conclusion as to whether the claim should be accepted. Secondly, the terms in the question are flexible, in that the term 'social context' can be operationalised in several different ways (as indeed can the term 'thwarted'). However, as a conceptual and/or historical issue in psychology, it can be assumed that the question is related to the issues discussed in this chapter.

Important points to include

The fact that social factors are important raises the issue of how psychology is related to other academic disciplines. Rather than discussing psychology on its own, it will be important to draw attention to how these topics overlap with other social science disciplines, and to the influences this overlap has had on the evolution of theory and methods in the relevant areas of psychology.

Make your answer stand out

While it is necessary to be even-handed in dealing with the various sides to these issues, it will also be important to present some evidence of being aware that things are not so evenly balanced in real terms within the discipline. In other words, while the implications of social context for epistemology are certainly of interest to psychologists, the vast majority of academic work in psychology is based on relatively orthodox scientific approaches. In presenting the material for your answer, it will be impressive if you can be relatively specific about this and to be able, for example, to describe with accuracy the relative prominence of different epistemological views and methodological approaches.

Explore the accompanying website at www.pearsoned.co.uk/psychologyexpress
→ Prepare more effectively for exams and assignments using the answer guidelines for questions from this chapter.
→ Test your knowledge using multiple choice questions and flashcards.
→ Improve your essay skills by exploring the You be the marker exercises.

Notes

Notes

The future of psychology

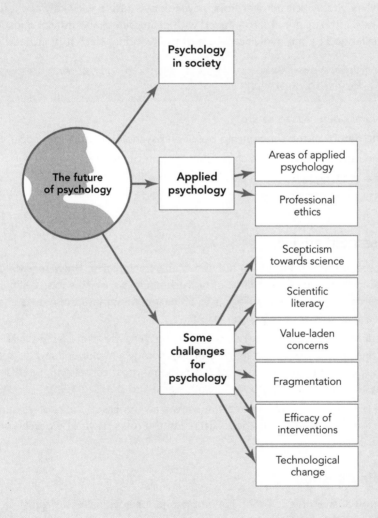

A printable version of this topic map is available from
www.pearsoned.co.uk/psychologyexpress

Introduction

Psychology has a very long and complex history, and continues to grow and evolve. Such growth and evolution relate not only to the continuing popularity of psychology as an academic subject and career choice, but also to the way scholarship in psychology provides new insights into the very nature of human thoughts, feelings and behaviour, thereby shifting the scope of the discipline by producing deeper as well as broader research agendas. One benefit of learning about the history and conceptual basis of a discipline is to enable an informed consideration of its future. As well as the ongoing research findings that will inevitably accrue over time, psychology's future will likely see it further integrated into society at large, faced with professional and ethical questions, and challenged by the evolving nature of the world in which it is situated.

→ Revision checklist

Essential points to revise are:
- ❏ The nature of the relationship between psychology and wider society
- ❏ The range of ways in which psychology can be applied
- ❏ The challenges that face psychology in the future

Assessment advice

- Discussions about the future are necessarily speculative. However, while not seeking to predict the findings of new research in specific subdisciplines, it is always wise for psychologists to at least contemplate the events and challenges that are likely to be faced.

- As such, when approaching assessments on this type of subject, it is advisable to consider not only the trajectory of psychology's evolution (and, as such, the aspects of its history that are most appear most consistent), but also the 'shape' of the discipline today in both social and practical terms.

- This will include the ability to demonstrate awareness of the professional structures in which psychology exists, and the roles played by psychologists in wider society.

Sample question

Could you answer this question? See opposite for a typical essay question that could arise on this topic.

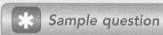

Sample question *Essay*

In the future, how will psychology change and how will it remain the same?

Guidelines on answering this question are included at the end of this chapter, whilst further guidance on tackling other exam questions can be found on the companion website at: **www.pearsoned.co.uk/psychologyexpress**

Psychology in society

Psychology is an extremely popular discipline. It is studied by large numbers of students at universities around the world, its professional training programmes are almost always over-subscribed, its subject matter is considered by most observers to be intrinsically interesting, and its practitioners are, in the main, held in high public regard. As such, unlike some of the less well-known sciences, psychology has a strong public profile. Accordingly, psychology is always likely to be influenced by its social context, and it might be assumed that society itself is likely to be influenced by psychology.

One way in which society influences psychology is by drawing attention to potential research topics of public concern. For example, much social policy is developed around issues that fall squarely within the realm of psychology, issues which receive almost daily coverage in the mass media. These include crime (and its causes), mental health, child-rearing, social conflict, education, political tension, use of drugs and alcohol, consumer behaviour and sexuality. Many psychologists will find themselves intrinsically motivated to help elucidate such matters, and to provide solutions to related problems. It is also of course true that, as these issues are subject to public policy attention, many psychologists will be engaged professionally to investigate them, both as staff of public agencies and as recipients of publicly funded research grants.

In addition, the public's interest helps prompt psychologists to study more existential matters, such as the nature of the human mind and whether it is grounded in physiology. To some extent, it might be argued that psychology now studies what for centuries had been the purview of mass morality movements, such as organised religions. As such, it is perhaps likely that popular fascination with mysticism and spirituality also contributes to interest in psychology.

As well as being influenced by society, psychology has served to leave its own impression on society in return. One way in which psychology can influence society is through the public profile of its academics and practitioners. By holding mainstream positions in universities, health services, industry and other settings, these professionals contribute to the embedding of the recognition of psychology (and its relevance) in the public consciousness. Indeed, it has frequently been suggested that society in general has been affected by a process of psychologisation, due to the growth of popular familiarity with psychological subjects. Psychology has provided a vocabulary of new terms that have been absorbed into general discourse (such as life stress, self-esteem and IQ), as well as adding refined technical meanings to old terms (such as empathy, depression and masculinity). One problem with this type of impact is that current understandings may be revised by future research, with the result that the use of particular terms in psychology changes over time. While the general public is certainly interested in psychological subject matter, it is unclear whether they fully appreciate how new research can serve to overwrite old, or the ways in which terms and concepts become obsolete. As the public profile of psychology grows, it is as yet unclear whether this problem will intensify or reduce in the future.

Example of how the use of psychological terms changes over time

As in any science, the way psychologists classify and explain concepts can be expected to evolve over time in response to new data, analyses and perspectives. However, as the subject matter of psychology is often of mass public interest, psychological terms can become widely used in society even after they have become obsolete within the discipline. One example of where this has occurred is in the psychology of intelligence. In the early 20th century, psychometricians used a three-category system to classify people who had below-average scores on IQ tests. Persons with the lowest scores were termed 'idiots', those in the next group were termed 'imbeciles', those in the next were termed 'morons'. These terms were introduced especially to describe the category of IQ score that they referred to, and were not intended to be controversial. The term 'idiot' comes from the Latin word for ordinary person; the term 'imbecile' comes from the Latin word for feeble; while the term 'moron' comes from the Greek word for blunt. The terms became widely used in general society, although they eventually became slang words with abusive connotations. Because of this, they were abandoned by mainstream psychology in the second half of the 20th century and are considered unacceptable for technical usage. Indeed, it would be generally regarded as highly offensive to use any of these terms to refer to a person with an intellectual disability. While the terms remain in common use as informal insults, it is likely that the majority of their users are unaware of their original technical meanings.

Test your knowledge

13.1 How has society affected psychology?

13.2 How has psychology affected society?

Answers to these questions can be found on the companion website at: www.pearsoned.co.uk/psychologyexpress

Sample question   *Essay*

> To what do you attribute the popularity of psychology: its processes or its products?

Applied psychology

Applied psychology refers to the use of formal psychological knowledge to address practical challenges in real-world settings, often in the context of specific professional roles. In this sense, it stands distinct from 'basic' psychology, which comprises the accumulated scientific practice and knowledge base within psychology (and primarily includes the subfields of cognitive psychology, biological psychology, personality theory, social psychology and developmental psychology). Some fields of applied psychology comprise those areas that most inform the public stereotype of psychology, where the psychologist works professionally to address people's mental health needs. These include clinical psychology (where the psychologist provides diagnoses, evaluations, treatment recommendations, direct therapy and advice on prevention) and counselling psychology (where the psychologist provides advisory and therapeutic services, especially to clients whose needs relate to problems of living rather than to psychiatric illness). Two other very common applied domains of psychology are educational psychology (where the psychologist provides services relating to learning and teaching in education contexts) and industrial or organisational psychology (where the psychologist provides services in the context of workplaces and other organisations). Some of the other areas of applied psychology are very well known but, in terms of the number of psychologists who work in them, are much smaller. These include forensic psychology (where psychology is applied in legal, criminological and correctional contexts), sport psychology (where psychology is applied to athletic participation and performance) and health psychology (where psychology is applied in the context of physical health, both in public health and clinical health areas).

Psychologists work in many different professional settings and roles, and receive the trust of a wide range of client groups. As with any profession, there is often a concern about how standards of professional conduct are maintained and how the general public can be protected. Psychology is typically characterised by a strong emphasis on professional ethics, and virtually all its professional bodies require members to undertake to adhere to a written ethical code. While the ethical aspect of psychology itself comprises a substantial area of study, it is nonetheless possible to concisely enumerate its main themes. Briefly, most formal ethical codes require psychologists to base their activities on principles such as respect (which includes interacting with others in a fair and courteous manner, maintaining confidentiality where it is called for, and obtaining informed consent from clients or others affected), competence (which includes maintaining adequate training, and being aware of the limits of one's competence), responsibility (which includes maintaining continuity of care, and protecting and debriefing research participants) and integrity (which includes being honest, avoiding conflicts of interest and maintaining professional boundaries). Although psychologists are required by their professional bodies (and in some cases by their employers) to be guided by ethics codes, it is certainly the case that the duty of behaving ethically rests with the individual psychologists. Whenever a psychologist is reported as being in breach of a particular code that he or she is covered by, the professional body concerned will have a procedure to investigate the case and, if deemed appropriate, to eject, suspend, or otherwise penalise the individual concerned.

Key terms

Professional ethics: refers to those ethical principles that pertain to the specialist knowledge or training of individuals who work in professions. In turn, professions are particular occupations that are characterised by a vocational ethos (i.e. a feeling of being personally drawn to the area), a high degree of specialised training, and – usually – membership of a formal body of fellow members of the same profession. Membership of such a professional body almost always involves the explicit endorsement of a code of professional ethics. While the term 'ethics' more broadly refers to the philosophical consideration of morality, in which dilemmas can be judged from a number of competing perspectives (such as utilitarianism and deontology), professional ethics tend to be by nature prescriptive. In other words, professional ethics are codified in a standardised way and are expected to be adhered to by all members of the profession, regardless of their individual moral judgements.

One issue with written ethical codes is that the principles they represent may not be consistent with the individual's own moral judgements. However, it is probably reasonable for professional bodies to acknowledge that allowing each psychologist to decide individually what constitutes ethical behaviour will not consistently serve to protect the public. As such, it is generally regarded as acceptable for standardised ethical codes to be operated as if binding. While doing so, professional bodies tend to acknowledge that psychologists should not only conform to their codified ethical principles, but should also reflect seriously about the ethical dimensions of their work and be intrinsically motivated to behave ethically. The British Psychological Society's (2009) code states that 'ethics is related to the control of power'. At their root, ethical codes serve to moderate the influence that psychologists have earned, and the status they are perceived as having by the general public.

Test your knowledge

13.3 What are the major areas of applied psychology?

13.4 What are the major areas typically covered by ethical codes for psychologists?

Answers to these questions can be found on the companion website at: **www.pearsoned.co.uk/psychologyexpress**

 Sample question   *Essay*

Is applied psychology really 'psychology'?

Some challenges for psychology

In the future, the challenges faced by psychology will be a mixture of the old and the new. Throughout its history, psychology has faced some perennial challenges which, given their consistency, might be expected to remain problematic. One longstanding set of difficulties for psychology results from the discomfort that many observers feel about psychology's standing as a science. This relates both to the values represented by science and to the complexities involved in the scientific approach. With regard to values, several psychologists (and students of psychology), although generally a minority, have questioned whether the human condition is best studied from the formal perspective of science. While the ethos of contemporary psychology is strongly scientific, there have historically always been movements within the discipline who aspire to offer an alternative approach. The continued interest in subjectivist approaches (such as psychoanalysis, phenomenology and humanism), as well as the recent infusion of relativist perspectives (such as might be represented by postmodernism and qualitative methodologies), may help indicate how debates within the discipline will continue to unfold in future years. On the other hand, the general public typically *underestimate* the degree to which psychology adopts a mainstream scientific ethos. One consequence of this is that public awareness of psychological concepts is usually not matched by an appreciation of the underlying evidence. Because scientific literacy is believed to be quite low in most societies, the resulting barriers to public understanding of psychology will presumably remain a significant challenge to psychology into the future.

> **Key term**
>
> **Scientific literacy**: refers to a person's capacity to understand scientific concepts and the processes of reasoning used in science, as well as their ability to use scientific principles to reason through problems. While there is no agreed single means of measuring scientific literacy, it is generally accepted that it includes awareness of major scientific facts (such as the fact that the world is round, that water boils at 100 degrees Celsius, and that nuclear radiation is poisonous) as well as some of the basic principles of the scientific method (such as the evidence-dependent nature of scientific theories). Scientific literacy is distinct from technological literacy (where a person exhibits adeptness in using technology), and is generally regarded as being low in most societies.

Another set of challenges for psychology that appears to have become perennial relates to the way it deals with spiritual and value-laden concerns. These may include relatively abstract notions (such as the mind–body problem and the nature of mortality) as well as highly charged controversies (such as the impact of abortion, the nature of homosexuality and the efficacy of criminal punishment). While the objectivity of science encourages psychologists to approach these topics in a neutral manner, it can be very difficult for them to leave aside their personal values when interpreting (and conducting) research. As such, the accumulated findings of psychology on these matters may be interpreted as in some way reflecting the 'value system' of psychology. This creates a double-edged problem. If psychologists as a whole *fail* to remain neutral, then the findings of psychology will become tainted by bias. However, if psychologists in general *succeed* in being neutral, then their research findings might be falsely interpreted as representing their moral beliefs, an outcome that could adversely affect some psychologists. For example, if valid psychological research were to reveal that the mental health impact of abortion on women is substantially less than has been suggested by some pro-life lobby groups, then this is the conclusion that should be relayed by psychologists. However, *individual* psychologists who are themselves opposed to abortion may feel that doing so in an authentically neutral fashion will lead others to question their moral integrity. To the extent that the public at large will continue to feel that psychology can usefully address important issues in society, this type of challenge is likely to remain with psychology long into the future.

A different type of perennial challenge that may continue to face psychology in the future relates to the fragmentation of the field. As well as the various areas of basic and applied psychology, the field is characterised by a number of significant theoretical schools, many of which present essentially incompatible worldviews. For example, while cognitivism emphasises the primary importance of cognitions, behaviourism argues that cognitions are of secondary importance at best. Similarly, while biological psychology seeks to emphasise the way that many psychological constructs are innately determined, the social learning perspective often suggests that the same constructs result from social influence (consistent with the nature–nurture distinction) and are not biological at all. It is often noted that the fragmentation of psychology into differing schools resembles what Kuhn described as the way sciences operate early in their histories, prior to the emergence of unifying paradigms. As such, the related future challenges for psychology could arise in two directions. On the one hand, psychology may continues to develop new explanatory schools of thought, which may eventually lead to the break-up of the discipline altogether. On the other hand, psychology may undergo a Kuhnian scientific revolution, in which the various current schools of psychology at last coalesce into a single unified worldview.

KEY STUDY

Psychotherapy and the 'dodo bird' conjecture

It has widely been understood for centuries that formal efforts to help people with problems such as depression and anxiety can be effective. More specifically, with the development of different theoretical paradigms within psychology during the 20th century, there emerged a view that specific types of therapies would be more or less effective than one another. However, there has always been a tradition of cautious scepticism among many psychologists toward the claims made for (some) psychotherapies. A number of studies have suggested that even when key features of a formal psychotherapy are removed or manipulated, efficacy outcomes remain unaltered. Wampold et al. (1997) published a major empirical review of the extant literature. These authors accumulated masses of statistical findings from previous studies of psychotherapies. What was novel about this analysis is that the research question was constructed as follows: *what is the average difference in efficacy between any two psychotherapies?* It was reasoned that if the claims made for different therapeutic paradigms were true, then some paradigms should prove to be more efficacious than others, not least because of the fact that the main paradigms in psychology are based on conceptually incompatible premises. Using meta-analysis to compare results across hundreds of published research studies, the authors found that the average difference in effect size between any two therapies was almost exactly zero. This was a startling discovery in that it suggested that, on average, the therapies offered by psychology – which are constructed on the basis of competing theoretical assumptions – appear not to differ in terms of their effects on mental health. As such, the various paradigms (behaviourism, cognitivism, humanism, psychoanalysis, etc.) can be said to have offered no unique benefit to the clients of therapy who were studied. Many commentators took this to imply a falsification of the very paradigms themselves, in that empirical comparisons of therapies based on such paradigms ought to amount to empirical tests of their predictive validity. Such findings have been reported frequently in psychology. Nonetheless, they have not had much impact on the professional practice of psychotherapy. This may offer an example of how a major empirical finding must wait for a receptive consensus to emerge among scientists before it can become generally accepted.

Source: Wampold, B. E., Mondin, G. W., Moody, M., Stich, F., Benson, K., & Ahn, H-N. (1997). A meta-analysis of outcome studies comparing bona fide psychotherapies: Empirically, 'all must have prizes'. *Psychological Bulletin, 122,* 203–215.

A final perennial challenge for psychology relates to the efficacy of its interventions. Generally speaking, while different types of psychological intervention and therapy are very popular and are utilised widely, there has always been a concern about the degree to which their efficacy can be supported by empirical evidence. Although much research has been conducted, and many individual studies of particular therapies have found them to be effective, several large-scale review studies have suggested that the overall body of research is disappointing. This relates not only to therapeutic interventions for mental health, but also to interventions relating to behaviour change, education, industry and other applied contexts. With society's increasing interest in such civic-minded principles as accountability, liability and value-for-money, it is likely that demand for psychological interventions to be empirically supported will increase over the coming years. This will create a challenge for psychology to develop ways of demonstrating its applied efficacy in clearer ways.

As well as the perennial challenges that will likely remain for psychology, it can be assumed that new challenges will also emerge. By its nature, predicting these new challenges is far from straightforward. Some of these challenges will be secondary to social change, while others will be secondary to technological change. As regards social change, it appears inevitable that both scholarship and practice in psychology will be affected by forces such as globalisation, climate change and geographical shifts in economic power and political influence. However, while such changes might bring uncertainty for psychology as a discipline, they may also bring benefits. For example, the production (and consumption) of psychological research conducted in diverse cultural settings will help to isolate the precise manner in which cultural variables shape and affect behaviour. Technological change will also influence the evolution of psychology. Advances in brain surgery and genetics may allow scientists to alter the psychological nature of individual humans, which if achieved would have profound implications for psychology as an explanatory science. Other impacts of technology will be more indirect. One example will relate to those advances in food production, public health and clinical medicine which have lengthened the human life expectancy. This creates a need for psychology to understand better the experiences of people who live longer lives, and who are physically healthier in old age. A second example is the way that social contact is increasingly facilitated by access to online resources. The fact that people can interact with social networks that are global in scope, that allow continuous personal access, and that afford opportunities for anonymity, will have great implications for the psychology of relationships, of self and of communities.

Test your knowledge

13.5 How does scientific literacy affect psychology?

13.6 In what way has psychology fragmented over time?

Answers to these questions can be found on the companion website at:
www.pearsoned.co.uk/psychologyexpress

 Sample question   *Essay*

How might public interest in psychology affect its development?

Chapter summary – pulling it all together

→ Can you tick all the points from the revision checklist at the beginning of this chapter?

→ Attempt the sample question from the beginning of this chapter using the answer guidelines below.

→ Go to the companion website at www.pearsoned.co.uk/psychologyexpress to access more revision support online, including interactive quizzes, flashcards, You be the marker exercises as well as answer guidance for the Test your knowledge and Sample questions from this chapter.

Further reading for Chapter 13	
Topic	*Key reading*
Psychology in society	Lilienfeld, S. O., Lynn, S. J., Namy, L. L., & Woolf, N. J. (2009). *Psychology: From inquiry to understanding.* London: Pearson.
Psychologisation	Ward, S. C. (2002). *Modernizing the mind: Psychological knowledge and the remaking of society.* Westport, Connecticut: Praeger.
Professional ethics	Parsons, R. D. (2000). *The ethics of professional practice.* London: Pearson.
BPS ethics code	British Psychological Society (2009). *Code of ethics and conduct: Guidance published by the Ethics Committee of the British Psychological Society.* Leicester: British Psychological Society.

Topic	Key reading
Values in psychology	Maio, G. R. (2002). Values: Truth and meaning – Spearman Medal Lecture. *Psychologist, 15,* 296–299.
Politics and psychology	Brewster Smith, M. (2000). Values, politics, and psychology. *American Psychologist, 55,* 1151–1152.
Efficacy of interventions	Wampold, B. E. (2001). *The great psychotherapy debate: Models, methods, and findings.* Mahwah, New Jersey: Erlbaum.

Answer guidelines

Sample question — Essay

In the future, how will psychology change and how will it remain the same?

Approaching the question

This question appears at first to offer you the opportunity to speculate in a relatively open-ended manner on the future of psychology. However, as this question is asked in an academic context, the requirements for scholarly argumentation still apply. This means that substantive points need to be supported by citations of authorities and/or evidence, and that points which are grounded in opinion need to be highlighted as such. Thus, when attempting to predict the future, one way to rationalise your points is to link them to events in the past and the present from which it is reasonable to extrapolate. An alternative approach is to emphasise the links between psychology and other activities whose future is more clearly predictable (such as the occurrence of technological progress). Finally, you should note that this is a double-barrelled question, and as such that both elements require treatment.

Important points to include

The question refers broadly to 'psychology'. Accordingly, it will be important to either (a) include coverage of psychology in its broadest sense, or (b) offer a rationale for selecting whatever area or areas of psychology you use as the subject matter for your answer.

Make your answer stand out

Although the question asks about the future, it would be helpful to attempt to show how considering these points helps us to decide what actions to take in the present. In so doing, an answer may wish to posit a number of different possible futures, each contingent on different immediate actions. This would facilitate (and perhaps necessitate) some kind of evaluative comparison, whereby you are then able to make recommendations about what actions should be pursued. Ultimately, such points help draw attention to the value of studying psychology from a historical and conceptual perspective.

Explore the accompanying website at www.pearsoned.co.uk/psychologyexpress

→ Prepare more effectively for exams and assignments using the answer guidelines for questions from this chapter.

→ Test your knowledge using multiple choice questions and flashcards.

→ Improve your essay skills by exploring the You be the marker exercises.

Notes

Notes

And finally, before the exam . . .

How to approach revision from here

You should be now at a reasonable stage in your revision process – you should have developed your skills and knowledge base over your course and used this text judiciously over that period. Now, however, you have used the book to reflect, remind and reinforce the material you have researched over the year/seminar. You will, of course, need to do additional reading and research to that included here (and appropriate directions are provided) but you will be well on your way with the material presented in this book.

It is important that in answering any question in psychology you take a research- and evidence-based approach to your response. For example, do not make generalised or sweeping statements that cannot be substantiated or supported by evidence from the literature. Remember as well that the evidence should not be anecdotal – it is of no use citing your mum, dad, best friend or the latest news from a celebrity website. After all, you are not writing an opinion piece – you are crafting an argument that is based on current scientific knowledge and understanding. You need to be careful about the evidence you present: do review the material and from where it was sourced.

Furthermore, whatever type of assessment you have to undertake, it is important to take an evaluative approach to the evidence. Whether you are writing an essay, sitting an exam or designing a webpage, the key advice is to avoid simply presenting a descriptive answer. Rather, it is necessary to think about the strength of the evidence in each area. One of the key skills for psychology students is critical thinking and for this reason the tasks featured in this series focus upon developing this way of thinking. Thus you are not expected to simply learn a set of facts and figures, but to think about the implications of what we know and how this might be applied in everyday life. The best assessment answers are the ones that take this critical approach.

It is also important to note that psychology is a theoretical subject: when answering any question about psychology, not only refer to the prevailing theories of the field, but also outline the development of them as well. It is also important to evaluate these theories and models either through comparison with other models and theories or through the use of studies that have assessed them and highlighted their strengths and weaknesses. It is essential to read widely – within each section of this book there are directions to interesting and pertinent papers relating to the specific topic area. Find these papers, read these papers and make notes from these papers. But don't stop there. Let them lead you to other sources that may be important to the field. One thing that an examiner hates to see is the same old sources being cited all of the time: be innovative and, as well as reading the seminal works, find the more obscure and interesting sources as well – just make sure they're relevant to your answer!

How not to revise

- **Don't avoid revision**. This is the best tip ever. There is something on the TV, the pub is having a two-for-one offer, the fridge needs cleaning, your budgie looks lonely . . . You have all of these activities to do and they need doing now! Really . . . ? Do some revision!
- **Don't spend too long at each revision session**. Working all day and night is not the answer to revision. You do need to take breaks, so schedule your revision so you are not working from dawn until dusk. A break gives time for the information you have been revising to consolidate.
- **Don't worry**. Worrying will cause you to lose sleep, lose concentration and lose revision time by leaving it late and then later. When the exam comes, you will have no revision completed and will be tired and confused.
- **Don't cram**. This is the worst revision technique in the universe! You will not remember the majority of the information that you try to stuff into your skull, so why bother?
- **Don't read over old notes with no plan**. Your brain will take nothing in. If you wrote your lecture notes in September and the exam is in May is there any point in trying to decipher your scrawly handwriting now?
- **Don't write model answers and learn by rote**. When it comes to the exam you will simply regurgitate the model answer irrespective of the question – not a brilliant way to impress the examiner!

Tips for exam success

What you should do when it comes to revision

Exams are one form of assessment that students often worry about the most. The key to exam success, as with many other types of assessment, lies in good preparation and self-organisation. One of the most important things is knowing what to expect – this does not necessarily mean knowing what the questions will be on the exam paper, but rather what the structure of the paper is, how many questions you are expected to answer, how long the exam will last and so on.

To pass an exam you need a good grasp of the course material and, obvious as it may seem, to turn up for the exam itself. It is important to remember that you aren't expected to know or remember everything in the course, but you should be able to show your understanding of what you have studied. Remember as well that examiners are interested in what you know, not what you don't know. They try to write exam questions that give you a good chance of passing – not ones to catch you out or trick you in any way. You may want to consider some of these top exam tips.

- Start your revision in plenty of time.
- Make a revision timetable and stick to it.
- Practise jotting down answers and making essay plans.
- Practise writing against the clock using past exam papers.
- Check that you have really answered the question and have not strayed off the point.
- Review a recent past paper and check the marking structure.
- Carefully select the topics you are going to revise.
- Use your lecture/study notes and refine them further, if possible, into lists or diagrams and transfer them on to index cards/Post-it notes. Mind maps are a good way of making links between topics and ideas.
- Practise your handwriting – make sure it's neat and legible.

One to two days before the exam
- Recheck times, dates and venue.
- Actively review your notes and key facts.
- Exercise, eat sensibly and get a few good nights' sleep.

On the day
- Get a good night's sleep.
- Have a good meal, two to three hours before the start time.
- Arrive in good time.
- Spend a few minutes calming and focusing.

In the exam room
- Keep calm.
- Take a few minutes to read each question carefully. Don't jump to conclusions – think calmly about what each question means and the area it is focused on.
- Start with the question you feel most confident about. This helps your morale.
- By the same token, don't expend all your efforts on that one question – if you are expected to answer three questions then don't just answer two.
- Keep to time and spread your effort evenly on all opportunities to score marks.
- Once you have chosen a question, jot down any salient facts or key points. Then take five minutes to plan your answer – a spider diagram or a few notes may be enough to focus your ideas. Try to think in terms of 'why and how' not just 'facts'.

And finally, before the exam . . .

- You might find it useful to create a visual plan or map before writing your answer to help you remember to cover everything you need to address.
- Keep reminding yourself of the question and try not to wander off the point.
- Remember that quality of argument is more important than quantity of facts.
- Take 30–60-second breaks whenever you find your focus slipping (typically every 20 minutes).
- Make sure you reference properly – according to your university requirements.
- Watch your spelling and grammar – you could lose marks if you make too many errors.

→ *Final revision checklist*

❑ Have you revised the topics highlighted in the revision checklists?

❑ Have you attended revision classes and taken note of and/or followed up on your lecturers' advice about the exams or assessment process at your university?

❑ Can you answer the questions posed in this text satisfactorily? Don't forget to check sample answers on the website too.

❑ Have you read the additional material to make your answer stand out?

❑ Remember to criticise appropriately – based on evidence.

Test your knowledge by using the material presented in this text or on the website: www.pearsoned.co.uk/psychologyexpress

Glossary

anecdotal evidence Purportedly corroborative information that has been relayed through word-of-mouth channels, most typically referring to an event or other information that was originally observed casually.

animism The view that physical entities are inherently capable of causing their own motion, perhaps with the assistance of an ethereal spirit or deity.

aphasia A disorder of language capabilities that results from damage to the brain.

authority A level of expertise which is popularly trusted or respected, or a person or institution perceived as possessing such expertise.

behaviourism The perspective that all human actions, both physical and mental, can be considered to be behaviours, which are subject to principles of learning and amenable to empirical observation.

biological determinism A theory asserting that people's psychological make-up is dependent on various aspects of their biology.

brain plasticity The principle that surviving parts of an injured brain are capable of assuming the specialised functions that would have subsequently developed in the injured areas had typical brain development been allowed to occur.

categorical measurement A system of measurement based on labelling entities as being either in or not in a given category.

classical conditioning A procedure for eliciting a physiological response to a neutral stimulus, based on repeatedly exposing the organism to the neutral stimulus together with a physiologically relevant one.

cognitive heuristics Mental shortcuts used in everyday reasoning that produce predominantly useful decisions, but which are also characterised in many contexts by systematic errors of judgement.

cognitivism An approach to psychology that emphasises mental processes.

combinatorialism The view that small cognitive processes can be combined to produce complex mental capabilities.

computation A process of decision-making based on the analysis of information, often numerical in form or content.

craniometry A now debunked technique used to measure features of human skulls, usually post mortem, in order to support inferences about psychological characteristics such as intelligence.

critical health psychology The application of critical psychology perspectives in the context of physical health.

critical psychology An approach to psychology that is based on the perspective of critical theory, namely, the view that researchers' personal perspectives will impede them from producing neutral scholarship.

critical realism An approach to scholarship based on the view that while reality certainly exists independently of our perceptions, our capacity to record it accurately is limited.

determinism The philosophical position that all events in the universe are caused by preceding events and that nothing in the universe can happen without a cause.

dualism The theory that the mind and body are separate entities.

empiricism The position that knowledge is best produced by experiences and observations.

environment In psychology, an individual person's surroundings.

epiphenomenon An event that occurs as the consequence of another.

essentialism The idea that concepts have single, unique and intrinsic definitions, in which every concept has an objectively verifiable essence amounting to the set of properties that it possesses.

evolutionary psychology An area of psychology focusing on how psychological attributes have been influenced distally by the principles of natural and sexual selection, and proximally by interactions between genetic predispositions and environmental contingencies.

experimentation The use of methods of research, known as experiments, that involve the comparison of different arrangements or procedures against one another in order to test a hypothesis.

folk psychology The beliefs about psychological subjects that emerge within general society in the absence of specific strategic or scientific attempts to establish relevant information or evidence.

generalisability The extent to which a particular finding can be considered valid in conditions other than those under which it was made.

generality The assumption that principles derived from one context can be applied in other contexts.

genome The full collection of genes in an organism, located in each cell and containing all the information needed to produce and develop the organism's body throughout its life.

Gestalt psychology A theory of psychology that emerged in the early 20th century, which argued that human thought could be understood only in terms of the interaction among perceptual phenomena, in the sense that the impact of the sum of these perceptions would exceed that of its individual parts.

grand narrative See 'metanarrative'.

heredity The sharing of characteristics by parents and offspring as a result of their biological relatedness.

hermeneutics The study of a subject based on processes of interpretation.

homogeneity In relation to a multiplicity of cases, the quality of lacking meaningful case-to-case differences.

humanistic psychology A movement in psychology that focuses on aspects of human nature said to be distinctively human, including aesthetics, morality, dignity, choice, meaning and self-worth.

hypothesis A tentative explanation for a conceivable phenomenon.

idealism The theory that reality, as we know it, consists only of our perceptions and ideas.

information In technical contexts, a quantity of symbols that form part of an ordered system reflecting the number of choices a user has when handling them.

information processing An approach in cognitive psychology that views thinking as the organising and interpreting of an ordered system of meaningful symbols.

interpretivism The position that scientific observations are required to be interpreted as well as recorded, that merely recording observations will not yield complete insight as to their meaning, that concepts only make sense in the wider context in which they are situated, and that understanding can occur only when the whole entity is considered.

interval measurement A system of measurement based on the use of numerical scores to represent the quantity of the feature being measured, in which differences between consecutive numerical scores are equal across the entire range of possible scores.

introspection A process of information gathering that requires people to report on their thoughts and perceptions at a given moment in time.

'just so' story A commonly believed explanation that is transmitted anecdotally but which cannot be verified retrospectively through direct observation.

law A generalisable principle derived from an accumulation of well-corroborated observations.

levels of measurement The formats, or scales, by which measurement types can reasonably be described, typically said to comprise 'nominal measurement', 'ordinal measurement', 'interval measurement' and 'ratio measurement'.

logical positivism The theoretical position combining principles of empiricism and rationalism, that knowledge is best arrived at by verifying hypotheses through observation.

materialism The theory that reality is grounded in physical objects, which exist independently and are available for us to perceive and think about.

mathematics The study of measurements, numbers and quantities, using symbolic representations.

mechanism The view that all entities in nature follow mechanical laws by which motion is caused by physical actions and forces such as pneumatics.

metanarrative An explanatory schema that seeks to provide a unifying account for all historical, social and cultural events.

metaphysics The branch of philosophy concerned with the study of existence, truth and knowledge, especially as is yielded by considerations that go beyond that which can be observed empirically, or analysed mechanically or physically.

mind-body problem The philosophical debate between dualism and monism.

model An explanation of a set of events in nature based on simplified patterns of relationships observed in data.

monism The theory that the mind and body are intrinsically part of the one entity.

nature–nurture debate The debate between, on the one hand, the view that behaviour can be said to be instinctive or innate, and, on the other hand, the view that behaviour is dependent on experience or learning.

nihilism The view that nothing can be truly knowable.

nominal measurement See 'categorical measurement'.

obscurantism The practice of deliberately making information obscure in order to impede it from being fairly scrutinised.

ontology The philosophical study of the nature of reality, concerned with explaining what reality consists of and the basis of deciding whether something can be said either to exist or to not exist.

ordinal measurement A system of measurement based on identifying where an entity falls when all entities in a sample are ranked according to the dimension being measured.

parsimony The principle of using the simplest available viable explanation, namely, one that relies on the fewest uncorroborated assumptions.

personality Broadly, those psychological characteristics of an individual that make up his or her distinctiveness.

phenomenology In psychology, the view that the best way to study the human condition is to examine immediate perceptual experiences.

philosophy of mind The branch of philosophy that examines the mind and mental phenomena, such as consciousness, with a particular focus on their relationship with the physical body.

phrenology A now debunked practice of inferring psychological characteristics from the topography of a person's head, based on the assumption that the shape of the underlying cranial surface reveals pertinent information about the brain.

polygenism A controversial theory of the origin of humans, which asserts that the different human races originally emerged on separate occasions and evolved along separate lineages.

positive psychology A relatively new subfield of psychology that focuses on the study of positive human functioning, including such constructs as achievement, optimism and happiness.

postpositivism The theoretical position that applies critical realism to logical positivism, asserting that all observation is fallible and all theories revisable.

professional ethics Those ethical principles that pertain to the specialist knowledge or training of individuals who work in professions.

pseudoscience A practice that has the superficial appearance of a science but which fails to meet the quality standards normally required of sciences.

psychiatrist A person who has received full medical training and who has gone on to specialise in mental health care.

psychoanalysis The theory of psychology proposed by Sigmund Freud, which emphasises the role of unconscious processes in human behaviour.

psychoanalyst A person who practices psychoanalysis (i.e. the advanced therapeutic activity related to the Freudian theory of the mind), and who has received the required psychoanalytic training to do so.

psychologisation The emphasis on psychological aspects of events in the absence of any particular justification.

psychologist A person who has been trained in the academic discipline of psychology.

psychometrics The various fields and practices within psychology concerned with the formal measurement of psychological attributes.

psychophysics The formal study of how the physical properties of a stimulus relate to a person's psychological perception of it.

psychotherapist A person who practices psychotherapy, taken to include therapies of all theoretical orientations.

quale An element of subjective conscious experience.

qualia Plural of 'quale'.

quantification The process of counting, measuring or indexing that assigns a systematic measure to an observed entity.

quasi-experiment An experiment in which it is impossible for the researcher to exert complete control over all the active variables so as to eliminate the risk of outcomes being determined (in part or wholly) by extraneous factors.

ratio measurement A system of measurement based on 'interval measurement', in which a score of zero denotes an actual absence of the feature being measured.

rationalism The position that knowledge is best produced by reasoning.

reliability The extent to which a measurement method succeeds in achieving consistency, regardless of accuracy.

realism The assumption that the universe has an independent existence separate from our consciousness.

recapitulation In developmental biology, the now debunked idea that the lifespan development of each individual human reflects the evolutionary development of the entire human species.

reductionism The epistemological view that complex systems can be adequately considered in terms of the sum of their constituent parts.

reflexivity In science, the confounding of cause and effect, ordinarily due to the presence of bidirectional influences between two entities.

reinforcer A stimulus that when presented after a specific behaviour increases the rate or probability of that behaviour.

relativism The idea that information is a function of perception and dependent on perspective.

representations Images, ideas, concepts, memories, words and strategies that occupy an intermediate conceptual level between the actual objects in the real world and the biological or neurological systems that underlie that which we call our 'minds'.

scepticism The view that it is reasonable to question and/or investigate any assertion purporting to describe factual information.

scientific literacy A person's capacity to understand scientific concepts and the processes of reasoning used in science, as well as their ability to use scientific principles to reason through problems.

social constructionism The view that all so-called objective knowledge, including all scholarly knowledge, is constructed by humans rather than discovered or inferred by them.

social constructivism The view that each individual constructs a personal understanding of the world through interacting with social environments.

social sciences A broad and heterogeneous group of academic disciplines that examine different aspects of the contexts in which humans live.

solipsism The view that there is no basis to believe in the existence of anything other than one's own immediate conscious experiences.

specialisation The separation of specific expertise and/or activities within a wider system of expertise and/or activities.

structuralism The view that all complex mental experiences can be understood in terms of combinations of small discrete perceptions and sensations.

subjective idealism The view that material entities exist only insofar as they are perceived by minds.

subjectivism The epistemological assumption that the most important (if not the only) source of knowledge is personal experience.

systematicity In science, the quality of being methodical and planned in ways that produces a coherent body of knowledge.

teleological argument A philosophical argument which states that the apparent orderliness of phenomena in the universe implies the existence of a sentient creator.

theory A proposed explanation for observed events that is composed of a collection of assumptions and hypotheses.

thought experiment An exercise where an investigator mentally considers the possible outcomes of an actual experiment, but without actually conducting the experiment in question.

top-down processing The use of prior knowledge, experience and assumptions to help organise and interpret new information.

truth relativism The view that assertions cannot be considered as being true or valid, but instead can only ever be seen as having ephemeral (and unreliable) subjective value based on each particular individual's perspective.

validity The extent to which a measurement method actually succeeds in producing an accurate measure of the entity it intends to measure.

References

Bering, J. M. (2006). The folk psychology of souls. *Behavioral and Brain Sciences, 29*, 453–498.

Bering, J. M., & Bjorklund, D. F. (2004). The natural emergence of reasoning about the afterlife as a developmental regularity. *Developmental Psychology, 40*, 217–233.

British Psychological Society (2009). *Code of ethics and conduct: Guidance published by the Ethics Committee of the British Psychological Society.* Leicester: British Psychological Society.

Coon, D. J. (1992). Testing the limits of sense and science: American experimental psychologists combat spiritualism, 1880–1920. *American Psychologist, 47*, 143–151.

Feyerabend, P. K. (1975). *Against method: Outline of an anarchistic theory of knowledge.* London: New Left Books.

Harding, S. (1986). *The science question in feminism.* Ithaca, New York: Cornell University Press.

Huxley, A. (1932). *Brave new world.* London: Chatto and Windus.

James, W. (1890). *Principles of psychology.* New York: Henry Holt.

Keller, E. F. (1978). Gender and science. *Psychoanalysis and Contemporary Thought, 1*, 409–433.

Kuhn, T. (1962). *The structure of scientific revolutions.* Chicago: University of Chicago Press.

Latour, B., & Woolgar, S. (1979). *Laboratory life: The construction of scientific facts.* Beverly Hills: Sage.

Leydesdorff, L., & Rafols, I. (2009). A global map of science based on the ISI subject categories. *Journal of the American Society for Information Science and Technology, 60*, 348–362.

Maslow, A. H. (1954). *Motivation and personality.* New York: Harper & Row.

Maslow, A. H. (1969). Toward a humanistic biology. *American Psychologist, 24*, 724–735.

Miller, G. A. (1956). The magical number seven, plus or minus two: Some limits on our capacity for processing information. *Psychological Review, 63*, 343–355.

Penfield, W. (1952). Memory mechanisms. *AMA Archives of Neurology and Psychiatry, 67*, 178–198.

Pinnick, C. (1994). Feminist epistemology: Implications for philosophy of science. *Philosophy of Science, 61*, 646–657.

Popper, K. (1959). *The Logical of Scientific Discovery.* London: Routledge.

Prilleltensky, I. (2003). Critical health psychology needs psychopolitical validity. *Health Psychology Update, 12*, 2–11.

QAA (2010). *Quality Assurance Agency benchmark for psychology.* London: Quality Assurance Agency.

Schachter, S., & Singer, J. E. (1962). Cognitive, social, and physiological determinants of emotional state. *Psychological Review, 69*, 379–399.

Valentine, E. R. (1992). *Conceptual issues in psychology* (2nd ed.). London: Routledge.

Wampold, B. E., Mondin, G. W., Moody, M., Stich, F., Benson, K., & Ahn, H-N. (1997). A meta-analysis of outcome studies comparing bona fide psychotherapies: Empirically, 'all must have prizes'. *Psychological Bulletin, 122*, 203–215.

Watson, J. B. (1913). Psychology as the behaviorist views it. *Psychological Review, 20*, 158–177.

Watson, J. B., & Rayner, R. (1920). Conditioned emotional reactions. *Journal of Experimental Psychology, 3*, 1–14.

Wood, D., Gosling, S. D., & Potter, J. (2007). Normality evaluations and their relation to personality traits and well-being. *Journal of Personality and Social Psychology, 93*, 861–879.

Index